Y0-BCU-300

Pro Expression
Blend 4

Andrew Troelsen

Apress®

Pro Expression Blend 4

Copyright © 2011 by Andrew Troelsen

All rights reserved. No part of this work may be reproduced or transmitted in any form or by any means, electronic or mechanical, including photocopying, recording, or by any information storage or retrieval system, without the prior written permission of the copyright owner and the publisher.

ISBN-13 (pbk): 978-1-4302-3377-0

ISBN-13 (electronic): 978-1-4302-3378-7

Printed and bound in the United States of America 9 8 7 6 5 4 3 2 1

Trademarked names, logos, and images may appear in this book. Rather than use a trademark symbol with every occurrence of a trademarked name, logo, or image we use the names, logos, and images only in an editorial fashion and to the benefit of the trademark owner, with no intention of infringement of the trademark.

The use in this publication of trade names, trademarks, service marks, and similar terms, even if they are not identified as such, is not to be taken as an expression of opinion as to whether or not they are subject to proprietary rights.

President and Publisher: Paul Manning
Lead Editor: Ewan Buckingham
Technical Reviewer: Andy Olsen
Editorial Board: Steve Anglin, Mark Beckner, Ewan Buckingham, Gary Cornell, Jonathan Gennick, Jonathan Hassell, Michelle Lowman, Matthew Moodie, Jeffrey Pepper, Frank Pohlmann, Douglas Pundick, Ben Renow-Clarke, Dominic Shakeshaft, Matt Wade, Tom Welsh
Coordinating Editor: Debra Kelly
Copy Editor: Bill McManus
Compositor: MacPS, LLC
Indexer: BIM Indexing & Proofreading Services
Artist: April Milne
Cover Designer: Anna Ishchenko

Distributed to the book trade worldwide by Springer Science+Business Media, LLC., 233 Spring Street, 6th Floor, New York, NY 10013. Phone 1-800-SPRINGER, fax (201) 348-4505, e-mail orders-ny@springer-sbm.com, or visit www.springeronline.com.

For information on translations, please e-mail rights@apress.com, or visit www.apress.com.

Apress and friends of ED books may be purchased in bulk for academic, corporate, or promotional use. eBook versions and licenses are also available for most titles. For more information, reference our Special Bulk Sales–eBook Licensing web page at www.apress.com/info/bulksales.

The information in this book is distributed on an "as is" basis, without warranty. Although every precaution has been taken in the preparation of this work, neither the author(s) nor Apress shall have any liability to any person or entity with respect to any loss or damage caused or alleged to be caused directly or indirectly by the information contained in this work.

The source code for this book is available to readers at www.apress.com. You will need to answer questions pertaining to this book in order to successfully download the code.

To the next little Troel

Contents at a Glance

■ Contents v

■ About the Author xiv

■ About the Technical Reviewer xv

■ Acknowledgments xvi

■ Introduction...xvii

■ Chapter 1: Learning the Core Blend IDE 1

■ Chapter 2: Vector Graphics and Object Resources............................... 33

■ Chapter 3: The Animation Editor 87

■ Chapter 4: Controls, Layouts, and Behaviors 119

■ Chapter 5: Styles, Templates, and UserControls 163

■ Chapter 6: Blend Data Binding Techniques 221

■ Chapter 7: Designing for Windows Phone 7 273

■ Chapter 8: Prototyping with SketchFlow.. 311

■ Index.. 347

Contents

■ **Contents at a Glance**... iv

■ **About the Author** xiv

■ **About the Technical Reviewer**..xv

■ **Acknowledgments**...xvi

■ **Introduction**..xvii

■ **Chapter 1: Learning the Core Blend IDE** 1

The Microsoft Expression Family 1

    The Role of Expression Web...2

    The Role of Expression Encoder...2

    The Role of Expression Design...2

    The Role of Expression Blend 3

The Expression Blend Project Templates...5

    WPF Project Templates 6

    Silverlight Project Templates 7

    Windows Phone Project Templates...8

A Guided Tour of the Core Blend IDE...8

    Loading a Blend Sample Project...9

    The Artboard and Artboard Controls 10

    The Objects and Timeline Panel...15

    The Properties Panel..16

    The Project Panel 19

    The Integrated Code Editor 20

    The Results Panel 21

    The Tools Panel..22

Handling and Implementing Events 28

Customizing the Options of the Blend IDE 30

Creating a Custom Workspace Layout 30

The Expression Blend Documentation System 31

Summary 32

■ Chapter 2: Vector Graphics and Object Resources 33

The Realm of Vector Graphics 33

Use of Graphical Data Is Pervasive 34

Exploring the Core Drawing Tools 34

Working with the Pencil Tool 35

Working with the Pen Tool 36

Working with the Rectangle, Ellipse, and Line Tools 38

Working with the Shapes Section of the Assets Library 39

Modifying a Shape Using the Appearance Editor 40

Coloring a Shape Using the Brushes Editor 42

Combining Geometries and Extracting Paths 47

Converting a Shape to a Path 49

Interacting with Shapes 50

Handling Events 50

Configuring "Pens" 52

Defining Pen Caps 52

Defining a Dash Pattern 53

Revisiting Visual Effects 54

Tweaking a Visual Effect 55

The Role of Expression Design 56

Preparing and Exporting a Sample Image 56

Creating a New Silverlight Application 60

Applying 2D Graphical Transformation 64

Building the Initial UI 64

Applying Transformations at Design Time 66

Applying Transformations in Code 68

Applying 3D Graphical Transformation 69

An Introduction to WPF 3D Graphics 69

An Introduction to Silverlight 3D Graphics 79

The Role of Object Resources 81

Summary 86

■ Chapter 3: The Animation Editor 87

Defining the Role of Animation Services 87

The Scope of Animation Services 88

The Blend Animation Workspace 88

Creating a New Storyboard 89

Managing Existing Storyboards 90

Adding Keyframes 91

Capturing Object Property Changes 92

Testing Your Animation 94

Viewing the Animation Markup 94

Configuring Storyboard Properties 94

Zooming the Timeline Editor 96

Interacting with Storyboards in Code 96

Further Details of the Storyboard Class 97

WPF-Specific Animation Techniques 98

Working with WPF Motion Paths 98

Controlling WPF Animations Using Triggers 102

Understanding Animation Easing Effects 109

Building the Initial Layout 110

Creating the Initial Storyboards 111

Applying Animation Easing Effects 111

Working with the KeySpline Editor 113

Executing the Storyboard at Runtime 114

Learning More About Animation Easing Effects 114

Controlling Storyboards in XAML via Behavior Objects.....................115

　　Modifying the SimpleBlendAnimations Example 115

　　Adding the ControlStoryboardAction Behavior...116

Summary..118

■ **Chapter 4: Controls, Layouts, and Behaviors** 119

A First Look at GUI Controls 119

　　Locating Controls Within the IDE...120

　　Configuring Controls via the Properties Panel 121

　　Learning About Control Details 121

Understanding the Control Content Model 123

　　Creating Composite Content 124

　　Handling Events for Controls with Composite Content 126

　　Reusing Composite Content..127

Understanding the Items Control Model 128

　　Adding ListBoxItems 128

　　Viewing the XAML 130

　　Finding the Current Selection 131

　　Working with the Tag Property 132

Working with Layout Managers 132

　　Additional Layout Types...134

　　Changing the Layout Type...134

　　Designing Nested Layouts...135

　　Grouping and Ungrouping Selected UI Elements 136

　　Repositioning a UI Element into a Layout Manager 137

Building a User Interface with Blend 138

　　Creating a Tabbed Layout System 138

　　Working with the Grid 141

　　Introducing the WPF Document API 147

　　Creating a ToolBar Control 149

Introducing Blend Behavior Objects...............................156

The MouseDragElementBehavior Object..159

Summary..161

■ **Chapter 5: Styles, Templates, and UserControls 163**

The Role of Styles 163

Creating a Simple Style by Hand..164

Assigning a Control's Style Property 165

Overriding Style Settings 167

Constraining a Style with TargetType 167

Subclassing Existing Styles 168

Defining Default Styles...169

Managing Existing Styles Using the Blend IDE...................................170

Creating New Styles Using Blend..172

Creating a New Empty Style 172

Working with WPF Simple Styles 175

The Role of Control Templates in Styles 180

Building a Custom Control Template by Hand....................................181

Storing Templates as Resources 182

Incorporating Visual Cues Using WPF Triggers 184

Understanding the Role of {TemplateBinding} 186

Understanding the Role of <ContentPresenter>..................................187

Incorporating Templates into Styles 187

Creating Control Templates Using Expression Blend 189

Creating a Copy of a Default Template 189

Creating a Stylized Template from a Graphic....................................193

Building Templates Using the Silverlight API 204

Working with the VSM via the States Panel......................................206

Viewing the Generated XAML...207

Establishing State Group Transition Timing 208

Defining Transition Effects...209

Configuring Individual Transitions 210

A Brief Word Regarding Custom States 211

Generating UserControls Using Blend 212

    Adding Visual States 215

    Transitioning States in Code 216

    Transitioning States in XAML 216

    VSM: Further Resources 218

Summary..219

Chapter 6: Blend Data Binding Techniques 221

The Role of Data Binding..222

Control-to-Control Data Binding..222

    Building the Example UI 222

    Creating New Data Bindings 224

    Viewing the Generated Markup 227

Converting Data Types 227

    Creating a Custom Data Conversion Class.....................................228

    Selecting a Conversion Class in Blend 229

Understanding Data Binding Modalities...232

    Configuring Data Binding Options with Blend..................................233

    Configuring a Two-Way Data Bind 234

Binding to Properties of Non-UI Objects 236

    Creating a Custom Collection of (Custom) Objects 236

    Defining an Object Data Source with the Data Panel..........................237

    Binding the Entire Collection to a ListBox 240

    Binding Individual Properties to ListBox Controls 243

    Binding the Collection to a DataGrid 243

    Manipulating the Collection at Runtime 245

Working with Data Templates...246

    Editing a Data Template...247

    Styling Items in a Data Template 247

    Defining Composite UI Elements for a Data Template 248

    Creating Control Templates Containing Data Templates 251

Defining a WPF XML Data Source **255**

Adding an XML Data Source 256

Binding XML Data to UI Elements via XPath...257

Creating a List Details Data Binding **259**

Creating the User Interface 259

Examining the Generated Markup...261

Exploring the Role of Sample Data **262**

Inserting Sample Data into a Project 263

Adding Additional Properties...264

Modifying the Data Types and Values...265

Binding Sample Data to the UI 266

Learning More About Sample Data 268

Data Binding: A Brief Word on Final Topics **269**

Binding to Relational Database Data...269

The Role of Blend Databound Project Templates (MVVM)...270

Summary...**271**

■ **Chapter 7: Designing for Windows Phone 7** **273**

Installing the Windows Phone 7 SDK...**273**

Examining the New Bits...276

Installing the Windows Phone 7 Documentation...278

Viewing the New Blend Projects 281

Viewing the New Visual Studio 2010 Projects 283

Exploring the Windows Phone Application Project Type...**284**

The Windows Phone Artboard...284

The Windows Phone System Styles 286

Creating a List-Details View with the Data Panel...287

Creating an Interactive Graphic 288

Creating a Custom Control Template 289

Handling the Click Event 291

Configuring the Emulator via the Device Panel...292

Exploring the Panorama Application Project Type 294

Examining the Initial Tree of Objects 294

Viewing the PanoramaItem Markup..295

Changing the Panorama Background 296

Adding a New PanoramaItem Object 299

Exploring the Pivot Application Project Type 300

Adding a New PivotItem...301

Designing the Pivot GUI Layout 302

Transforming the Grid 303

Controlling the Storyboard in XAML 304

Learning More About Windows Phone Development 306

MSDN Windows Phone Sample Projects..306

The App Hub Web Site 309

Summary...310

■ **Chapter 8: Prototyping with SketchFlow... 311**

The Role of Application Prototyping...311

The Role of SketchFlow 312

Examining a SketchFlow Prototype Sample 314

Exploring the SketchFlow Map Panel...315

Testing the Prototype with the SketchFlow Player 320

Creating a Silverlight Prototype 326

Examining the Project Files..327

Creating a Component Screen 329

Creating Additional Screens...332

Replicating the Navigation GUI...334

Using the NavigateToScreenAction Behavior..334

Incorporating Prototype Interactivity...337

Using the PlaySketchFlowAnimationAction Behavior 340

Packaging a Prototype 341

Moving a Prototype into Production..343

Modifying the *csproj Files 343

Updating the Root Project Assembly References...343

Modifying the App.xaml.cs File 344

Summary...346

■ Index.. 347

About the Author

Andrew Troelsen fondly recalls his very first computer, an Atari 400 complete with a tape deck storage device and a black-and-white TV serving as a monitor (which his parents permitted him to have in his bedroom—thanks guys!). He also is grateful to the legacy *Compute!* magazine, a B.A. degree in mathematical linguistics, and three years of formal Sanskrit. All of these artifacts have greatly influenced his current career.

Andrew is employed with Intertech (www.intertech.com), a .NET and Java training and consulting center. He has authored a number of books, including *Developer's Workshop to COM and ATL 3.0* (Wordware Publishing, 2000), *COM and .NET Interoperability* (Apress, 2002), and *Pro C# 2010 and the .NET 4.0 Platform* (Apress, 2010).

About the Technical Reviewer

 **Andy Olsen** is a freelance consultant and trainer based in the UK. Andy has been working with .NET since the days of the first beta, and has been involved with WPF and Silverlight since they first landed on our desktops (and in our browsers). Andy lives by the sea in Swansea with his wife, Jayne, and children. Andy enjoys running along the seafront (with regular coffee stops along the way), skiing, and following the Swans and Ospreys. Andy can be reached at andyo@olsensoft.com.

Acknowledgments

I have been lucky to work with the staff of Apress for close to 10 years, and I can say that each book I have written has benefited greatly due to their efforts.

Huge thanks to Andy Olsen, Ewan Buckingham, Debra Kelly, and the entire copy editing team for helping transform my initial ramblings into a cohesive text. I am deeply grateful, and look forward to working with all of you again in the future.

Introduction

Confessions of an XAML Jockey

Perhaps my story sounds familiar...when I first started programming with Windows Presentation Foundation (WPF), and later when I dove into Silverlight 2.0, I was one of "those" programmers who figured I would build my applications by typing all of the necessary markup by hand.[1] After all, a copious amount of typing is part of the job description for any software engineer. When I was defining layouts with grids, stack panels, and controls, life was good. However, once I dove deeper and began working with animations, data templates, control templates, and custom graphics, I soon realized just how unproductive my days were becoming.

I knew of a Microsoft tool named Expression Blend, but as far as I was concerned, this was a tool for *graphical artists*. I will admit to anybody that I am not a graphical artist by any stretch of the imagination, and given this, I avoided Blend like the plague. In fact, I will also admit that I was a tad put off by the Blend IDE early on. The designer looked nothing like Visual Studio, the organization of the properties editor made no sense to me, and the earlier versions of Blend had no code editors (which is thankfully no longer the case).

However, there was one fateful day that I decided to roll up my sleeves and give Expression Blend a real, honest look. To my surprise, *I liked it*. The more time I spent learning the tool, *the more I liked it*. These days, I cannot imagine working on a WPF, Silverlight, or Windows Phone 7 project without it...quite honestly, I'd feel like I was typing with one hand tied behind my back.

With my newfound understanding, I attempted to spread the word to fellow programmers; however, I found that they were in the same boat that I was in initially. They felt that the Blend IDE was too complex, and (they now would say) Visual Studio 2010 has solid support for XAML-based development these days anyway...so why bother? Nowadays, when I hear this sort of reaction, I concur that Visual Studio 2010 is a step in the right direction, but I quickly point out that Blend dwarfs Visual Studio 2010 in terms of productivity. For example, with Expression Blend, you can do the following:

- Generate a control template from a vector graphic with a single menu selection
- Author complex animations using an integrated editor
- Visually edit data templates
- Incorporate visual cues into a custom template using integrated graphical editors
- Build a "list-details" data view with two mouse operations
- Prototype a WPF or Silverlight application and record client feedback in real time[2]

---

[1] You may recall that Visual Studio 2005 had no real support for WPF to begin with, beyond an experimental technology preview designer surface.

[2] Via SketchFlow, if you have a copy of Expression Studio Ultimate (see Chapter 8).

Simply put, I wrote this book to help my fellow software engineers learn the ins and outs of the Blend IDE. I honestly feel that this tool is a critical part of any production-level WPF, Silverlight, or Windows Phone 7 development effort, and that once you are comfortable with the tool, you will feel the same way. Of course, Visual Studio 2010 is also important and downright mandatory when you need to debug your code (and test your code, expand code snippets, etc.). As you will see, Expression Blend is intended to be a *complement* to your Visual Studio 2010 IDE, not a *replacement*.

This Is Not a Programming Book...

All of the previous books I've written have been squarely focused on *code*, and lots of it. I have always purposely authored technology books in such a way that I spent as little time as possible talking about menu options of an IDE, wizards, and so forth. In my opinion, when you are learning a new language or platform, you need to dive into the code and type away. Once you are comfortable with the "raw code," then the use of visual development tools is a welcomed bonus.

In this book, I had to take the exact opposite approach (which I must admit was very weird). This book is a book that *does* talk all about menu selections, integrated wizards, dialog boxes, and IDE configuration choices. To be sure, screenshots, not code samples, are the crux of this text.

In fact, if I were to scrape out all of the C# code found in this book, I bet I could capture it on ten printed pages. Likewise, if I were to cut out all of the XAML code examples, I can't image it would be more than ten additional printed pages.

So, please be very aware that the mission of this book is *not* to cover all of the programmatic details of building WPF, Silverlight, or Windows Phone 7 applications. I will not be covering how to build custom dependency properties or bubbling routed events. I will not dive into the details regarding which virtual methods to override when building a class that extends UIElement.[3] These topics (as well as many others), while important, are not the focus of this text.

... and Graphical Artists Are Welcome!

Given that this book will not focus on complex code, this text is also intended to help graphical artists learn how to use Expression Blend to construct professional UIs for a WPF, Silverlight, or Windows Phone 7 project. As you will see, Blend can be used in conjunction with a related tool named Expression Design. Using Design, you can build complex vector-based graphics and export the image data into a format that can be used within Blend. This one-two punch radically simplifies how programmers (and designers) can build interactive graphics.

If you are a graphical artist, you should find that the little C# code found in this book will be quite manageable (and if you would rather not type it yourself, you can simply download the solution projects from the Apress web site). On a final note, if you are a graphical artist by trade, please don't laugh too loudly when you view my primitive graphical renderings....

---

[3] You may wish to consult the latest edition of my C# or VB books for such information, where you will find a number of chapters devoted to WPF programming topics (many of which apply directly to Silverlight and Windows Phone 7).

Chapter Overview

This book consists of eight chapters, which ideally will be read from beginning to end, as each chapter builds on concepts from the previous chapters. Here is a quick rundown of what is covered.

Chapter 1: Learning the Core Blend IDE

This chapter sets the foundation for the remainder of the book, by giving you a guided tour of the core aspects of the Blend IDE. You will learn about the artboard, the integrated XAML and code editors, and the role of several key "panels" such as the Objects and Timeline panel, the Properties panel, the Tools panel, and so forth. You will also learn about the various project types supported by Expression Blend and the role of the Assets library. To illustrate these important concepts, you will examine and modify one of the intrinsic sample projects that ship with Expression Blend.

Chapter 2: Vector Graphics and Object Resources

Experienced WPF and Silverlight developers know that graphics are a key part of any project. In this chapter, you will learn how to use the intrinsic graphic design tools of Blend, including the Pen and Pencil tools, the various "shape assets," the Brushes editor, and other items of interest. In addition, this chapter will explore how to use Blend to establish graphical transformations of UI elements, how to create and manipulate 3D graphics, and how to define and package up *object resources*, which are basically named blobs of XAML that you want to reuse throughout your projects.

Chapter 3: The Animation Editor

Animations are also a key part of a WPF and Silverlight project, as you use them extensively when building control templates, data templates, and other forms of "visual eye candy." In this chapter, you will learn about the integrated animation editor of Expression Blend. You will learn how to define and configure storyboards and keyframes, control the pacing of an animation, and apply various physical effects (spring, bounce, snap, etc.) to an animation cycle using *easing effects*. You will also be given your first look at a Blend *behavior object*, which will be further explored in Chapter 4.

Chapter 4: Controls, Layouts, and Behaviors

The goal of Chapter 4 is to illustrate a number of techniques used when working with UI controls within the Blend IDE. You will explore the control content model, learn how to customize ListBox controls with intricate list items, learn how to capture user input with the InkCanvas control, and explore the role of the WPF Document API controls. As well, this chapter will introduce the topic of *behaviors*. As you will see here (and in other chapters of the book), a behavior object allows you to apply complex runtime functionality to a user interface element, in a visual manner (with no code required).

Chapter 5: Styles, Templates, and UserControls

When you are building WPF and Silverlight applications, the *style mechanism* allows you to ensure that related UI elements have the same look and feel. This chapter begins by examining how the Blend IDE can simplify the creation and management of styles. Next, you will learn about the role of *control templates*, which take the style concept to the next level. As you will see, when you define a custom control template, you can completely replace the default look and feel of a control with your own set of rendering instructions. The chapter wraps up with a quick look at using Blend to create new custom UserControl objects with the click of a mouse.

Chapter 6: Blend Data Binding Techniques

Chapter 6 walks you through the numerous tools of the Blend IDE that facilitate data binding operations. You will learn how to configure control-to-control data bindings, how to bind to collections of custom business objects, and how to bind to data contained in XML documents. In addition, this chapter will illustrate how to use Expression Blend to create customized *data templates*, which allow you to stylize how a data binding operation will be display within the application.

Chapter 7: Designing for Windows Phone 7

While I was authoring this book, Microsoft formally unveiled its Windows Phone 7 family of handheld devices and, with this, the official version of the Windows Phone 7 Software Development Kit (SDK). In this chapter, you will learn how to download and install the necessary tools to build Windows Phone 7 applications using Expression Blend (and Visual Studio 2010). Then, you will explore several new topics, including the role of panorama and pivot device displays, the Blend Device panel, and the integrated Windows Phone emulator. As you will be happy to see, just about everything you learned during the first six chapters of this book apply directly to the construction of Windows Phone 7 projects.

Chapter 8: Prototyping with SketchFlow

Ironically, the final chapter of this book addresses what is often the very first aspect of a new development project! Specifically, Chapter 8 examines how to create WPF and Silverlight prototypes using SketchFlow. As you will see, the SketchFlow component of Expression Studio Ultimate Edition allows you to quickly mock up prototypes in real time, capturing stakeholder feedback as you go. You will learn about the various SketchFlow-centric aspects of Blend, including the Map panel, the Sketch Styles, the user annotation viewer, and the "mini" animation editor. As well, this chapter illustrates how you can transform a SketchFlow prototype into a real WPF or Silverlight project.

Obtaining the Sample Projects

Every chapter of this book will give you a chance to learn how to use the numerous features of the Expression Blend IDE by building various sample projects. I *really* can't stress enough how important it is that you roll up your sleeves and create (and expand upon) these applications as you read the text. To be sure, Blend is a product that is best learned by *doing* and not simply reading a book and looking at various screenshots.

While this is true, you can download each sample project from the Apress web site. Simply navigate to www.apress.com, click the Source Code link, and look up this title by name (in the list) or by ISBN (using the Find Source Code search tool). Once you are on the home page for *Pro Expression Blend 4*, you may download a self-extracting *.zip file. After you unzip the contents, you will find that the projects have been partitioned on a chapter-by-chapter basis.

On a related note, be aware that you will find Source Code notes like the following in the book's chapters, which are your visual cue that the example under discussion may be loaded into Expression Blend (or, for that matter, Visual Studio 2010) for further examination and modification:

■ **Source Code** This is a Source Code note referring you to a specific directory in the *.zip archive!

To open a solution into Expression Blend, use the File ➤ Open Project/Solution menu option, and navigate to the correct *.sln file within the correct subdirectory of the unzipped archive.

Obtaining Updates for This Book

As you read through this text, you may find an occasional error (although I sure hope not). If this is the case, my apologies. Being human, I am sure that a glitch or two may be present, despite my best efforts. If this is the case, you can obtain the current errata list from the Apress web site (located once again on the home page for this book) as well as information on how to notify me of any errors you might find.

Contacting Me

If you have any questions regarding this book's sample projects, are in need of clarification for a given example, or simply wish to offer your thoughts regarding the Blend IDE, feel free to drop me a line at the following e-mail address (to ensure your messages don't end up in my junk mail folder, please include "Blend Book" in the Subject line somewhere):

atroelsen@intertech.com

Please understand that I will do my best to get back to you in a timely fashion; however, like yourself, I get busy from time to time. If I don't respond within a week or two, do know I am not trying to be a jerk or don't care to talk to you. I'm just busy (or, if I'm lucky, on vacation somewhere). So, then! Thanks for buying this text (or at least looking at it in the bookstore while you try to decide if you will buy it). I hope you enjoy reading this book and putting your newfound knowledge to good use.

CHAPTER 1

■ ■ ■

Learning the Core Blend IDE

The point of this first chapter is to examine the nuts and bolts of the Microsoft Expression Blend integrated development environment (IDE). You will begin with a brief overview of each member of the Microsoft Expression family of products, and see their place within a Windows Presentation Foundation (WPF) and Silverlight development effort. Next, you will examine the various project templates of Expression Blend, come to know the key workspace areas (the artboard, the Objects and Timeline panel, the Properties panel, etc.), and understand the interplay between Expression Blend and Microsoft Visual Studio 2010. The chapter concludes with coverage of how to customize the layout of the IDE to suit your personal preferences.

The Microsoft Expression Family

The Microsoft Expression family of products was first demonstrated during the 2005 Professional Developers Conference (PDC), but it was not until 2007 that Microsoft released the first edition of the tools to the world at large. The Expression product lineup is a set of applications aimed at the professional graphical artist; however, it is increasingly common for software developers to use the products as well.

At the time of this writing, the Expression family consists of four[1] products (Expression Web, Expression Encoder, Expression Design, and Expression Blend), which may be purchased via the acquisition of Microsoft Expression Studio Ultimate. You'll be happy to know that if you or your company has an MSDN subscription, Expression Studio Ultimate is part of your current package. If you do not have a valid MSDN subscription, you will be equally happy to know that you can download a 60-day trial edition of Expression Studio Ultimate from the following web site:[2]

www.microsoft.com/expression/try-it

Strictly speaking, this book only requires you to have access to a copy of Expression Blend. However, if you wish to explore how to incorporate complex vector graphics into a WPF or Silverlight application (see Chapter 2), I suggest that you install a copy of Expression Design. As

---

[1] Or five products, if you include Expression Media, which has recently been acquired by Phase One A/S. Expression Media is a commercial digital asset management (DAM) cataloging program for Microsoft Windows and Mac OS X operating systems.

[2] On a related note, the Microsoft Expression home page (www.microsoft.com/expression) provides supporting links to a rich online community. You can find numerous video tutorials, case studies, technology previews, and so forth. Take a moment to check out this site; it's definitely worthy of a browser bookmark.

far as the other members of the Microsoft Expression family are concerned, we will not be making use of them in this text. Nevertheless, you may want to explore them on your own, so the following quick tour describes the high-level nature of each member of the Microsoft Expression family.

The Role of Expression Web

Expression Web is a tool that allows you to visually create production-ready (and standards-based) web sites. Even though this is a *Microsoft* web development tool, you are *not* limited to the use of ASP.NET or ASP.NET AJAX (although support for the .NET platform within Expression Web is excellent). If you wish, you can use the integrated page designers and source code editors to construct web sites using PHP, HTML/XHTML, XML/XSLT, CSS, JavaScript, as well as Adobe Flash and Windows Media components.

Expression Web also ships with a companion product named *SuperPreview*. This aspect of Expression Web (greatly) simplifies the testing of your web site across several popular web browsers (for both Windows and Mac). If you are a web-savvy developer, you know that ensuring a web page renders and behaves properly across diverse environments is a constant source of irritation. Using Expression Web and SuperPreview, you have a solid set of tools to help with this endeavor.

The Role of Expression Encoder

Although we will not use Expression Encoder for this book, be aware that this tool provides a platform to import, edit, and enhance video media, encoded in a wide variety of formats including AVI, WMV, WMA, QuickTime MOV files (if installed), MPEG, VC-1, and H.264.

By way of an example, using Expression Encoder, you could create a professional training video configured to stream within a Silverlight (or WPF) application. As well, Expression Encoder can be used to create media that seamlessly integrates into a WPF/Silverlight application via bookmarks and customizable skins.

The Role of Expression Design

Expression Design is a Microsoft tool that stands in direct competition with Adobe products such as Illustrator and Photoshop (in fact, Expression Design, as well as Expression Blend, can import file formats from each of these designer-centric applications). In a nutshell, Expression Design is a tool that enables graphical artists to generate rich, vector-based graphics.

As you would expect, Expression Design allows a graphical designer to save their work in a variety of standard image formats (PNG, JPEG, GIF, TIFF, etc.). In addition, and for our purposes more interestingly, Expression Design also allows you to save your graphical data in WPF or Silverlight *XAML*.

As you may know, the Extensible Application Markup Language (XAML) is an XML-based grammar used to describe the state of a .NET object (graphically based or otherwise). For example, the following markup describes the look and feel for the vector image shown in Figure 1–1. Notice that we are able to create a pleasing drop shadow effect and a complex radial gradient brush used to fill the interior of the circle using just a few lines of XAML:

```
<Ellipse x:Name="shadowCircle" HorizontalAlignment="Left"
        Height="117.5" Margin="99,58,0,0" Stroke="#FF0B17D6"
        VerticalAlignment="Top" Width="117.5"
        StrokeThickness="7">
  <Ellipse.Effect>
    <DropShadowEffect Color="#FFB7B8E0" BlurRadius="6"
```

```
                        ShadowDepth="11"/>
    </Ellipse.Effect>
    <Ellipse.Fill>
      <RadialGradientBrush GradientOrigin="0.38,0.304">
        <GradientStop Color="#FF111EE0" Offset="0"/>
        <GradientStop Color="#FFC5C7E0" Offset="1"/>
        <GradientStop Color="#FF4750DA" Offset="0.526"/>
      </RadialGradientBrush>
    </Ellipse.Fill>
  </Ellipse>
```

Figure 1–1. The rendered output of the example XAML

By providing the ability to save a vector-based graphic as XAML, Expression Design makes it very simple for a developer to incorporate professional-looking graphics into an existing application, and interact with the data through code. For example, a graphical artist could create a stylized 2D maze for an interactive video game. Once saved as XAML, this data can be imported into an Expression Blend (or Visual Studio 2010) project and stylized further with animations, hit-testing support, and other features. You'll see how this is possible in Chapter 2.

The Role of Expression Blend

Now, as they say, on to the good stuff! Expression Blend is a key component for building a production-level WPF or Silverlight application. This tool will generate a vast amount of the XAML required by your programs. While you *could* author the same markup manually using numerous development tools (ranging from Notepad to Visual Studio 2010), you will most certainly suffer from massive hand cramps due to the verbose nature of XML-based grammars.

Well beyond the relatively simple XAML editing support provided by Visual Studio 2010, Expression Blend supplies sophisticated tools to lay out and configure controls, author complex animation sequences, create custom styles and templates, generate new UserControl[3] classes from existing vector graphics, visually design data templates, assign behaviors and visual states to user interface (UI) elements, and perform a host of other useful operations.

As you progress through the book, you will learn a great deal about using Expression Blend to build extremely expressive user interfaces for the Web (via Silverlight), the desktop (via WPF), and Windows Phone 7 (using, surprise!, Silverlight).

---

[3] A "user control" is a .NET class (with the associated XAML) that represents a chunk of reusable UI elements. You'll learn how to generate user controls via Expression Blend in Chapter 5.

Expression Blend Is Typically Only One Side of the Coin

While Expression Blend does ship with a simple, lightweight C# and VB code editor (seen later in this chapter), you most likely would not want to author all of your .NET code within this IDE as it is fairly limited in scope (for example, no debugging support). As luck would have it, an Expression Blend project has the *exact* same format as its Visual Studio counterpart. Thus, you could begin a new project with Expression Blend and design a fitting UI, and then open the same project in Visual Studio 2010 to implement complex code, interact with the debugger, and so forth.

To be sure, a vast majority of your WPF/Silverlight applications will make use of each IDE during the development cycle.[4] You'll examine the integrated code editor of Expression Blend and see the interplay with Visual Studio 2010 later in this chapter.

The Role of SketchFlow

In addition to providing the tools required to build rich user interfaces, Expression Blend also includes a suite of tools that enables you to rapidly prototype applications using *SketchFlow*.[5] This aspect of Expression Blend allows you to quickly and effectively mock up and define the flow of an application UI, screens layout, and application state transitions. Figure 1–2 shows a SketchFlow project loaded within the Expression Blend IDE.

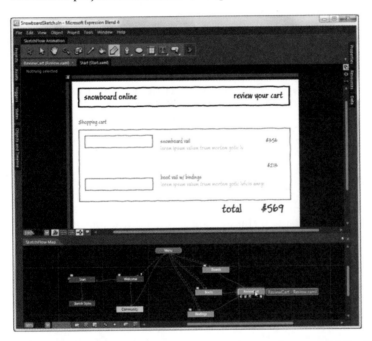

Figure 1–2. SketchFlow enables rapid prototyping of WPF and Silverlight applications.

---

[4] An Expression Blend project is able to integrate within the Visual Studio Team Foundation source control management system.

[5] SketchFlow is only included with Expression Studio Ultimate Edition.

Because SketchFlow is intended to be used during application prototyping, you can build UI mock-ups without being concerned with lower-level details, and can quickly adapt your prototypes in real time based on client feedback. This is made even easier given the freely distributable SketchFlow player, which ensures your prototypes can be demonstrated effectively to your client. Perhaps best of all, a SketchFlow project can become the starting point for a "real" WPF or Silverlight application. You will learn how to work with this facet of Expression Blend in Chapter 8.

The Expression Blend Project Templates

Now that you understand better the overall purpose of the members of the Microsoft Expression family, we can turn our attention to the various types of projects supported by the Expression Blend IDE. When you launch Expression Blend, you'll be greeted by default with the Blend Welcome Screen. Figure 1–3 shows the contents of the Help tab.

Figure 1–3. The Expression Blend Welcome Screen

As you can see, this Welcome Screen is divided into three tabs, Projects, Help, and Samples. For the time being, select the Projects tab, and click the New Project option. Once you do, you'll be presented with the New Project dialog box, shown in Figure 1–4.[6]

---

[6] Notice in Figure 1–4 that the mouse cursor is located over a vertical UI element that allows you to show or hide the leftmost project template tree view.

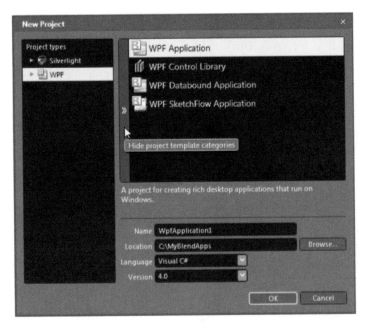

Figure 1–4. The Expression Blend New Project dialog box

Regardless of which project template you select, you will find that the New Project dialog box allows you to specify a name and location for your new project, as well as select between a C# or VB code base. Last but not least, you are able to configure your new project to target a specific version of the .NET (for WPF projects) or Silverlight platform.

■ **Note** In this book, I will assume you are making use of C# as you work through the various examples. If you would rather use VB, you should not have any difficulties mapping the minimal C# code into the syntax of VB.

WPF Project Templates

If you are interested in creating a new, rich desktop application for the Microsoft Windows operating system, chances are you'll be starting with a new WPF application. As of Blend 4, the WPF node of the New Project dialog box provides four starter templates, each of which is documented in Table 1–1.

Table 1–1. WPF Project Templates of Expression Blend

WPF Project Template	Meaning in Life
WPF Application	This template is for building a traditional desktop WPF executable.
WPF Control Library	This template is for creating reusable .NET class libraries that contains custom WPF controls. You will learn about building custom user controls (and styles/templates) in Chapter 5.
WPF Databound Application	This template is also for building a traditional desktop application, but it uses `View` and `ViewModel` objects (and the MVVM design pattern) to provide loose coupling between your presentation and data logic[7].
WPF SketchFlow Application	This template allows you to prototype a new WPF desktop application using SketchFlow (see Chapter 8).

Silverlight Project Templates

Table 1–2 documents the web-centric Silverlight project templates of Expression Blend, which can be viewed by clicking the Silverlight node of the New Project dialog box. As you can see, they are similar to their WPF counterparts.

Table 1–2. Silverlight Project Templates of Expression Blend

Silverlight Project Template	Meaning in Life
Silverlight Application + Website	This template is for creating a new Silverlight application and a corresponding web site project that hosts it.
Silverlight Application	This template is for creating a new Silverlight application. You will not get a full web site project with this option, but Blend will autogenerate a simple HTML test page (`Default.html`) when you run your project.
Silverlight Databound Application	This template is also for creating a Silverlight application, but it uses `View` and `ViewModel` objects (and the MVVM design pattern) to provide loose coupling between your presentation and data logic.
Silverlight Control Library	This template is for creating reusable .NET class libraries that contain custom Silverlight controls. You will learn about building custom user controls (and styles/templates) in Chapter 5.
Silverlight SketchFlow Application	This template allows you to prototype a new Silverlight application using SketchFlow (see Chapter 8).

---

[7] Chapter 6 will briefly examine this project type; however, detailed coverage of the MVVM design pattern is beyond the scope of this book.

Now, the good news is that a majority of the Blend IDE will remain the same, regardless of which of the project templates you select. Of course, always remember that WPF and Silverlight are not perfect carbon copies of each other. While they are both forged from the same technologies (XAML, a control content model, etc.), their codebases are not 100 percent compatible.

By way of one simple example, the WPF API provides support for full 3D vector graphics, whereas Silverlight ships with only simple (but still very useful) 3D perspective graphics. As well, WPF supports a deeper (or as some would say, more complex) model to handle UI cues via markup using triggers *or* the Visual State Manager (VSM), whereas Silverlight opts to deal with UI cues in XAML using the VSM (almost) exclusively.

Windows Phone Project Templates

At the time of this writing, Microsoft is preparing to launch the Windows Phone 7 family of mobile devices.[8] As you might already know, the native development platform of Windows Phone 7 is in fact Silverlight! Given this point, be aware that the Blend IDE (as well as Visual Studio 2010) can be updated to support a variety of Windows Phone 7 project templates via a free web download.

I'm sure that the next release of Expression Blend will ship with these templates preinstalled. In any case, Chapter 7 will introduce you to the topic of using Blend to build UIs for Windows Phone 7 devices, and at that time, I'll show you how to download and install the required SDK and project templates if they are not already on your development machine.

■ **Note** You will be happy to know that almost everything you will learn about using Blend to build a WPF or Silverlight project applies directly to a Windows Phone 7 project.

A Guided Tour of the Core Blend IDE

You will begin to build your own Expression Blend projects beginning in Chapter 2. For the time being, I will give you a tour of the key aspects of the IDE by loading one of the supplied sample projects. I feel this will be helpful in that you will be able to see a "real" project as you learn the lay of the land, and you will also have a much better idea of what sorts of applications you can create with WPF and Silverlight.

Assuming the New Project dialog box is still open on your screen, press the Esc key on your keyboard to return to the Blend Welcome Screen (if you already dismissed the New Project dialog box, you can open the Welcome Screen once again using the Help ➤ Welcome Screen menu option). In any case, click the Samples tab, shown in Figure 1–5, and notice you have a set of built-in sample projects.

---

[8] Consult www.microsoft.com/windowsphone for more information regarding Windows Phone 7.

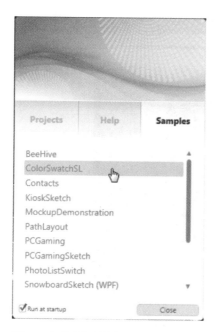

Figure 1–5. The Welcome Screen allows you to open a number of sample projects.

The exact list of sample projects you will see varies between different versions of Expression Blend, so don't be too alarmed if your list does not match Figure 1–5 to a tee. For this portion of the chapter, I will be using the Silverlight **ColorSwatchSL** sample project; however, you are free to load any project you wish to explore.

Loading a Blend Sample Project

Before we dive into the IDE, let me tell you how to run a Blend project so you can test how the application is coming along. When you press the F5 key, or the Ctrl+F5 keyboard combination, Blend will build and run your current project. If you are building a WPF application, the end result will typically be that a new window appears on your desktop. On the other hand, if you are building a new Silverlight application, you will find that your web browser will load up and display the hosting web page.

Go ahead and run the **ColorSwatchSL** project now. Notice that as you move your mouse over any of the colored strips, they pop forward via a custom animation. If you click any colored strip, a "details" area springs into view using another animation sequence. Figure 1–6 shows a possible test run.

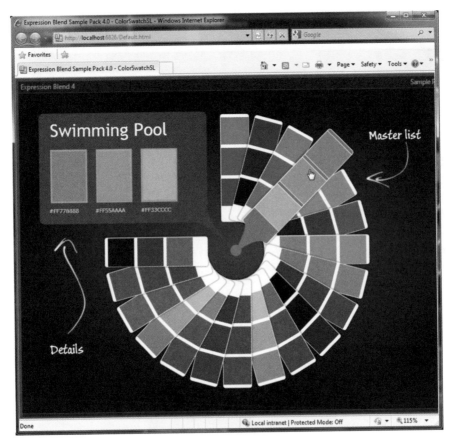

*Figure 1–6. The running **ColorSwatchSL** application*

Once you have finished testing the sample program, close your browser and return to Expression Blend.

The Artboard and Artboard Controls

The "artboard," located in the center of the IDE, is perhaps the most immediately useful aspect of Expression Blend, in that you will use this visual designer to create the look and feel of any WPF window or Silverlight user control. Figure 1–7 shows the artboard for the `MainControl.xaml` file of the current sample project.

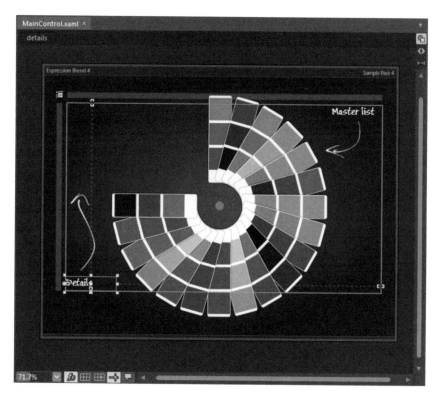

Figure 1–7. The artboard allows you to visually design the UI of a WPF or Silverlight application.

Mounted on the lower left of the artboard is a set of controls (not surprisingly, called the *artboard controls*; see Figure 1–8) that allows you to alter the general display of the designer surface.

Figure 1–8. The artboard controls allow you to configure basic aspects of your artboard designer.

Here is a rundown of the functionality found within the artboard controls area (and a few other important artboard tools).

Zooming the Artboard Display

Starting with the leftmost item in the artboard controls, we find a *zoom control*, which can be used to scale the size of the designer surface. As you play around with this control, you'll notice it is a fancy combo box that allows you to type in a specific value, select from a predefined list of values, and set the scale with the mouse by clicking and holding your left mouse button when the cursor is within the scale value (much like a scrollbar thumb). You will find that the ability to scale your current artboard is very useful when creating controls with custom content, creating data binding templates, and building custom styles (among other tasks).

Showing and Hiding Rendering Effects

The next item in the artboard controls looks like a mathematical function notation (fx) and can be used to turn off or on any "rendering effects" placed on a UI element on the designer. As you will see later in this book, Expression Blend ships with a large number of predefined visual effects (such as the drop shadow effect seen previously in Figure 1–1). As you are building rich UIs, you may occasionally want to hide such visual effects at design time, to more easily configure the basic UI. Given that this particular project is not making use of any visual effects, clicking this button will appear to do nothing (however, we will add a visual effect a bit later in this chapter).

Tweaking UI Positioning with Snap Grid

Next, we have three controls that allow you to set how the artboard should respond to item placement. If you click the "Show snap grid" button, a positioning grid will be overlaid on the designer surface. You can then toggle two related buttons on the artboard control, "Turn on snapping to gridlines" and "Turn on snapping to snaplines."

If snapping to gridlines is turned on, as you drag an object onto the artboard designer, the object will snap (or pull) toward the closest horizontal and vertical gridlines. This can be useful when you want to align a set of controls against a horizontal or vertical position.

The snapping to snaplines option is useful when you wish to ensure that two or more UI items are positioned relative to each other in a meaningful way. For example, if you have enabled snapping to snaplines, you could ensure that the text in two controls is positioned on the same horizontal line. This feature also allows you to "snap" controls into cells of a grid layout manager, or "snap" to a specified padding or margin value between related items.

Figure 1–9 shows an arbitrary example of working with the snap grid view and the snapping to snaplines option. To try things out first-hand, simply select the Master list text area on the designer and move it around the designer. Note how the designer behavior changes when you toggle on and off the various "snap-centric" options.

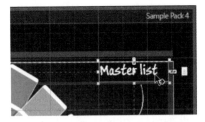

Figure 1–9. The snap-centric artboard controls allow you to establish how content is positioned within a layout manager.

Viewing Annotations

The final button on the artboard control area is used to view or hide Blend annotations. You can think of annotations as a Blend programmer's version of a sticky note. Using annotations, you can add textual notes to your current design, which can be particularly useful during the prototyping phase (see Chapter 8).

Currently, the **ColorSwatchSL** sample project does not have any annotations; go ahead and add one using the Tools ➤ Create Annotation menu option. Once you do, you can type in any sort of textual data (see Figure 1–10). After you have added a note or two, try toggling the Annotations button to view the end result.

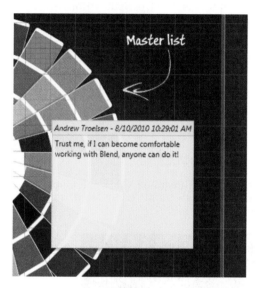

Figure 1–10. *Blend annotations allow you to document notes within your current design.*

Be aware that annotations are never visible when your program is running. Also, do know that the annotations you add to a Blend project will not be shown on the Visual Studio 2010 WPF or Silverlight designers, although a determined programmer can see the raw XAML that represents the annotation data. That's right, even annotations are stored as XAML. For example, the note shown in Figure 1–10 is realized as the following markup:

```
<Anno:AnnotationManager.Annotations>
  <Anno:Annotation AuthorInitials="AT" Author="Andrew Troelsen"
    Left="765.43" SerialNumber="1" Top="262.179"
    Timestamp="08/10/2010 15:30:55"
    Text="Trust me, if I can become comfortable working with Blend,
        anyone can do it!"/>
</Anno:AnnotationManager.Annotations>
```

On a final note, be aware that if you have a UI element selected on the designer *before* adding a new annotation, the annotation will be "connected" to the selected element. This will be useful when you want to make comments on (for example) a specific UI control or graphical data item. If you do not have a particular item selected before adding an annotation (meaning you have clicked an empty location on the artboard), it will serve as a "general" note that is not tied to a given UI element.

Viewing and Editing the Underlying XAML

If your primary role at your company is that of a graphical artist, you may not be terribly interested in viewing the XAML that Expression Blend is creating on your behalf. However, if you are a software developer who is making use of Blend, you'll be happy to know that the Blend IDE does provide a sophisticated XAML editor. Before you can view and modify this markup, you need to toggle from the Design button to either the XAML or Split button, which are all mounted on the upper-right area of your artboard (see Figure 1–11).

Figure 1–11. You can view your artboard data in design, XAML, or split mode.

Activate the Split view option. Once you do, you'll see the integrated XAML editor appear on the bottom of your artboard. As you can see in Figure 1–12, the XAML editor supports code completion and IntelliSense and provides useful help information.

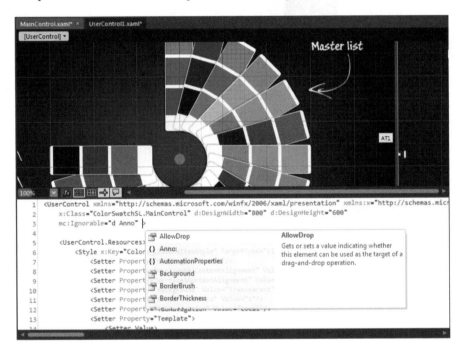

Figure 1–12. The Expression Blend XAML editor is quite feature rich.

That wraps up our look at the Expression Blend artboard. Next up, let's examine ways to view and configure the UI elements that populate the designer area.

The Objects and Timeline Panel

The next important aspect of the Blend IDE to consider is the *Objects and Timeline panel*, which is mounted on the left side of the IDE by default. This one panel serves two specific purposes. First and foremost, this panel shows you a visual treelike representation of the XAML for a given window or user control on the designer. The top node of the tree represents the entirety of the window (via the `<Window>` element) or user control (via the `<UserControl>` element), while the immediate child node represents the root layout manager, called `LayoutRoot` by default. Within this layout manager, you will find any number of contained UI elements that represent your current artistic vision (see Chapter 4 for details regarding layout managers and controls).

In Figure 1–13, notice that each node within the Objects and Timeline panel has an "eyeball" icon to the right, and to the right of the eyeball, a small circle. The eyeball control can be toggled to on or off, to show or hide aspects of your UI in the designer. This can be helpful when you have a complex nested layout system and only wish to see a smaller collection of controls. Understand that if you hide part of the UI, this is only realized on the Blend designer! You will always see the full markup rendered when running your project.

The small circle to the right of any given eyeball provides a way to lock an object (and any contained objects) in place, so that it cannot be edited on the visual designer. As you might guess, this can be useful when you have created the "perfect" UI element and want to make sure you do not accidentally alter it.

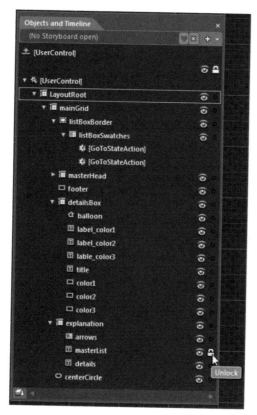

Figure 1–13. UI elements can be selectively hidden and locked.

Selecting Objects for Editing

Beyond simply viewing a tree of markup in a visual manner, the nodes in the Objects and Timeline panel provide a quick and easy way to select an item on the designer for editing. Take a moment or two to click various nodes within the tree and see which part of the artboard is selected for editing. Go ahead and do so now...I'll wait...this is actually a very important aspect of the panel and you will need to be comfortable using it.

Regarding the "Timeline" Aspect

Okay, that covers the "Objects" part of this panel, so what about the "Timeline" aspect? As it turns out, the Objects and Timeline panel also allows you to create *storyboard objects*, which contain animation instructions. Using this aspect of the panel, you can select a node in the tree and modify it in various ways (change its location, color, etc.). While you are doing so, your actions are recorded via the Expression Blend animation tools. The animation editor is very sophisticated and will be fully examined in Chapter 3. Until that point, we will only use the Objects and Timeline panel to view our markup, and select items for editing on the artboard.

The Properties Panel

Now that you understand how to select a UI element via the Objects and Timeline panel, you are ready to examine the *Properties panel*, which is located on the right side of the IDE by default. Similar to the Visual Studio 2010 Properties window, this aspect of the Blend IDE allows you to modify the selected item in a variety of manners. On a related note, if you modify a selected item on the artboard via your mouse (for example, relocating a control via a drag-and-drop operation), the related properties on the Properties panel are updated in turn. In either case, the underlying XAML is modified automatically by the IDE.

The Properties panel is broken up into various property categories, each of which can be expanded or collapsed independently. Now, the exact categories you will find in the Properties panel will change dynamically based on what you have currently selected on your designer.[9] For example, if you select the entire window or user control, you will see a good number of categories such as Brushes, Appearance, Layout, and Common Properties (among others). Figure 1–14 shows the categories (most of which I have collapsed) in the Properties panel if you select the topmost UserControl object within the Objects and Timeline panel.

---

[9] Also be aware that the exact categories seen in the Properties panel will differ based on which type of project you are working with (WPF, Silverlight, or Windows Phone 7).

Figure 1–14. *The Properties panel allows you to change the characteristics of the currently selected item.*

Naming and Finding Objects

Take a moment to look at the very top of the Properties panel, and you will find a Name text field. As you would suspect, this allows you to provide a value to the Name property of a given XAML element, so that you are able to manipulate it in your code. Right below this, you will find a very helpful Search text area, which will help you quickly locate a property by name (rather than hunting manually in each property category). To test this searching aspect out first-hand, begin to type in the value **height**. As you type, you will find all items that have a full or partial match (see Figure 1–15). When you clear the Search area of all text, you'll find that all property categories reappear[10].

---

[10] Friendly reminder: always clear a search when you are finished. I can't tell you how often I'd forget to do so and wonder why the Properties panel was showing me incorrect choices for a selected item on the artboard.

Figure 1–15. The Properties panel can be easily searched.

An Overview of Property Categories

As you work through the chapters of this book, you will be exposed to a number of important aspects of the Properties panel within the context of a given topic (graphics, layout and controls, animation, etc.). However, to whet your appetite, Table 1–3 documents the nature of some very common property categories, listed alphabetically.

Table 1–3. Common Categories of the Properties Panel

Blend Property Category	Meaning in Life
Appearance	This category controls general rendering settings, such as opacity, visibility, and the application of graphical effects (blurs, drop shadows, etc.).
Brushes	This category provides access to the visual brush editor.
Common Properties	This category contains properties common to most UI elements, including tool tips, tab index values, and the location of a data context (for data binding operations).
Layout	This category is used to edit properties that configure a control's physical dimensions (height, width, margins, and so on).
Miscellaneous	This category is basically the "everything else" section of the Properties panel. Most importantly, this category allows you to establish which style or template to apply to a selected item.
Text	This category enables you to configure textual properties for a selected item, such as font settings, paragraph settings, and indentations.
Transform	This category allows you to apply graphical transformations (rotations, angles, offsets, etc.) to a selected item.

Viewing Advanced Configuration Options

As you continue examining the Properties panel, you will notice that some of the categories have an expandable area mounted on the bottom. When you click this area, the category will expand to show you further (often times, more advanced or lesser used) properties of that category. Consider for example the expanded version of the Text category shown in Figure 1–16.

Figure 1–16. Some categories provide expandable subsections.

Speaking of advanced settings, you may have also noticed that some properties (in any given category) have a small square located to their extreme right side (see Figure 1–17). You can click this small square, called the Advanced options button, to open yet another editor for advanced settings for a *single property*. This is useful when you are working with data binding operations and object resources, and will be examined in later chapters of this book.

Figure 1–17. Some properties support advanced subsettings.

That should be enough information to orient you to working with the Properties panel. Again, you will be given many more details in the chapters ahead.

The Project Panel

The Project panel (located on the far left side of the IDE by default) will be very familiar to you if you have experience with the Microsoft Visual Studio IDE. Each time you make a new Expression Blend project, the tool will create a set of starter files (XAML files and code files) and automatically reference a set of necessary .NET libraries (aka assemblies). As you are creating your projects, you are free to insert additional types of files into your project and add references to additional .NET libraries. Furthermore, you can add new folders to a given project to contain related artifacts such as image files, sound clips, video files, and XML documents.

If you have loaded the **ColorSwatchSL** project, as I have, you will notice that your Project panel actually contains two projects. The first project contains the code files and libraries for the Silverlight application, while the second contains the files for the related hosting web page. Just like Visual Studio, Expression Blend uses a solution/project metaphor. A single solution can contain multiple projects, which collectively represent the application you are constructing. Consider Figure 1–18, which shows items for both projects and also illustrates the process of adding new items to a given project via a standard right-click mouse operation (we are not really adding anything to either project right now; I just wanted to illustrate the insertion operation).

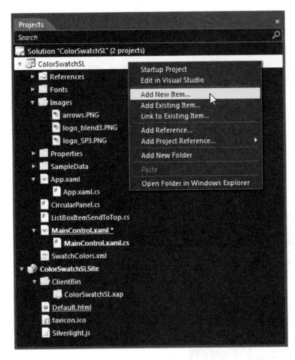

Figure 1–18. *The Project panel shows you a project-by-project and file-by-file breakdown of your current solution.*

The Integrated Code Editor

While XAML allows you to do some amazing things without ever writing a single line of C# or VB code, your projects will eventually need some code to drive their functionality. Earlier editions of the Expression Blend IDE did not ship with any sort of integrated code editor. Thus, if you were to double-click a given C# (`*.cs`) or VB (`*.vb`) code file within the Projects panel, Blend would automatically launch Visual Studio (or Notepad if Visual Studio was not installed).

Nowadays, Expression Blend does indeed have a useful code editor. To view this for yourself, double-click the `ListBoxItemSendToTop.cs` code file (or any code file of your choosing) found within the Project panel. The Blend code editor is useful when you wish to add some simple "stub" code for event handlers or author some simple test code during development and prototyping (as you will be doing for much of this book!).

As useful as this feature is, the Blend code editor is nowhere near as powerful as Visual Studio (nor should it be). For example, Blend does not provide an integrated debugger. It has no support for C# or VB code snippets, no support for code refactoring, and no support for the visual construction of class hierarchies. On the plus side, the Blend code editor does indeed support IntelliSense and code completion, as demonstrated in Figure 1–19.

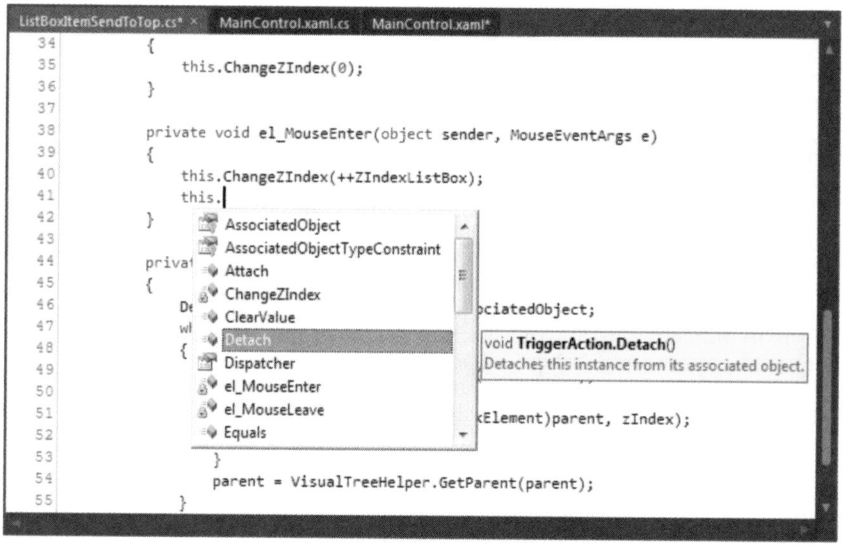

Figure 1–19. The Blend code editor allows you to add code during program creation.

Although this book is not focused on the construction of full-blown WPF or Silverlight applications, you will occasionally need to author code as you work through the examples to come. The code you will write will not be terribly complicated, but if you find the need for more assistance (such as an integrated debugger), don't forget that Blend and Visual Studio use the exact same solution/project format. You can very easily open a Blend project into Visual Studio to set breakpoints and author more sophisticated code.

The Results Panel

As you are manually typing code or markup, you may of course author some incorrect statements (misspell a keyword, forget to close an XAML element, use the wrong capitalization, or what have you). If you attempt to run your Blend application (via F5 or Ctrl+F5), the Results panel will show you a list of your current offences. If you double-click any error, Blend will open the related file and position your mouse at the location of the offending line of code or markup. Figure 1–20 shows my Results panel, identifying some errors I intentionally added to the **ColorSwatchSL** project.

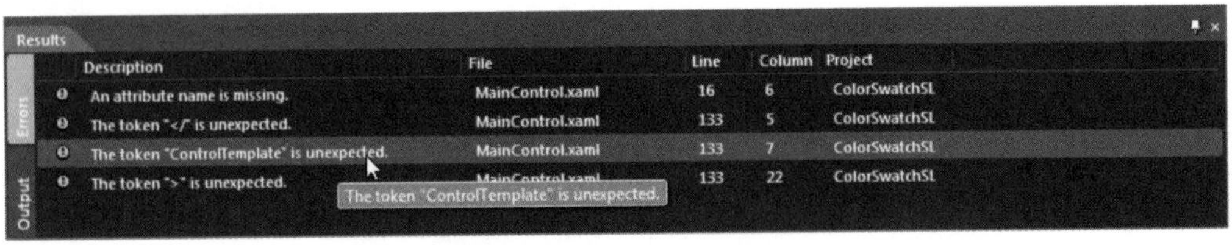

Figure 1–20. The Results panel will show you the error of your ways...

The Tools Panel

Now, close the current code file (if you are following along) and make sure you have opened an XAML file (such as `MainWindow.xaml`). By default, on the extreme left of the Blend IDE, you will find a vertical strip of buttons that may remind you of the Visual Studio toolbox (if you have background working with this product). This area is termed the *Tools panel*, and represents a collection of common UI elements (controls, layout managers, simple geometries, and so on) that you can select in order to build your user interfaces.

You will notice that some of the sections of the Tools panel have a small white triangle on the lower right. This is an indication that if you click and hold the topmost item, you will see a selection of related items. For example, in Figure 1–21, you can see that when I click and hold on the Rectangle tool, the Ellipse and Line tool pop up as additional options (be aware that the Tools panel looks slightly different depending on whether you are working on a WPF or Silverlight project. Also note I have mounted my Tools panel to the top of my IDE, not the left-hand side).

Figure 1–21. Some items on the Tools panel group related options.

As you work through the next few chapters, you will have a chance to work with a number of different tool items, during examination of various topics. For the time being, I'd like to focus on the following aspects of the Tools panel:

- The Selection and Direct Selection tools

- The Zoom and Pan tools

- The Assets library

Basically, we will be looking at the aspects of your Tools panel that are shown in Figure 1–22; I blurred out the buttons that we will not examine, for the time being. The first tools of the Tools panel we will examine are the selection tools. However, to understand the difference between a "select" and "direct select," we first need to add a bit of new content to the current **ColorSwatchSL** sample project for illustrative purposes.

Figure 1–22. We will examine these aspects of your Tools panel over the next few sections.

Adding Custom Content to the Sample Project

To begin adding custom content to the sample project, select the LayoutRoot node of the tree in the Objects and Timeline panel, as you will be adding a new object on the main layout manager. Next, locate the Pencil tool on your Tools panel, which can be found as a subitem under the Pen tool (see Figure 1–23; you can also press the Y key as a hot key to select the Pencil tool).

Figure 1–23. Select the Pencil tool from the Tools panel.

Use your mouse to draw a random, enclosed geometric shape somewhere on an open area of the designer (any shape, size, and location will be fine). Ensure that your new geometric shape is selected in the Objects and Timeline panel (it will be defined in the tree as a [Path] node), and then use the Properties panel to give your new shape a proper name via the Name text field at the top of the Properties panel (I called mine myPolygon). Finally, use the Brushes editor (located in the Brushes properties category) to give your shape a solid color. To do so, just click the color editor directly (Chapter 2 will examine the Brushes editor in detail). Figure 1–24 shows one possible rendering.

Figure 1–24. A simple polygon rendered with the Pencil tool

We will interact with this object through code in just a bit, but for now, you'll learn more about the Tools panel itself.

The Selection and Direct Selection Tools

The Tools panel contains two different tools for selecting an item on the artboard, specifically the Selection tool and the Direct Selection tool.[11] If you are like me, I am sure you are already wondering why we have two tools to "select" an item. Well, if you are simply trying to select an item on the artboard so that you can reposition it within your window or user control, or wish to change the size of the item using the designer's pull handles, you want to use a *selection* (i.e., the first, black pointer; press V as a shortcut to activate the Selection tool). Activate the Selection tool now, and verify you can move and resize your custom graphical data around the artboard.

In contrast, if you want to select the *individual segments* that constitute a geometric shape, or if you want to edit complex internal content of a `ContentControl` derived class (see Chapter 3), you want a *direct selection* (i.e., the second, white pointer). Press the shortcut key for the Direct Selection tool (the A key), and notice that you can now alter each segment of your polygon (see Figure 1–25).

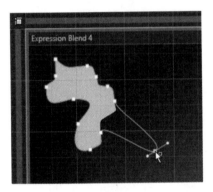

Figure 1–25. *A direct selection allows you to edit segments of a path, or complex content of a control.*

Once you have modified your geometry, click the Selection tool again, to verify you can now move your shape around the designer surface once again. Next, go back into Direct Selection mode, change a segment, and return to Selection mode. Get used to this back and forth toggle of Selection (V shortcut key) and Direct Selection (A shortcut key)—you'll be doing this a lot!

The Zoom and Pan Tools

Earlier in the chapter, you learned that you can use the mouse wheel to zoom the data in the artboard. You also learned that the artboard control area provides an alternative method to zoom the data on the artboard. Now for a third approach: the Zoom tool (Z is the shortcut key).

Select this item on the Tools panel (it's the one that looks like a magnifying glass), and then click anywhere on your artboard to zoom in. If you hold the Alt key while clicking, you will zoom back out. Finally, if you double-click the Zoom tool on the Tools panel, the data in the artboard will rescale to the original size as defined in the XAML definition.

---

[11] I must admit, when I first started to work with Expression Blend, I spent far too much time trying to figure out the difference between these two selection tools. It really drove me crazy!

The Pan tool (the one that looks like a hand) provides an alternative to using the Ctrl key and mouse wheel combination, in that when you select this tool (H is the shortcut key), you can click and drag your artboard around to position the area rendered in the artboard. The Pan tool is most useful when you have zoomed deeply into some complex graphical data, and need to move to a specific location to edit embedded content.

The Assets Library (and the Assets Panel)

The Blend Tools panel does not show you every single possible WPF or Silverlight control that could be used to create a UI. When you are looking for additional UI elements, you will want to use the Assets library, which you can open by clicking the final (rightmost) button in the Tools panel (which looks like a double greater-than sign, >>). As shown in Figure 1–26, the Assets library organizes its contents into several high-level categories.

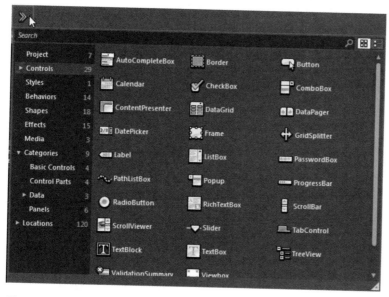

Figure 1–26. The Assets library shows you a number of WPF and Silverlight assets.

Table 1–4 explains the overall role for each category.

Table 1–4. Categories of the Blend Assets Library

Assets Library Category	Meaning in Life
Project	This category shows all of the custom assets that you have added to your current application (image files, custom styles, sound files, video files, etc.).
Controls	This category displays all WPF/Silverlight UI controls that you can use to build a user interface.
Styles	This category shows you any custom styles that you have created for the current project.
Behaviors	This category contains behaviors, which are objects that allow you to capture common events in your markup without the need to author custom C# or VB code. You'll learn about behaviors beginning in Chapter 3.
Shapes	This category contains prerendered geometries that you can add to a program (hexagons, callouts, stars, etc.). They can help you add standard shapes more quickly than when working with the Pen and Pencil tools.
Effects	This category contains effects, which allow you to alter the look and feel of a UI element in various manners. Recall that the *fx* button of the artboard controls area allows you to toggle effects on or off.
Media	This category is similar to the Project category in that you can view your custom project assets, but the Media category only shows image, audio, or video files.
Categories	This category groups all the assets of your current project by subcategories. This allows you to quickly view (for example) all the controls used by the project, all controls using data binding, and so forth.
Locations	This category shows you all the .NET libraries (assemblies) that contain the various assets used by WPF and Silverlight projects.

Because working with assets is so common, the Blend IDE actually provides a second way to view the exact same information, named the Assets panel (see Figure 1–27). Personally, I find myself using the Assets panel more than the Assets library, as this area is always on the screen and will not hide from view like the Assets library, but you should use whichever approach you find most useful.

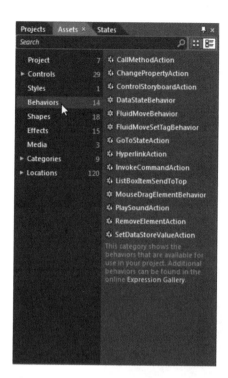

Figure 1–27. *The Assets panel is another way to locate items in the Assets library.*

Let's take the Assets panel (or Assets library) out for a spin. First, use the Objects and Timeline panel and ensure that the LayoutRoot object is selected in the tree. Now, select the Star object in the Shapes category of the Assets panel, and draw a small star next to your custom geometry (see Figure 1–28), and use the Properties panel to name your object myStar.

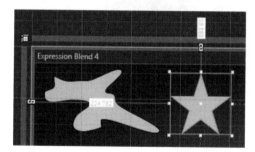

Figure 1–28. *Adding a second geometry to the layout manager*

Now, select your LayoutRoot object in the Objects and Timeline panel once again, and locate the Ripple effect in the Assets panel (remember, you can type in the name of an item in the Search area to quickly locate it). Drag the Ripple effect onto the LayoutRoot node using a standard drag-and-drop mouse operation (see Figure 1–29).

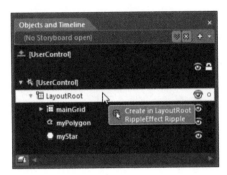

Figure 1–29. Adding a "ripple effect" to the entire layout manager and all its child objects

Once you add this effect, the artboard shows a very different view of the UI layout (see Figure 1–30)!

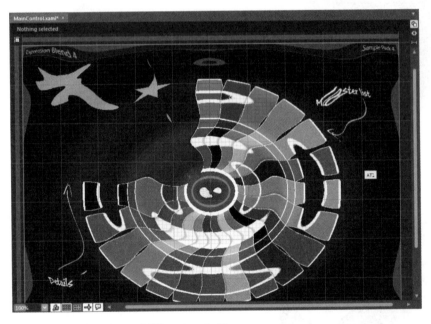

Figure 1–30. Showing or hiding visual effects

To be sure, you will use the Assets library as you work through this text, so don't bother trying to memorize each category. Next up, let's see how we can use the integrated code editor to add some interactivity.

Handling and Implementing Events

To wrap up our modification of the **ColorSwatchSL** sample project, locate the myPolygon object in the Objects and Timeline panel. Next, go to the Properties panel and click the Events button at the top of the editor (look for the button with the lightning bolt symbol; see Figure 1–31) to open the Events editor.

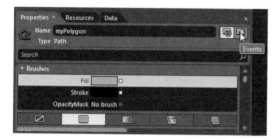

Figure 1–31. You can handle events for objects via the Properties panel.

Once you have clicked the Events button, locate an event named MouseLeftButtonDown. Type in the name of a method that will be called when the user clicks the left mouse button within your custom polygon (myPolygonMouseDown is a good name; see Figure 1–32).

Figure 1–32. Entering the name for an event handler

Once you type in your name, press the Enter key on the keyboard. This will open the code editor window. Update your code with the following logic, which will disable the visual effect on the layout manager:

```
private void myPolygonMouseDown(object sender,
  System.Windows.Input.MouseButtonEventArgs e)
{
  // Remove the ripple visual effect.
  LayoutRoot.Effect = null;
}
```

Now, handle the LeftMouseButtonDown event on the star geometry using the same series of steps, but this time call your method myStarMouseDown. Update the starter code with the following:

```
private void myStarMouseDown(object sender,
  System.Windows.Input.MouseButtonEventArgs e)
{
  // Try adding a different effect!
  LayoutRoot.Effect =
    new System.Windows.Media.Effects.BlurEffect();
}
```

Next, run your application (press F5 or Ctrl+F5). When the application first runs, you will find the "ripple" effect. However, if you click either of your two geometries, you can toggle between no visual effects or a blur visual effect. Not bad for two lines of code! Of course, few of your WPF or Silverlight applications will need to ripple or blur out the entire UI. You'll see how visual effects can help you build more useful projects later in the book.

■ **Source Code** The ColorSwatchSL_Modified project can be found under the Chapter 1 folder.

Customizing the Options of the Blend IDE

I'd like to point out a few ways in which you can customize the Blend IDE. First of all, the Tools ➤ Options menu can be used to establish general preferences for the Blend IDE, such as the font to use in the code editor, the default settings for a new artboard, default names and initials for annotations, and other basic settings. One setting in particular you may be interested in can be found in the Workspace section of the Options dialog box, which allows you to pick between a "light" or "dark" theme for the Blend IDE (see Figure 1–33).

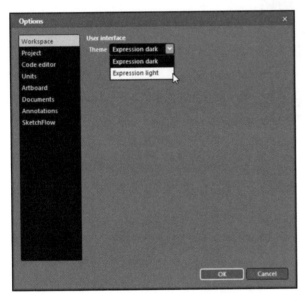

Figure 1–33. The Options dialog box allows you to configure various IDE settings.

Creating a Custom Workspace Layout

Beyond tweaking options in the Options dialog box, also be aware that every panel of the Blend IDE (Tools, Properties, Objects and Timeline, etc.) can be positioned anywhere within the IDE. For example, if you want to have the Tools panel mounted on the top of the IDE (rather than on the left side), all you need to do is position your mouse on the "grab area" above the selected panel, and attach it to the top part of your IDE using a standard mouse drag-and-drop operation (try to do that now).

Other panels don't have a "grab area," but they can also be repositioned by clicking and dragging the tab of the panel. For example, click (and hold) the Properties tab of the Properties panel and drag it to one of the sides of the IDE (or to another panel tab to integrate it within a current set of tabs). Again, give it a try.

Once you have positioned your panels in a way that suits your fancy, you may wish to save it as a custom workspace using the Window ➤ Save as New Workspace menu option. Once you select this menu item, you can give your workspace a name (via the resulting dialog box) and then find it from the list of workspaces under the Window ➤ Workspaces menu option (see Figure 1–34).

Figure 1–34. Locating and loading a custom workspace

You'll notice that the top two choices of the Window ➤ Workspaces menu option list the two standard workspaces of Blend, Design and Animation. If you ever lose your way, and make your IDE fantastically confusing, you can "roll back" to the out-of-the-box look and feel simply by selecting the Design workspace.

The Expression Blend Documentation System

To wrap up this first chapter, I must point out that the Expression Blend product ships with a dedicated User Guide, which you can access using the Help ➤ User Guide menu option. This documentation system will be a very useful companion as you work through this text. For example, in the User Guide, you can find a section that documents each and every keyboard shortcut (highlighted in Figure 1–35), read tutorials on various aspects of the IDE, learn the details of SketchFlow, and more.

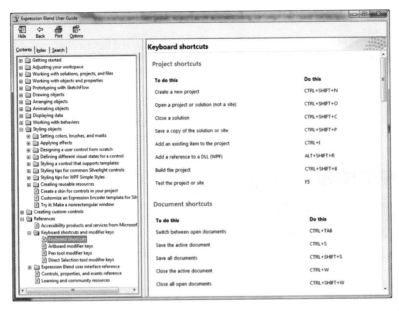

Figure 1–35. The Blend documentation is very useful, and should be consulted often!

I'll point out various aspects of the help system throughout the book, but you should do yourself a favor and take the time to dig into the Expression Blend documentation on your own. You will thank yourself later!

Summary

That wraps up the introductory look at the Blend IDE. The point of this chapter was to get you comfortable with the key components of the Blend IDE (as they say, the journey of a thousand miles begins with a single step). First, you learned the role of each member of the Expression line of produces (Web, Encoder, Design, and Blend). After that, we quickly moved into an initial exploration of the Blend IDE through the use of a canned sample project.

The artboard panel is the primary designer area for any new WPF or Silverlight project. Using the Tools panel, Assets library (or the related Assets panel), and Properties panel, you can add UI elements to the root layout manager and configure them.

The Objects and Timeline panel is a very key aspect of working with the Blend IDE, in that it shows you the underlying XAML markup in a familiar tree-like visual display. Recall that you can select a node in the tree to quickly select it on the artboard for editing. Later in this book, you will learn how you can use the Objects and Timeline panel to create sophisticated animation sequences.

Blend has two integrated code editors. If you switch to the XAML editor, you can manually type in markup to describe your UI, or simply tweak the XAML generated by the IDE. If you double-click a C# or VB code file within the Projects panel, you can open the source code editor, which can be very useful when you wish to add some simple starter code for generated event handlers. Remember, however, that a majority of the C#/VB code will most likely be authored using Visual Studio 2010, which has the exact same format as a Blend project.

In the next chapter, you will explore the role of interactive vector graphics, which will be a key ingredient for any WPF or Silverlight application.

CHAPTER 2

■■■

Vector Graphics and Object Resources

This chapter explores the various tools that Expression Blend provides to help you create interactive, vector-based graphics. You will begin by learning about the core drawing tools of the Blend IDE (Pen, Pencil, the Brushes editor, etc.). Along the way, you will also learn how to stylize the "pen" used to render the border of a geometric rendering, how to apply visual effects, and how to incorporate graphical data authored via Expression Design.

Next, you will explore various tools and techniques that allow you to work with graphical transformations and 3D graphics within the Blend IDE. At this time, you will quickly notice that WPF and Silverlight both support various degrees of 3D graphic processing, and you will evaluate each option.

The chapter wraps up with a seemingly unrelated topic, that of *object resources*. As you will see, object resources are named blobs of markup, which can be reused across applications. The Blend IDE has a number of ways to manage your resources, edit existing resources, and create new resources. While vector graphics are one of the most common types of object resource, as you work through the remainder of this book, you will also learn how to capture other types of graphical content (styles, templates, etc.) as reusable object resources.

The Realm of Vector Graphics

WPF and Silverlight applications render all graphical data using *vector-based graphics*. Use of vector graphics is not limited to custom geometric patterns that you construct using the Pen or Pencil tool, however. As it turns out, each of these APIs renders user interface controls (buttons, text boxes, menus, grids full of data, etc.) and textual information using vector-based graphics as well.

Vector graphics provide numerous benefits, the first of which is resolution independence. When you build a WPF or Silverlight application, you can rest assured that the UI data (as well as your custom graphical data) will be viewed clearly regardless of the size of the viewing screen. For example, if your Silverlight application is running on a Windows Mobile 7 phone, the UI will scale appropriately for the small screen. If this same Silverlight application is running out of the browser on a user's desktop, it will scale cleanly regardless of specific monitor resolution settings.

Use of vector-based graphics for UI controls (and the layout managers that contain them) is especially powerful. For example, you could define with just a few lines of markup a `StackPanel` of controls that is rendered at a 45-degree angle, or upside down, or on a 3D plain. As well, WPF and Silverlight both support numerous visual effects (drop shadows, swirls, blur effects, etc.) that can be applied to vector-based data, with no fear of degrading the final rendered output.

As you work through this chapter, you will see that Expression Blend supports a number of tools to create, modify, and transform vector-based graphics. While many of your WPF and Silverlight applications may only require the drawing tools Blend provides, you might need to create highly detailed graphical data, which could be quite tedious if you were using Blend alone. Thankfully, Expression Design (examined later in this chapter) provides a full set of powerful graphical rendering tools, similar in scope to Adobe Illustrator. As you will see, it is possible for a graphical artist to export Expression Design data as XAML and incorporate (and interact with) the markup in a Blend (or Visual Studio 2010) project.

Use of Graphical Data Is Pervasive

If you are coming to WPF or Silverlight from a different UI framework, such as Windows Forms, ASP.NET, or whatnot, you might wonder if you *really* will need to work with graphical data. For example, you may think that a typical business application (full of menu systems, grids of data, and custom dialog boxes) will not need too much graphical flare. While this might be somewhat true, be very aware that the use of vector graphics runs deep in WPF and Silverlight, and will pop up in unexpected places.

For example, understanding how to manipulate graphics is essential if you need to build a custom style for a set of controls. You will also use graphics (and animations) if you intend to create control templates, customize a data binding operation (via a data binding template), or incorporate visual cues for your end user (such as a glowing effect for the active text entry area). Furthermore, as you will see later in this book, Expression Blend provides a number of techniques to generate custom controls on-the-fly using a vector graphic as a starting point.

So, although you may not need to define a random green circle (or what have you) too often in your WPF and Silverlight applications, understanding how to manipulate graphical data is the foundation for many real-world operations. To get the ball rolling, let's see how we can use Expression Blend to generate custom vector-based geometries using a set of core drawing tools.

Exploring the Core Drawing Tools

The Blend IDE defines a set of five basic tools that allows you to create simple vector-based geometries; specifically, this set includes the Pen, Pencil, Ellipse, Rectangle, and Line tools, all of which you can find on your Tools panel (see Chapter 1). To illustrate these tools (and a number of related topics, such as the Brushes editor), launch Expression Blend and create a new WPF application or Silverlight application project named **BlendDrawingTools**. It really does not matter which type of project you create, as these basic drawing tools work identically for WPF and Silverlight projects. For this example, I will opt for a WPF application (see Figure 2–1).

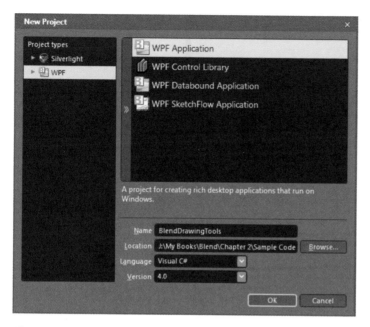

Figure 2–1. Creating a new WPF application project

Working with the Pencil Tool

In the previous chapter, you examined the Pen and Pencil tools from a high level. Recall that the Pencil tool allows you to create a freehand line drawing. The Pen tool, on the other hand, allows you to create arcs and a set of connected points. Locate these tools on your Tools panel (see Figure 2–2) and select the Pencil tool (Y is the shortcut key for the Pencil tool).

Figure 2–2. The Pen and Pencil tools

Using the Pencil tool, draw a random geometry or two on the artboard by holding down the left mouse button and moving your mouse cursor. You'll notice that a pixel is rendered wherever the Pencil tool is placed. You can use this tool to define a random unconnected geometry, or to connect the starting and ending points to create a unique polygon.

Once you are finished drawing a few shapes of your liking, enable the Direct Selection tool (A is the shortcut key). Recall from Chapter 1 that when you "direct select" a shape, you are able to modify the individual points that represent the overall graphic (see Figure 2–3). In contrast, recall that the Selection tool (V is the shortcut key) allows you to select an item as a whole to reposition, resize, or transform the selected UI element.

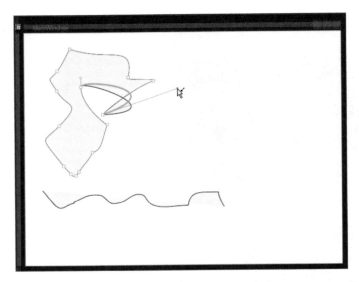

Figure 2–3. Recall that the Direct Selection tool allows you to modify path points of a geometry.

Working with the Pen Tool

Whereas working with the Pencil tool is quite straightforward, working with the Pen tool is surprisingly more sophisticated. Select the Pen tool using the P shortcut key. The key difference between the Pen and Pencil tools is that the Pen tool will *not* record pixel data with each mouse movement. Rather, you use the Pen tool to create a set of connected line segments, each based on a single mouse click.

To illustrate, find an empty area on your artboard and click five or six times with the Pen tool. You'll see that each click-point results in a new line segment. Once you have rendered a set of line segments, you can use the Pen tool in a few additional ways to modify the path. For example, if you hold down the Alt key while using the Pen tool, you can select (and hold) an existing click-point and transform a line segment into an arc segment while moving your mouse (again, with the Alt key pressed; try this out yourself, as shown in Figure 2–4).

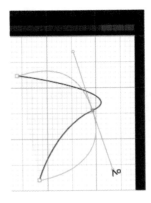

Figure 2–4. Using the Pen tool + Alt allows you to change line segments to arcs.

Also be aware that if you select the Pen tool and place the mouse cursor on top of an existing click-point, the Pen cursor will change to show a small minus symbol. When you click a point, it will be removed from the path. If you wish to add an additional click-point to a geometry, simply click a given location of the current line segment.

The Pen tool responds to a number of other keystroke operations that allow you to further modify a path. Look up the topic *Pen tool, modifiers* using the Index tab of the Expression Blend User Guide for full details (see Figure 2–5).

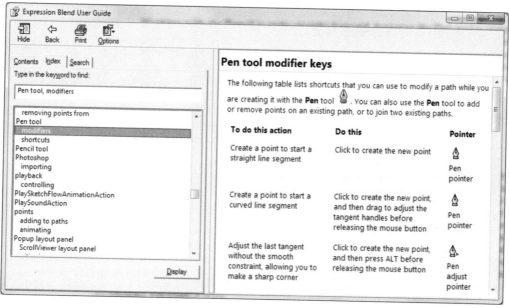

Figure 2–5. *The full set of Pen tool modifiers is documented in the Expression Blend User Guide.*

The Result of Using the Pen and Pencil Tools

When you create new geometries using the Pen and Pencil tools, Blend captures your mouse and keyboard operations to build a new `Path` object. WPF and Silverlight both provide a set of classes that represent common geometric shapes; all of these classes are located within the `System.Windows.Shapes` namespace. The `Path` class defines a property named `Data`, which ultimately contains a collection of various "geometry objects," which define the size and shape of a given item. For example, WPF and Silverlight both provide classes such as `RectangleGeometry`, `EllipseGeometry`, `PathGeometry`, and so forth.

However, if you view the underlying XAML for the `Path` objects Blend has created, you will *not* find these expected geometry objects, but instead will find that the `Data` property is set to a lengthy string value (containing several alphabetic tokens such as `M`, `C`, and `Z`) such as the following:

```
<Path Data="M254,101 C297.83333,110.83333 330.5,191.50008 385.5,130.5
    440.5,69.499921 456.83333,142.5 492.5,148.5 419.5,159.83333
    229.5,236.5 273.5,182.5 317.5,128.5 242.83333,164.5 227.5,155.5 z"
    Fill="#FFF4F4F5" Margin="227.5,101,130.5,0"
    Stretch="Fill" Stroke="Black" Height="101.57"
    VerticalAlignment="Top"/>
```

This lengthy string is a very compact form for describing the geometry objects used to render a `Path` object (often termed the "path mini-language"). Mercifully, you never need to manually tinker with this string data. All you need to know is that within this terse string are a number of rendering instructions that the `Path` object will use to render its output[1].

■ **Note** When you export custom graphical data using Expression Design, the XAML does not use the path modeling language, but instead uses the larger object model. Typically, this is exactly what you require, as the geometry objects can be easily manipulated in code.

Working with the Rectangle, Ellipse, and Line Tools

While you could use the Pen and Pencil tools to create any sort of geometry, Blend does provide a set of tools that generates some standard shapes. Using the Rectangle (M shortcut key), Ellipse (L shortcut key), and Line (\ shortcut key) tools is very straightforward, but note the following points of interest:

- If you hold the Alt key after selecting one of these drawing tools, the center point of the geometry will be at the first point where you click, rather than the top-left corner.

- If you hold the Shift key when drawing with the Rectangle tool or Ellipse tool, the height and width values will be identical.

- If you hold the Shift key when using the Line tool, the angle of the line will be constrained to multiples of 15 degrees. This makes it easy to draw a perfectly straight line at various angles.

Once you have rendered a geometry with any of these tools, you can use the Selection and Direct Selection tools to modify its size and position. As well, if you place the mouse cursor just outside of a given "pull point," you can apply some simple transformations (skews and rotations in particular). I'll talk more about graphical transformations later in this chapter; however, consider Figure 2–6, which illustrates how you can rotate a rendered `Rectangle` object via the corner pull point.

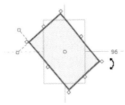

Figure 2–6. The artboard allows you to apply various transformations to selected items.

---

[1] If you are so interested, the .NET 4.0 SDK documentation describes the details of the path mini-language. Simply do a search for *path markup syntax*.

Working with the Shapes Section of the Assets Library

In addition to using the Rectangle, Line, and Ellipse tools to create the corresponding standard shapes, you can use the Assets library's (see Chapter 1) Shapes section,[2] which defines a number of useful preset geometries. As you can see in Figure 2–7, you can select various arrows, callouts, and other common shapes (triangles, pentagons, etc.).

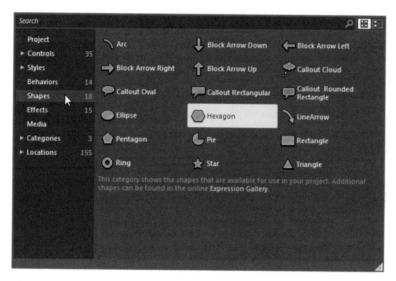

Figure 2–7. The Assets library provides a number of additional stock geometries.

By way of a simple test, select the Star tool within the Assets library. You will then find that this tool appears in the "last selected" area of the Tools panel (see Figure 2–8).

■ **Note** Chapter 1 first introduced the role of the Assets library on your Tools panel (the >> icon). However, allow me to repeat the previous point: When you select an item from the Assets library, the previously selected item will appear directly after the >> icon. This is a handy way to nab an item of interest for further use.

Figure 2–8. Items selected in the Assets library appear in the "last selected" area of the Tools panel.

---

[2] This is a new feature of Blend 4. Earlier versions of this tool did not contain a set of common shapes.

When you use these additional shapes, you will indirectly add a reference to a new library named `Microsoft.Expression.Drawing.dll`. This library defines some additional classes for these specialized geometries. For example, the Star tool uses a class named `RegularPolygon`. The various "callout" shapes are represented by the `Callout` class. Thus, if you were to add a star and a rectangular callout to your artboard, you would find that the new items highlighted in Figure 2–9 appear in the Objects and Timeline panel.

Figure 2–9. The shapes within the Assets library are represented by unique classes.

■ **Note** The Expression SDK assemblies can be referenced within a Visual Studio project as well via the .NET tab of the Add References dialog box. Furthermore, the Expression Blend SDK assemblies will be deployed as private assemblies by default, so your output directory will contain local copies of these libraries.

Modifying a Shape Using the Appearance Editor

All of the shapes we have examined so far (rectangle, star, line, etc.) can be selected and configured using the Blend Properties panel. Of course, based on which item you select on the artboard, you will see a set of unique properties. While this is true, the Properties panel does have a few settings that are common to all geometries.

For example, let's say you drew a shape using the Star tool. If you select this item on the designer and locate the Appearance section of the Properties panel, you will see ways to configure the stroke thickness to be used to render the border and the level of transparency (via the `Opacity` property). For the star geometry, you will also see some specific properties such as `PointCount` and `InnerRadius` (see Figure 2–10).

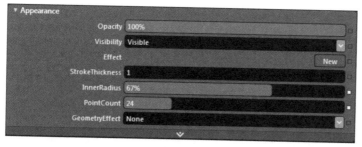

Figure 2–10. The Appearance editor shows you a number of common, and object-specific, properties.

If you were to select a rectangular callout object on the artboard, you would see that the Appearance editor now shows various properties for this particular class (such as CalloutStyle). Figure 2–11 shows customized star and callout objects after changing various settings within the Appearance editor.

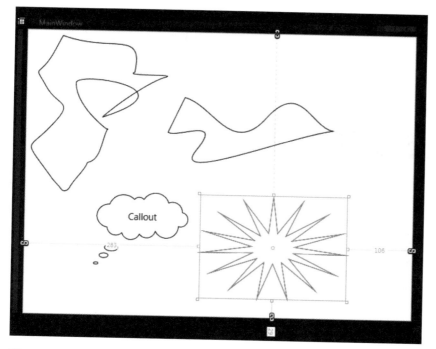

Figure 2–11. Some customized shapes

To be sure, the Appearance editor will change its contents based on which item you select on the artboard. This is true for each editor within the Properties panel. As you work through this text, you'll see a number of settings you can tweak using the Properties panel; however, the best advice I can give you is to select an item of interest on the artboard, and examine your configuration options in the Properties panel first-hand.

■ **Note** If you select multiple items on the artboard via a Shift+click operation, you will only see the common properties of the selected items. This can be handy when you want (for example) to set identical height and width values for multiple items.

Coloring a Shape Using the Brushes Editor

The Brushes editor of the Properties panel allows you to configure the colors to use when drawing the border of a UI element as well as the color to use to fill the interior of a UI element. This editor can be used for any UI element, including shapes, controls, layout managers, or an entire WPF `Window` object or Silverlight `UserControl` object. Regardless of which type of item you are configuring, the overall operations of the Brushes editor remain the same, so for this example, let's assume we are interested in modifying the colors used to render a hexagon added to the artboard via the Shapes section of the Assets library.

Viewing Brush-Centric Properties

The topmost area of the Brushes editor will show a list of "brush-centric" properties for the item selected on the artboard. In Figure 2–12, you can see that the hexagon (or, more specifically, the underlying `RegularPolygon` object) supports three such properties, `Fill`, `Stroke`, and `OpacityMask`. You can click any one of these properties to configure the related brush to be used.

Figure 2–12. *The topmost area of the Brushes editor shows you brush-centric properties of the selected item.*

Selecting the No Brush Option

Directly below this area, you will find five selectable tabs (see Figure 2–13 for a visual), which allow you to pick a general brush type. Starting at the left is the No brush option, which you can use to configure a brush-centric property to use what is essentially a transparent brush. If you select this option, the item selected on the artboard will show the elements beneath it in Z-order.

Defining a Solid-Colored Brush

Next to the No brush option is the "Solid color brush" option, which allows you to set a single solid color for the selected property using an intuitive color editor. Figure 2–13 illustrates using this solid-colored brush editor to set the `Fill` property of the hexagon to a shade of aqua.

Figure 2–13. Configuring a solid-colored brush

Be sure you take a moment or two to tinker with the various aspects of this solid-colored brush editor. For example, the Color Eyedropper tool mounted on the lower right of the color editor (see Figure 2–14) allows you to capture the color of any item you click, even items outside of the Blend IDE! For example, let's say you wanted to get the color of a given folder on your Windows desktop. You could select the Color Eyedropper tool and then click the item of interest directly on your desktop.

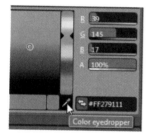

Figure 2–14. The Color Eyedropper tool allows you to pick up the color of any item you click.

Defining a Gradient Brush

The next brush type is a *gradient brush*. This allows you to define a brush that is composed of a set of colors, which blend together to paint the surface. Select one of your shapes on the artboard, and then pick the `Fill` property on the Brushes editor. From here, click the Gradient brush option (see Figure 2–15).

Figure 2–15. The gradient brush editor

By default, you will be given two gradient stops (which represent the first two colors; black and white by default) for any gradient brush, both of which are represented by the thumb-slider controls mounted on either end of the gradient stop editor. If you click either thumb, you can change the color to use for that portion of the gradient using the color selector. As well, you can move any thumb along the gradient stop editor to control the starting and stopping values of the gradient. Consider Figure 2–16, which shows one possible configuration for these first two gradients.

Figure 2–16. Configuring gradient stops

If you wish to add additional gradient stops, simply click anywhere within the gradient stop editor. Figure 2–17 shows a gradient brush that now makes use of four gradient stops, each configured to use a unique color.

Figure 2–17. To add additional gradient stops, simply click in the gradient stop editor.

■ **Note** If you want to delete a gradient stop, click (and hold) the offending thumb and drag it off the gradient stop editor.

Another aspect of the gradient stop editor to be aware of is that, mounted on the lower left, you have two buttons that allow you to select a radial or linear gradient brush. As you would guess, these buttons control whether the colors blend in a circular or linear manner. Directly next to these buttons is a final button that allows you to reverse all existing gradient stops (handy!). See Figure 2–18.

Figure 2–18. Additional options of the gradient brush editor

The last major aspect of the gradient brush editor is the Gradient tool mounted on your Tools panel (G is the shortcut key). To illustrate, select a shape on the artboard (which has a Fill property using a gradient brush) and then press the G key. At this point, you can control the gradient origin, as well as reposition each gradient stop using the Gradient tool. Figure 2–19 shows the final version of my particular brush.

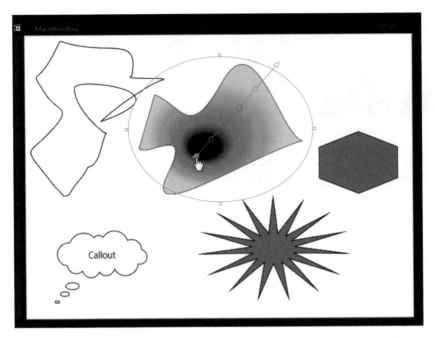

Figure 2–19. The Gradient tool allows you to configure the origin of a gradient brush.

If you were to look at the XAML that represents your custom brush, you would find something similar to the following (which shows a `RadialGradientBrush` based on my brush configuration; if you are not using a radial brush, you'd find a `LinearGradientBrush` object instead):

```
<RadialGradientBrush RadiusY="0.587" RadiusX="0.587"
                     GradientOrigin="0.386,0.662">
  <GradientStop Color="#FFCE1DD8" Offset="0.458"/>
  <GradientStop Color="#FFB0BBE9" Offset="0.747"/>
  <GradientStop Color="#FF2B022D" Offset="0.153"/>
  <GradientStop Color="#FFDF8064" Offset="0.522"/>
</RadialGradientBrush>
```

Defining a Tile Brush

The last brush option we will examine at the moment is the Tile brush editor. This type of brush allows you to paint an area based on image data located in a given external graphics file (*.bmp, *tif, *.jpeg, and so on). Select another one of your geometric shapes (or render a new one on the artboard), select it, and then click the Tile brush option. Now, set the `ImageSource` property using the "Choose an image" button (see Figure 2–20).

Figure 2–20. Selecting a source for the tile brush

At this point, you can use the resulting dialog box to navigate to the location of any image file on your computer. Once you select an image file, it will automatically be added to your project *and* the image data will be used to build your new brush. Figure 2–21 shows one of my geometries that is filled based on the graphical data within a *.bmp file.

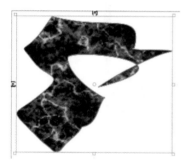

Figure 2–21. Tile brushes allow you to build a brush based on image data.

Great! At this point you (hopefully) feel confident building brushes to set various brush-centric properties (Fill, Stroke, etc.) using the Blend IDE. Next up, you will examine some ways to combine geometries to form new Path objects.ew Path objects.

Combining Geometries and Extracting Paths

Expression Blend provides a number of operations that allow you to create new Path objects by combining existing shapes in a variety of ways. The first step to activating these tools is to select multiple items on your artboard—more specifically, multiple items that in some way overlap. Use the Selection tool to arrange two or more items on your artboard so that they do indeed overlap. Now, perform a Shift+click operation to select each item.

■ **Note** Blend will use the brush of the *last item* selected when generating the new `Path` object! Therefore, make sure you select last the shape that has the brush you wish to use. Of course, you can always use the Brushes editor to change the brush to use after combining items.

Next, right-click the selected items and navigate to the Combine menu. Here you will find a number of useful operations, as shown in Figure 2–22.

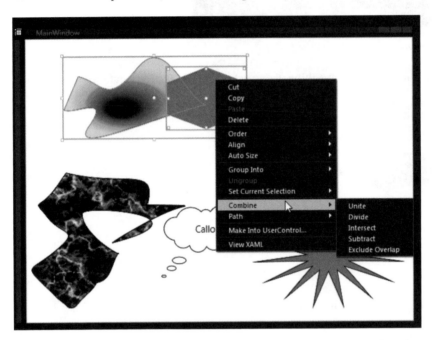

Figure 2–22. The Combine menu allows you to create new Path objects based on existing geometries.

Here is a breakdown of each Combine menu option:

- *Unite*: Combines all shapes or paths into one single object
- *Divide*: Cuts the shapes or paths based on where they intersect but leaves all the pieces intact
- *Intersect*: Keeps the overlapping areas of the objects and removes the nonoverlapping areas
- *Subtract*: Cuts all other selected shapes out of the last selected shape
- *Exclude Overlap*: Keeps the nonoverlapping areas and discards the overlapping areas

If you test each option, you'll see that each operation is fairly intuitive. Take a moment or two to try out each option, and don't forget that Blend does support standard undo (Ctrl+Z) and redo (Ctrl+Y) keyboard commands.

Converting a Shape to a Path

Expression Blend provides a second way to generate a new Path object, using the Convert to Path option. This can be useful if you have created a geometry using the basic drawing tools (such as the Ellipse, Rectangle, or some other specialized shape option selected from the Assets library) and want to further modify its individual line segments.

For example, consider the star shape seen earlier in this chapter. If you were to view the XAML, you would find something such as the following:

```
<ed:RegularPolygon Fill="#FF279111" InnerRadius="0.302"
    PointCount="15" Stretch="Fill" Stroke="Black"
    Margin="0,114,18,168"
    HorizontalAlignment="Right" Width="235"/>
```

Right-click this shape on the designer (or a similar shape on your artboard) and choose the Path ➤ Convert to Path menu option. Once you do, the previous RegularPolygon will be converted to a Path object such as the following:

```
<Path Data="M117.5,0.5 L124.7254,57.65331 L165.35032,7.4490627
L137.92686,61.669108 L204.92688,27.094695 L147.59633,69.006338
L229.38655,56.039988 L152.06187,78.396325 L234.50001,89.280037
L150.55135,88.215455 L219.38311,121.06734 L143.32595,96.765911
L186.64969,145.90558 L131.63501,102.56924 L141.95966,159.49999
L117.5,104.622 L93.040342,159.49999 L103.36499,102.56924
L48.350318,145.90558 L91.674053,96.765911 L15.616902,121.06734
L84.448655,88.215455 L0.49999996,89.280037 L82.938135,78.396325
L5.6134615,56.039988 L87.403677,69.006338 L30.073123,27.094695
L97.073147,61.669108 L69.649686,7.4490627 L110.27461,57.65331 z"
Fill="#FF279111" HorizontalAlignment="Right"
Margin="0,114.25,18.25,168.25" Stretch="Fill" Stroke="Black"
Width="234.5"/>
```

After the new Path object has been selected, you can perform a Direct Selection and modify each aspect of the geometry (see Figure 2–23, which shows my greatly modified star shape).

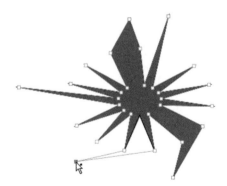

Figure 2–23. Converting a shape to a path is useful when you need to modify line segments.

■ **Note** This usage of Direct Selection would not have been possible when it was a regular polygon, because a regular polygon doesn't expose its individual path points for adjustment.

Interacting with Shapes

It is always important to remember that any shape you render on the artboard using Expression Blend is a true object and can be interacted with in code. For example, shapes (rectangles, paths, ellipses, lines, callouts, etc.) support a number of events that you can handle in your programs to interact with the geometries in various ways.

The first step in interacting with shapes from code is to give them a name, using the Name field on the Properties panel. If you are following along, try the following. Select each shape in turn using the Selection tool, and then name each shape via the Properties panel. The exact name you give each item is unimportant, but you should pick useful monikers such as myCallout, myStar, and so on. Figure 2–24 shows the name (fancyShape) of one of my geometries.

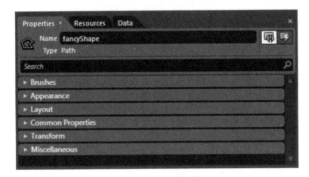

Figure 2–24. Naming objects is the first step in interacting with them.

When you give an object a name, you will find that the x:Name attribute is added to the XAML definition of the item. For example:

```
<Path x:Name="fancyShape" ... />
```

Handling Events

Now, select any one of your shapes on the designer, and click the Events button of the Properties panel, which you will find in the upper right (look for the lightning bolt icon). Find the MouseEnter event and type in a method named **InsideAShape** (see Figure 2–25).

Figure 2–25. Handling an event for a given item

As soon as you press the Enter key, the Blend IDE will generate an event handler in your corresponding code file:

```
private void InsideAShape(object sender,
                          System.Windows.Input.MouseEventArgs e)
{
    // TODO: Add event handler implementation here.
}
```

For this example, I have handled the MouseEnter for each one of my shapes in the current project (a total of five—your number may differ), specifying the exact same method (InsideAShape) each time. Because the same method will be called regardless of which shape has been entered, you can use the first incoming parameter (an object named *sender*), to determine which one of the geometries sent the event (meaning, which shape we are inside of).

If you are a programmer by trade, the following code should make sense. Here, I am casting the incoming object to the UIElement parent class (all visual shapes and controls in WPF/Silverlight inherit from the UIElement class), and then changing the Opacity property value to 50 percent.[3] If you are not a programmer, simply type in what you see (and remember, C# is a case-sensitive language!):

```
private void InsideAShape(object sender,
                          System.Windows.Input.MouseEventArgs e)
{
    // Make the currently selected shape appear to be transparent.
    ((UIElement)sender).Opacity = .5;
}
```

If you run your application now (by pressing the F5 key), you should see that when you move your mouse within the boundaries of any shape, it becomes semitransparent.

---

[3] If you are using VB to build the current example, you will want to use the DirectCast statement, as opposed to the C# casting operator.

■ **Note** If you downloaded the code for this book from the Apress web site, you will find that I also handled the MouseLeave event for each shape. Inside of the shared MouseLeave event handler, I reset the Opacity property to the value 1.0. In this way, each shape "resets" when the mouse cursor leaves its border.

Configuring "Pens"

So far you have been using the Brushes editor to create customized brushes to fill the interior of geometries via the Fill property. In addition, it is possible to configure the "pen" used to draw the border of a given UI element. By default, when you draw a shape on the artboard, the border will be rendered using a one-pixel thick, black-colored brush.

If you wish to change this default setting, the first option you have is to change the brush used for the Stroke property by using the Brushes editor as previously described. You can also change the StrokeThickness property found under the Appearance section of the Properties panel. In addition, you have a number of "stroke-centric" properties that can be found under the advanced options area of the Appearance editor (see Figure 2–26).

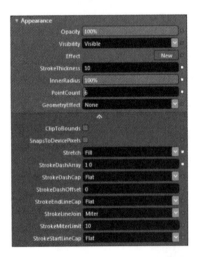

Figure 2–26. The Appearance editor has a number of properties that allow you to control how borders and lines are to be rendered

Defining Pen Caps

While any UI element can be configured using these various stroke properties, some of them (such as StrokeStartLineCap and StrokeEndLineCap) are only useful when you are rendering lines. Using the Pen or Line tool, add a line to your current artboard and change the StrokeThickness property to 10. Now, change the StrokeStartLineCap and StrokeEndLineCap properties to use to one of the available "pen caps" (Flat, Square, Round, or Triangle). In Figure 2–27, you can see the effect of using a Round start line cap and Triangle end line cap.

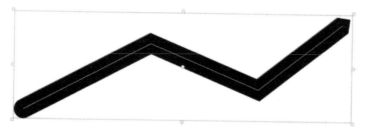

Figure 2–27. Pen caps allow you to control how to render the starting and ending portion of a line.

■ **Note** Depending on the size of your line, you may need to zoom into the geometry to view the pen cap effect (recall from Chapter 1 that you can use the mouse wheel, or the artboard controls, to zoom into or out from the artboard).

Defining a Dash Pattern

Now, locate the `StrokeDashArray` property in the Appearance editor, which is currently set to the value `1 0`. This property allows you to control how the pen should be configured with regard to any *dash pattern*. The first value (`1`) represents the length of a dash, while the second value (`0`) represents the length of the gap. Thus, the value of `1 0` basically represents a solid line, containing no gaps. If you were to change this value to `1 1`, you would be able to define a dashed line, as shown in Figure 2–28.

■ **Note** You can separate the numbers used to set the `StrokeDashArray` property with commas as you type in the value (`1, 1` as opposed to `1 1`). Blend will strip out the comma once you press the Enter key in the property editor.

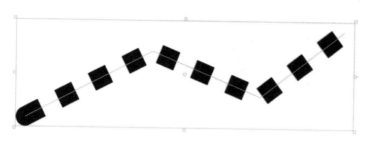

Figure 2–28. A dashed line

The value assigned to the `StrokeDashArray` property need not be limited to one pair of numbers. You can create more elaborate dash combinations by defining sets of pairs, each member representing part of the dash operation. Consider the following `StrokeDashArray` value for a new object drawn with the Line tool:

```
StrokeDashArray="0.5 1 2 1"
```

In this case, our line begins by drawing half of a dash, followed by a blank space, followed by a double dash, followed by a single blank space. This pattern repeats for the remainder of the line rendering, leaving us with the line shown in Figure 2–29.

Figure 2–29. *A fancy dashed line*

I'll leave it in your hands to tinker with the remaining stroke-centric settings found in the Appearance section of the Properties panel. If you need more information for a specific property, consult the Expression Blend User Guide.

Revisiting Visual Effects

Chapter 1 had you apply a visual effect to a Blend sample application; however, I do want to remind you that the Assets library (or Assets panel, which I find easier to use for drag-and-drop operations) of Blend provides a number of built-in visual effects that you can add to any UI element seen within the Objects and Timeline panel. Figure 2–30 shows the Effects section of the Asset library.

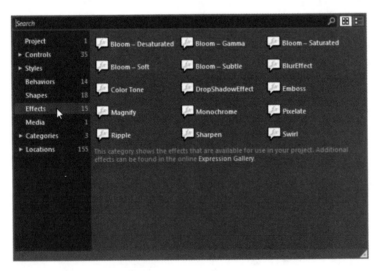

Figure 2–30. *Visual effects can be added to any UI element.*

To apply a visual effect, you can either drag the item onto a given node of the Objects and Timeline panel, or drag the item directly onto the target item on the artboard. Figure 2–31 shows my Objects and Timeline panel after applying various visual effects to some of my geometries (I've highlighted the effects).

Figure 2–31. Various visual effects

■ **Note** You can download many additional visual effects (and other items of interest) free of charge by visiting the Microsoft Expression Gallery online (`http://gallery.expression.microsoft.com`).

Tweaking a Visual Effect

Once you have added a visual effect to a UI element, you can select it in the Objects and Timeline panel and view any configurable properties. Each visual effect has its own set of specific properties. If you take some time to experiment with these properties, you should not have any problems creating some interesting graphical effects. By way of one example, Figure 2–32 shows the properties that can be set for the DropShadowEffect object.

Figure 2–32. Each visual effect can be configured using the Properties panel.

You should be aware that a vast majority of the visual effects supported by Expression Blend have been bundled into a .NET assembly named `Microsoft.Expression.Effects.dll`. If you happen to create a new WPF or Silverlight project using Visual Studio 2010, do know that you can manually reference this library using the Add References dialog box (you will find it listed alphabetically under the .NET tab). Also, if you need to refer to these effects in code, you'll typically need to import the `Microsoft.Expression.Media.Effects` namespace.

■ **Note** Recall from Chapter 1 that the Blend artboard provides the "Turn off rendering of Effects" button to disable visual effects during development. Look for the *fx* button on the lower left of the artboard controls.

That wraps up our examination of the core drawing tools of Expression Blend. Next up, we examine how you can import graphical data created using Expression Design, and why you might want to do so.

■ **Source Code** The **BlendDrawingTools** project can be found under the Chapter 2 subdirectory.

The Role of Expression Design

As useful as the Blend drawing tools are, it would be quite challenging for a graphical artist to create a complex, vector-based image using the techniques we have just examined. As luck would have it, Microsoft Expression Design can be used to create much more sophisticated graphical data, which can then be exported into a variety of file formats, including XAML. If the data has been exported as XAML, it can easily be imported into a WPF or Silverlight application. At this point, you can manipulate the objects using the Objects and Timeline panel, using all of the tricks you have seen thus far (apply visual effects, interact with the data in code, etc.).

■ **Note** Detailed coverage of Expression Design is beyond the scope of this book (and to be honest, outside of my skill set). If you are interested in learning more about using Expression Design to create your own custom graphics, consult the Expression Design User Guide using the Help menu.

Preparing and Exporting a Sample Image

To begin our next project, launch Expression Design. Now, if you happen to have some graphical skills, you could draw a custom graphic for this example. However, if you are like myself and are a bit artistically challenged, simply activate the Help ➤ Samples menu option. Here, you will find a number of different `*.design` files you can load, such as `bear_paper.design` (see Figure 2–33).

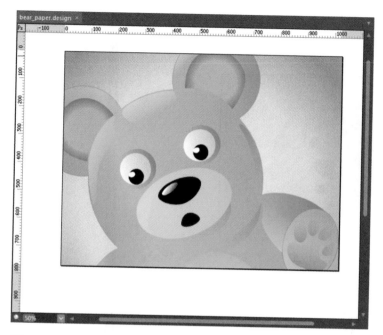

Figure 2–33. The "teddy bear" sample graphic

■ **Note** If you do not have a copy of Expression Design, I've included the exported `bear_paper.xaml` file in the Chapter 2 subdirectory.

Before we export this image data as an XAML file, let's make a few adjustments to the graphical data. Currently, it appears as if the entire image consists only of the face and one paw of our furry friend. In reality, the graphical data you are seeing is a small *viewport* of a much larger graphic.

To see this first-hand, press the Ctrl+A keyboard command to select all of the graphical data in this `*.design` document. As you can see in Figure 2–34, the entire body of the teddy bear has been defined outside of the current viewport. Also notice in Figure 2–34 that my mouse cursor is hovering over the upper-right pull-point of the viewport boundary.

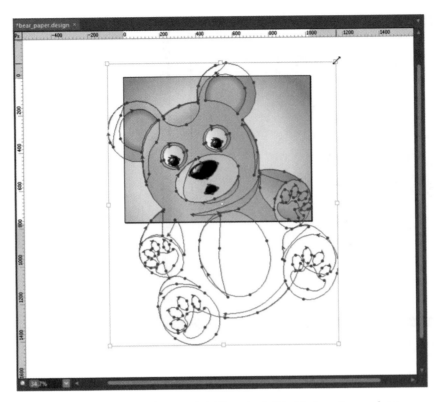

Figure 2–34. *The current viewport is hiding the full teddy bear image data.*

Now, put *your* mouse cursor over the upper-right pull-point of the viewport, and reduce the height and width by about 50 percent via the mouse (don't worry about the exact reduction of size; we just want a smaller image to export). Once you have done so, you can select the image data with the mouse and move it back over the blue background. Once you are finished, you should see something similar to Figure 2–35.

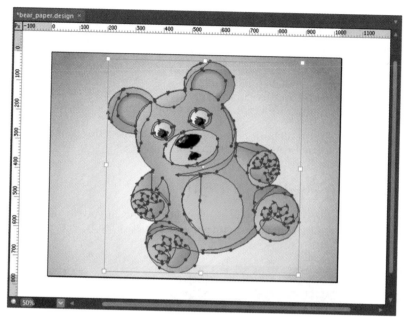

Figure 2–35. The resized teddy bear graphic data

Now that the graphical data has been finalized, you can export the data using the File ➤ Export menu option. The Format drop-down list box offers a number of popular file formats, but for this example we are interested in the XAML Silverlight 4/WPF Canvas option (see Figure 2–36), so select that.

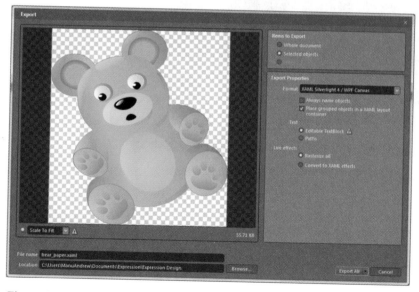

Figure 2–36. Exporting the "teddy bear" sample graphic as XAML

Once you have selected the correct XAML file format, uncheck the "Always name objects" option. Recall that when an element has an x:Name attribute, you can interact with the item in code. However, this teddy bear will be described using a great number of XAML elements. If we were to tell the tool to name every possible object, we would end up with a large number of member variables added to our C# (or VB) code base, which we are not really going to use (and this can increase the size of the final compiled application).

Also, make sure you select a location for this exported data (bear_paper.xaml) that will be easy to find later (such as on your Windows desktop). All other options can be left to their defaults.

When you are ready, click the Export All button, and, lo and behold, the teddy bear image data is captured as XAML! You can close Expression Design at this point.

Creating a New Silverlight Application

Now we are ready to import this data into a WPF or Silverlight application. Again, you can pick either project type. Here, I will create a new Silverlight application named **InteractiveTeddyBear** (see Figure 2–37).

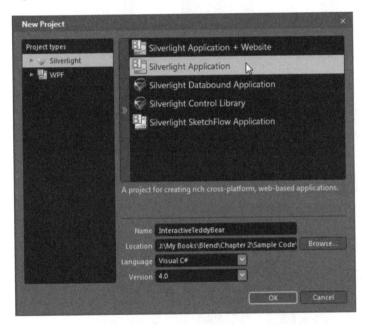

Figure 2–37. Creating a new Silverlight application with Expression Blend

Select the Silverlight UserControl in the Objects and Timeline panel, and then increase the size of this object by a fair amount. The exact size does not matter, but I've set my Height and Width properties to 800, using the Layout section of the Properties panel.

Importing the Sample Data into a Blend Project

Now for the fun part! Activate the Project ➤ Add Existing Item menu option of Blend and, using the resulting dialog box, navigate to the location of your bear_paper.xaml file (or the copy I've provided in the Chapter 2 folder of your code download). Once you click the OK button, you'll find that this XAML file has been added to your project (which you can verify by examining the Projects panel; see Chapter 1).

Double-click this file from the Projects panel, in order to view your image data within the Blend IDE (be sure to click the Split view option of the artboard so you can also see the underlying XAML; see Figure 2–38).

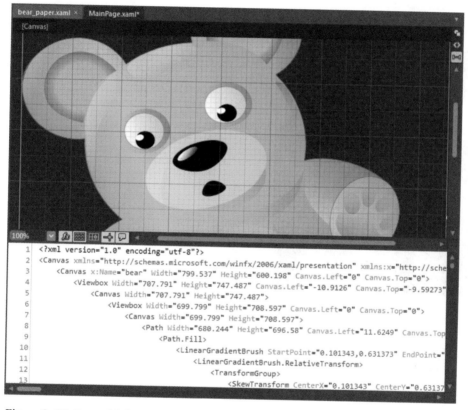

Figure 2–38. *Our teddy bear XAML data in Expression Blend*

Now, by viewing the Objects and Timeline panel of the bear_paper.xaml file, you will see that each XAML element is present and accounted for. The goal here is to locate the *left eyeball* and *right inner ear* of the bear and give each item a name. While you could manually hunt for the correct objects (which would be very tedious), simply activate the Selection tool and click these items. This will automatically highlight the correct node in the Objects and Timeline panel. Select the left eyeball and use the Properties editor to name this object **leftEye**. Select a portion of the right ear (whichever part you wish to select) and name it **rightEar**. Figure 2–39 shows the selected left eyeball.

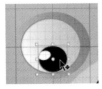

Figure 2–39. *Locating objects via the Selection tool*

Now, right-click the `bear` node in the Objects and Timeline panel and select the Copy menu option (see Figure 2–40).

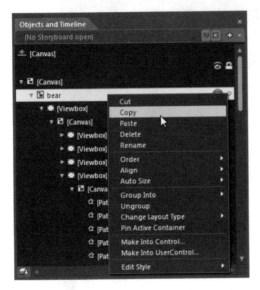

Figure 2–40. *Copying the bear node to the clipboard*

At this point you can close the `bear_paper.xaml` file. Switch back to the artboard for the `MainPage.xaml` file, right-click the `LayoutRoot` object in the Objects and Timeline panel, and paste in the clipboard content. You will now see that the bear object is located in your `Grid` as a nested `Canvas` named `bear`!

■ **Note** You might find it more difficult than expected to resize or move the bear `Canvas` within the `Grid`. This is because the original Expression Design sample data made use of numerous graphical layers arranged by Z-order.

Interacting with the Bear

At this point, you can handle events for the `leftEye` and `rightEar` objects, just like you handled events for the simple shapes in the previous example of this chapter: Select each object on the designer in turn, activate the Events section of the Properties panel, and enter event handler names as required. For the current example, handle the MouseLeftButtonDown event for each object (leftEye and rightEar), specifying a unique method name each time.

Here is some simple C# code that will change the look and feel of each object once clicked (if you don't feel like typing all the code shown here, you could simply add a MessageBox.Show() statement for each handler, and display a fitting message):

```csharp
private void leftEye_MouseLeftButtonDown(object sender,
  System.Windows.Input.MouseButtonEventArgs e)
{
  // Change the color of the eye when clicked.
  leftEye.Fill = new SolidColorBrush(Colors.Red);
}

private void rightEar_MouseLeftButtonDown(object sender,
  System.Windows.Input.MouseButtonEventArgs e)
{
  // Blur the ear when clicked.
  System.Windows.Media.Effects.BlurEffect blur =
    new System.Windows.Media.Effects.BlurEffect();
  blur.Radius = 80;
  rightEar.Effect = blur;
}
```

Now, run your application (press the F5 key). Your Silverlight application will load into your web browser. Go ahead and click the bear's left eyeball. You will be happy to see the results, shown in Figure 2–41.

Figure 2–41. Yikes! Poor bear…

So there you have it! You now understand the process of importing complex graphical data created with Expression Design into an Expression Blend project, and more importantly, how to interact with the graphical data in code.

Later in this book, you will examine how to use the animation editors of Expression Blend. You might want to revisit this example at that time to do something even more interesting, such as spinning the eyeball of the bear in a circle, shrinking the size of the ear, or what have you.

■ **Source Code** The **InteractiveTeddyBear** project can be found under the Chapter 2 subdirectory.

Applying 2D Graphical Transformation

Silverlight and WPF both support the ability to transform a UI element in a variety of ways. Each API provides a number of common graphical transformations, including rotations, skews, flipping operations, and scaling operations. Mind you, *any* object can be the target of a graphical transformation. For example, you could define a complex layout of controls that can be radically re-rendered based on user input (for example, rotate a set of controls based on mouse input).

As you work with the Blend IDE, you'll find that transformations can be animated and incorporated into custom templates to create some very slick visual effects. For the time being, I'd like to walk you through a new example of how to work with the basic transformation tools of Expression Blend.

Building the Initial UI

Begin by creating a new WPF application named **Transformations** (a Silverlight application would also be fine, but I recommend creating a WPF project, as I will talk about a few options that are not found within the Silverlight API). Now, to give you a somewhat interesting example, the first task of this example is to define a *nested layout system* for the Window at hand. Again, Chapter 4 will walk you through the details of building UIs with layout managers and controls, so just stick it out for now.

First, split your initial grid into two rows by selecting the LayoutRoot node of the Objects and Timeline panel and then clicking the outer blue grid editor to make a new row. The exact size does not matter, but make the first row considerably smaller than the second. Next, ensuring that your Grid object is still selected in the Objects and Timeline panel, locate the StackPanel control within your Tools panel (see Figure 2–42).

Figure 2–42. The StackPanel control

Once you have selected this StackPanel, double-click the icon on the Tools panel to add this to your Grid object and stretch it out to take up the entire space of the first row. Select your new StackPanel in the Objects and Timeline panel. Now, locate the Button control in your Tools panel (see Figure 2–43).

Figure 2–43. The Button control

Double-click the Button control three times. This should add three Button objects to the nested StackPanel. Next, select all three Button controls in your Objects and Timeline panel (via a standard Shift+click) and use the Properties panel to set a Width value of 100 (look in the Layout section) and a bottom Margin value of 10 (also found in the Layout section; see Figure 2–44).

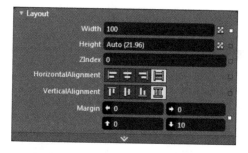

Figure 2–44. Configuring the Button controls

Now, select each Button one at a time (via a Selection operation) and change the Content property (located in the Common Properties section of the Properties panel) to the values Skew, Rotate, and Flip. As well, use the Name field of the Properties panel to given each button a proper name, such as btnSkew, btnRotate, and btnFlip. Click the Events button (lightning bolt icon) of the Properties panel and then handle the Click event for each Button.

■ **Note** Remember, you can also simply double-click in the text area for a given event to generate a default event handler, which takes the form *NameOfElement_NameOfEvent*. Thus, if you handle the Click event for btnFlip, the handler will be named btnFlip_Click.

To finalize the UI, create a shape of your choosing (using any of the tools presented in this chapter) from the Tools panel, and add it to the second row of the grid (remember, the Layout section of the Properties panel contains properties that you can use to assign an item to a given grid cell, but you can also drag an item into a grid cell via the mouse). Name your new UI element **myShape**. Figure 2–45 shows the final layout.

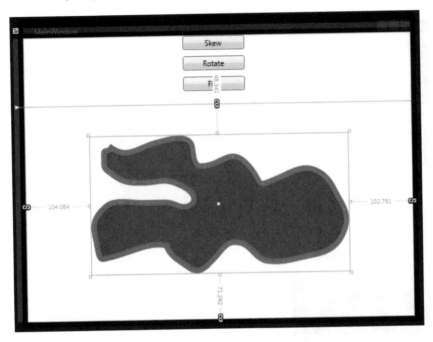

Figure 2–45. Our WPF layout

■ **Note** Here, I am using a basic graphic as the target of our transformations to simplify the current example, but remember, any UI element (including layout managers containing controls) can be transformed using the techniques presented here.

Applying Transformations at Design Time

Before we add code to our event handlers, we'll look at how to apply graphical transformations at design time using the Blend Transform editor. Select your custom shape via a Selection operation, and locate the Transform section of the Properties panel (see Figure 2–46).

Figure 2–46. The Transform editor

Similar to the Brushes section, the Transform section provides a number of tabs to configure various types of graphical transformation for the select item in the Objects and Timeline panel. Table 2–1 describes each transformation option, listed in the order of evaluating each tab from left to right.

Table 2–1. Blend Transformation Options

Transformation Option	Meaning in Life
Translate	Allows you to offset the location of an item on an X, Y position.
Rotate	Allows you to rotate an item on a 360-degree angle.
Scale	Allows you to grow or shrink an item on an X, Y position.
Skew	Allows you to skew the bounding box containing the selected item on an X, Y position.
Center Point	When you rotate or flip an object, the item moves relative to a fixed point, called the object's center point. By default, an object's center point is located at the object's center. This transformation allows you to change an object's center point in order to rotate or flip the object around a different point.
Flip	Flips a selected item based on an X or Y axis.

I suggest that you test each of these transformations using your custom shape as a target (just press Ctrl+Z to undo the previous operation). Like many other aspects of the Blend Properties panel, each transformation section has a unique set of configuration options, which should become fairly understandable as you tinker. For example, the Skew transform editor allows you to set the X and Y skew values using two slider controls, the Flip transform editor allows you to flip on the X or Y axis, and so forth.

RenderTransform or LayoutTransform?

If you look at the Transform section of the Properties panel, you'll notice that there is an advanced settings area. If you expand this area, you will see a secondary transformation editor, which looks more or less identical to what you have already seen. The distinction is that the transformations in the top set are considered *render transformations* while the transformations in the bottom set are considered *layout transformations* (see Figure 2–47).

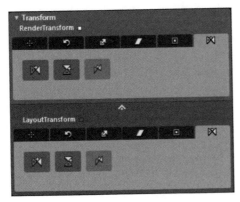

Figure 2–47. The Transform editor has two possible ways to apply a transformation.

■ **Note** Silverlight elements can only be transformed using the `RenderTransform` options. `LayoutTransform` options are only valid in a WPF application.

While both transformation editors will ultimately change the way a selected item is displayed on the screen, the difference is *when* the transformation is applied. The optimal way to set a transformation is using render transformations. With this approach, transformations are applied after an item has been rendered on the `Window`/`UserControl`, and typically offer better performance.

As an alternative, `LayoutTransform` operations occur in memory during the layout process and before any UI elements are realized on the screen. While this can hurt performance a tad, the benefit of layout transformations is that the parent object (typically a layout manager) can alter the transformation for child objects dynamically (possibly affecting the Z-order).

Applying Transformations in Code

The implementation of each `Click` event handler will be more or less the same. We will configure a transformation object and assign it to the `myShape` object. Thus, when you run the application, you can click a button to see the result of the applied transformation. Here is the complete code for each event handler (notice I am setting the `LayoutTransform` property, so the shape data remains positioned relative to the parent container):

```
private void btnFlip_Click(object sender,
    System.Windows.RoutedEventArgs e)
{
    myShape.LayoutTransform  = new ScaleTransform(-1, 1);
}

private void btnRotate_Click(object sender,
    System.Windows.RoutedEventArgs e)
{
    myShape.LayoutTransform = new RotateTransform(180);
}
```

```
private void btnSkew_Click(object sender,
  System.Windows.RoutedEventArgs e)
{
  myShape.LayoutTransform  = new SkewTransform(40, -20);
}
```

When you run this program (press F5), you will be able to dynamically change the layout of the custom shape with the click of a button. So far, so good! The next section examines a much more grandiose type of graphical transformation, that of 3D space.

■ **Source Code** The **Transformations** project can be found under the Chapter 2 subdirectory.

Applying 3D Graphical Transformation

Both of the example projects that you have created so far in this chapter have made use of 2D graphical data. Expression Blend also defines a dedicated set of tools that allows you to create, manipulate, and import 3D graphics. However, the way Blend handles 3D graphics will differ quite a bit based on whether you have created a WPF application or a Silverlight application. Recall that WPF is a technology that is limited to the Windows OS, and because of this, the API is able to leverage OS-specific graphical services such as Microsoft DirectX. Given this, WPF is able to support a full-fledged 3D framework. Silverlight, on the other hand, is a cross-platform, browser-centric API. Thus, the Silverlight API is unable to support a full 3D framework, but rather makes use of a lighterweight alternative termed *perspective 3D graphics*.

Because each API has different levels of 3D support, Expression Blend provides unique 3D-centric tools for each framework. Therefore, the next example will introduce the basic ins and outs of working with 3D graphics within the context of a WPF project. You'll examine Silverlight's 3D support a bit later in this chapter.

■ **Note** You are free to skip over this section if you are interested exclusively in Silverlight development, but I do hope you will at least open the sample solution for each project so that you can see the possibilities.

An Introduction to WPF 3D Graphics

Expression Blend does not have any way to generate a full-blown 3D model using integrated drawing tools. However, it does provide ways to import a 3D object model generated through dedicated (third party) tools. Before I describe one such tool (ZAM 3D), we will begin with an example that illustrates how we can map a 2D image into a 3D plane, and then manipulate it on the artboard as well as through code.

■ **Note** A comprehensive examination of 3D modeling is well beyond the scope of this book. If you have not worked with 3D graphics before, the following pages will give you a very good idea about what is possible to do using Expression Blend and WPF. If you require a deeper understanding of the topic, navigate to www.msdn.com and search the term **WPF 3D**. You will find numerous links for further study.

Mapping a 2D Image to a 3D Plane

Begin by creating a new WPF application named **Wpf3DExample**. Your next task is simple: find an image file on your computer that you wish to map to a 3D coordinate system. Once you have found a fitting image, open your Projects panel, right-click your project, and select the Add Existing Item menu option. Use the resulting dialog box to navigate to your image. Once you are done, you will see that a copy of the file has been placed into your project (see Figure 2–48; note that if you hover over an image file, Blend gives you a small thumbnail view of the graphical data[4]).

Figure 2–48. Adding an image file to your WPF project

■ **Note** If you add a very large image file to your project, Blend will recommend that you embed the image data into your compiled executable. For this example, it does not matter either way.

Now, via a standard mouse drag-and-drop operation[5], drag your image file node from the tree view in the Projects panel onto your artboard. Resize the image so that it takes up about half of the upper part of the WPF widow. Before moving on, take a peek at the generated XAML; you see that the IDE automatically added an Image control, which has a Source property set to a value pointing to the image data file (or, alternatively, the location of the embedded image data):

---

[4] The image you see here is a picture of the "CoCoLoCo." This adult beverage packed quite the punch. Once you finish this project and rotate the image in a 3D plane, you will have a good idea of how I felt after I finished drinking it.

[5] The Silverlight Image control only supports JPEG or PNG file formats.

```
<Image Height="481" Margin="79.215,0,-284.215,-464"
       Source="pack://siteoforigin:,,,/CoCoLoCo.tif"
       Stretch="Fill" VerticalAlignment="Bottom"/>
```

■ **Note** The odd value assigned to the `Source` property is a special syntax used to locate an embedded image resource. If the image data was not embedded into the executable, you would simply see `Source="CoCoLoCo.tif"`.

Select the `Image` control in the Objects and Timeline panel, and then activate the Tools ➤ Make 3D Image menu option of the Blend IDE. Although there will not appear to be any changes on the designer itself, if you look at the generated XAML, you will find that your once simple `Image` control has been completely transformed into a rather complex `Viewport3D` object, part of which is a new `ImageBrush` object that was constructed based on the initial image file. Here is a breakdown of the core items.

The Elements of Viewport3D

The amount of XAML to represent a `Viewport3D` object is quite large, so I won't show it here. However, if you examine the Objects and Timeline panel, you can see that this `Viewport3D` object consists of four subelements, specifically `Camera`, `ModelContainer`, `AmbientContainer`, and `DirectionalContainer`. Expand the `Camera` node, select the `[PerspectiveCamera]` subnode, and use the Properties panel to name this object **my3DCamera**. Figure 2–49 shows the result of the renaming operation (with all subnodes selected).

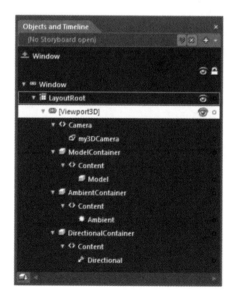

Figure 2–49. The Viewport3D element enables 3D mapping of data.

Each aspect of the Viewport3D object allows you to control various aspects of how the data will be rendered in 3D space (location, lighting, etc.). You'll be introduced to each aspect over the next few pages. Table 2–2 provides a quick breakdown of each component to get you started.

Table 2–2. Viewport3D Subelements

Viewport3D Subelement	Meaning in Life
Camera	Provides a way to control the location of the camera's viewing location, as well as the location point of the image being viewed
ModelContainer	Shows the raw 3D model that is being used to display the 3D view port
AmbientContainer	Allows you to add, remove, and manage "materials" that control how the 3D viewport will render lighting effects on the front and back of the image
DirectionalContainer	Allows you to add, remove, and manage additional "materials" that control the direction of an external light source projected on your 3D image

Transforming the 3D Viewport with the Camera Orbit Tool

Once you select your Viewport3D object in the Objects and Timeline panel, you can activate the Camera Orbit tool on the Tools panel (see Figure 2–50).

Figure 2–50. The Camera Orbit tool allows you to transform a 3D viewport via the mouse.

Once you click this tool, you can place your mouse cursor over any selected Viewport3D object and change the X, Y, and Z axes for the item in question (just click and hold the left mouse button while you move your mouse cursor; see Figure 2–51).

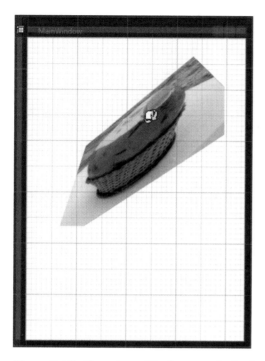

Figure 2–51. Changing a 3D viewport via the Camera Orbit tool

Changing Camera Settings Using the Properties Panel

Using the Camera Orbit tool is useful when you want to quickly transform data in a 3D space using rough measurements. If you require a higher level of precision, you can use the Camera section of the Properties panel. To locate the Camera section, you must first select the `Camera` node of a `Viewport3D` node using your Objects and Timeline panel (remember, we named this object `my3DCamera`). Once you select this item, the Camera section presents itself in the Properties panel (see Figure 2–52).

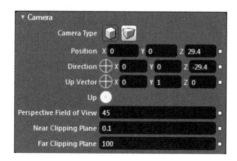

Figure 2–52. The Camera section of the Properties panel

As you play around with these settings, you'll see that you can change the same general settings that you can change using the Camera Orbit tool (viewport location, camera location, and look direction). As well, this editor allows you to pick between two types of cameras, specifically a *perspective camera* or an *orthographic camera*.

By default, the camera for a new `Viewport3D` object will be a perspective camera, which works just like a normal camera you would use to take pictures: as the object gets farther from the camera, it appears smaller and smaller. Your other choice, the orthographic camera, will *not* render view port data at a smaller scale as the camera moves farther away from the object. This can be useful if you want to transform an image on a 3D space while retaining the general height and width of the original viewing area.

■ **Note** To see the differences between these two camera choices, toggle between your options and use the Camera Orbit tool at design time. This will clearly illustrate what the printed page cannot!

There are some other settings in the Camera editor that you might want to explore at your leisure (controlling the field of view of a perspective camera, controlling clipping locations, etc.), but I won't cover them here. Do know, however, that the remaining settings will change based on your selected camera type.

Changing the 3D Viewport Using the Artboard Tools

In addition to the Camera Orbit tool and the Camera editor, you can also activate a 3D positioning tool directly on the artboard. To activate this tool, locate and select the `Model` node under the `ModelContainer` node (see Figure 2–53).

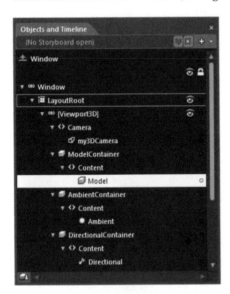

Figure 2–53. The ModelContainer node allows you to activate the artboard 3D editor.

At this point, you will see the 3D location tool appear on the artboard. Using the mouse, you can freely rotate the view port on an X, Y, or Z axis using the various grab handles. To get a rotation, grab hold of the red, green, or blue arcs (representing rotations around each axis; see Figure 2–54).

Figure 2–54. *Changing the view port via the artboard*

Changing 3D Lighting Effects Using the Light Editors

The final components of the Viewport3D node (AmbientContainer and DirectionalContainer) allow you to control how your view port will render itself based on various lighting effects. The role of *ambient light* is to cast light on the view port as if it is coming from all directions; it can be used to light all parts of objects evenly. If you select the current Ambient node via the Objects and Timeline panel (see Figure 2–55), a Light section will open on the Properties panel. By default, the ambient light is a neutral gray, but you can change this via the built-in color editor, as shown in Figure 2–56.

Figure 2–55. Ambient lighting is applied in a uniform manner.

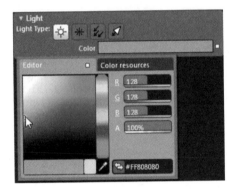

Figure 2–56. Changing ambient light settings

If you select the `Directional` subnode in the `DirectionalContainer` node (also visible in Figure 2–55), you can change the location of the light source. Notice in Figure 2–57 that the Direction settings can be changed collectively by clicking the "directional icon" and dragging your mouse cursor.

Figure 2–57. Changing the light location

That wraps up your introductory look at the general ways to configure a 3D view port using Expression Blend. To complete this current example, let's add a bit of code to control the camera.

Controlling the Camera in Code

In the code download for this book, you can open the provided **Wpf3DExample** project into Blend to save yourself some time (and possibly confusion) since we really have not talked about manipulating controls in the Blend IDE (but we will, starting in the next chapter). Essentially, I've added three Slider controls (and a few descriptive Label controls) to the main Window, which allow the user to change the X, Y, and Z positions of the camera location.

■ **Note** Be sure to view the XAML definitions for each Slider control in the solution code to see some valid minimum and maximum ranges for each axis.

Within the C# code file, I've defined three private member variables named xVal, yVal, and zVal, all of type double. As well, I've handled the ValueChanged event of each Slider control. Within the event handlers, I simply update the correct X, Y, or Z value and call a private helper function named ChangeCamera(). For example:

```
private void sliderXChange_ValueChanged(object sender,
    System.Windows.RoutedPropertyChangedEventArgs<double> e)
{
  // Change the X look direction.
  xVal = e.NewValue;
  ChangeCamera();
}
```

The ChangeCamera() method sets the Position and LookDirection properties of the perspective camera object, which I suggested you name my3DCamera:

```
private void ChangeCamera()
{
  this.my3DCamera.Position = new
    System.Windows.Media.Media3D.Point3D(-xVal, -yVal, -zVal);
  this.my3DCamera.LookDirection = new
    System.Windows.Media.Media3D.Vector3D(xVal, yVal, zVal);
}
```

If you run the sample code, you will find that my image of the CoCoLoCo drink (yikes!) spins and twirls as you move each slider. Figure 2–58 shows the final application in action.

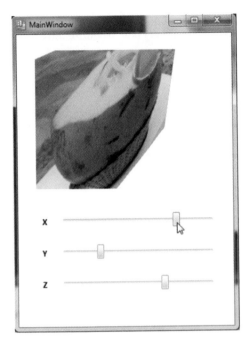

Figure 2–58. *Driving the camera in code!*

A Brief Word on ZAM 3D

The ability to map 2D images into a 3D space is really quite impressive. However, the techniques we have seen so far cannot be considered "true" 3D, in that the 2D image data does not have full 3D renderings. For example, you may have noticed that the image data does not show a full rotation of the image as you flip to the "back side" when you flip the camera a full 180 degrees.

As mentioned, Expression Blend does not have any internal support to build full-blown 3D models. Fortunately, other, third-party tools do provide such functionality. One popular tool is named ZAM 3D.[6] This product allows you to create full-blown 3D graphics, apply numerous effects to the graphical data, and export it as XAML. This XAML (as you would guess) can then be imported into a WPF Blend application, after which you can use the same 3D tools we have just examined to manipulate the image at design time and drive it through code. Figure 2–59 shows a simple 3D ring created with ZAM 3D and imported into a new WPF Blend application.

---

[6] You can download an evaluation copy of ZAM 3D from http://www.erain.com.

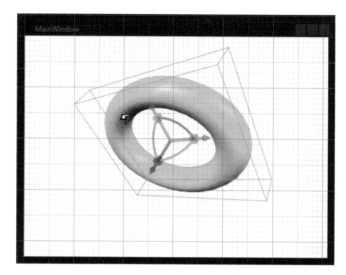

Figure 2–59. Blend can manipulate full 3D object models (it just cannot create them).

I won't be examining how to use ZAM 3D here (that would require a dedicated book!). But if you are interested in learning more, again, I encourage you to download the free trial edition of the tool and take a look.

■ **Source Code** The **Wpf3DExample** project can be found under the Chapter 2 subdirectory.

An Introduction to Silverlight 3D Graphics

The Silverlight API also has support for manipulation of 3D data, and produces very similar results as those found in our WPF example where we mapped a 2D image to a 3D plane. However, Silverlight does not currently offer full-blown 3D support (as WPF does), but rather opts for a more lightweight 3D perspective framework.[7]

Specifically, rather than working with Viewport3D elements and the assorted camera and lighting objects, any Silverlight object that derives from the UIElement base class can change its X, Y, and Z positioning via the Projection property. This property may be set to a PlaneProjection object, which is a very lightweight version of Viewport3D. In its simplest form, the PlaneProjection object can be configured with RotationX, RotationY, and RotationZ properties. It is also possible to control the center point of the rotation (via CenterOfRotationX, CenterOfRotationY, and CenterOfRotationZ properties) as well as global and local offsets.

As you would hope, the Blend IDE provides an editor in the Properties panel that will fully configure a PlaneProjection object and connect it to a UIElement. To illustrate, open the

---

[7] This is not to say that Silverlight cannot be used to build very exotic 3D renderings. If you want to see what can be done, be sure to open the Zune3D sample project that ships with Blend 4. However, be aware that much of the functionality of this example is driven by a considerable amount of code, not XAML, and therefore is a bit out of scope for this book.

Silverlight3DExample project located in the Chapter 2 subdirectory of this book's downloadable code. As you might suspect, this project moves the CoCoLoCo adult beverage image to the Web. Because of some differences between the WPF and Silverlight APIs, the image data has been saved to a *.png file, as the Silverlight Image control only supports JPEG and PNG file formats. Beyond that, the layout of the UserControl mimics what we created in the WPF version of this project.

If you select the Image control on the artboard, you will see that the Transform section of the Properties panel supports a Projection subsection (see Figure 2–60). This area can be used to set the Projection property of any selected item on the artboard.

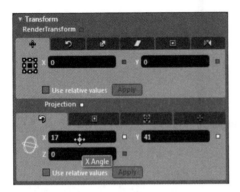

Figure 2–60. In Silverlight, the Projection editor is used to map 2D data to a 3D plane.

Like other range-centric controls of the Properties panel, you can use your mouse to adjust the values for the X, Y, and Z projection settings (just click and hold on a range control and move your mouse). Again, rather than seeing a Viewport3D, you will see XAML such as the following:

```
<Image x:Name="imgCoCoLoCo" Margin="162,18,162,185"
       Source="/CoCoLoCo.png" Stretch="Fill">
  <Image.Projection>
    <PlaneProjection RotationX="46"
                     RotationY="12" RotationZ="-29"/>
  </Image.Projection>
</Image>
```

Driving a Projection in Code

The code representing this Silverlight UserControl is somewhat similar to the previous WPF example. We are still defining three double member variables to represent the current X, Y, and Z values controlled by the Slider objects, and each ValueChanged event handler is still calling the ChangeCamera() helper function. This time, however, the implementation configures a PlaneProjection object and sets the Projection property of the Image control (imgCoCoLoCo):

```
private void ChangeCamera()
{
  PlaneProjection pp = new PlaneProjection();
  pp.RotationX = xVal;
  pp.RotationY = yVal;
  pp.RotationZ = zVal;
```

```
  if(imgCoCoLoCo != null)
    this.imgCoCoLoCo.Projection = pp;
}
```

If you run this project within the Blend IDE, you'll once again be able to spin and rotate the image data, this time from a hosting web browser.

■ **Source Code** The **Silverlight3DExample** project can be found under the Chapter 2 subdirectory.

The Role of Object Resources

To wrap up your look at the graphical capabilities of Expression Blend, I'll close this chapter with our first look at the role of object resources. When you are using Blend to generate visual assets (custom brushes, styles, control templates, etc.), you are bound to run into a situation where you want to reuse a particular item. Say, for example, you have created "the perfect gradient brush," which took a good amount of tinkering time. It would be quite painful if you needed to re-create the same actions on the Brushes editor to generate the XAML once again. Worse, you might decide that you need a brush you created a few weeks back, and have forgotten exactly how you manipulated the Brushes editor in the first place. True, you *could* copy and paste the markup between projects, but this is cumbersome at best.

Thankfully, both WPF and Silverlight support the concept of an *object resource*, also known simply as a *resource*. Essentially, a resource is a named blob of XAML that is stored in your current project. When UI elements want to refer to this named blob, they can select it by this assigned name. Expression Blend has a number of tools that allow you to define, manage, and reuse resources. In this example, I'll show you how to manage a custom brush object; you'll see other types of resources (styles, etc.) in upcoming chapters. The good news is that regardless of the type of resource, Blend provides a consistent designer experience.

Creating Resources in Blend

To keep things as modular as possible, let's create a new WPF application named **BlendResources** (however, you could use any of this chapter's examples as a starting point). Render a geometric shape on your current artboard via the Pencil tool, and set the Fill property to a custom, complex, gradient brush of your choosing. Once you are done, look to the right of the Fill property (or any of the brush-centric properties) in the Brushes editor. You'll notice a small square icon, which, as you might recall from Chapter 1, is the Advanced options button and provides some advanced settings when clicked. Once you click this button, you will see a menu option named Convert to New Resource (see Figure 2–61).

Figure 2–61. Extracting a Brush resource

When you select this option, you will be presented with a dialog box asking you for a few important bits of input. First and foremost, you need to give your object resource a fitting name, which I'll assume is myBrush. Next, you need to specify a location for the resource to reside. You have three choices, which are described in Table 2–3.

Table 2–3. Blend Resource Location Options

Resource Location	Meaning in Life
Application	The resources will be moved into the App.xaml file of your project. This will allow any part of a WPF or Silverlight project to use the resource.
This document	The resource can be reused within the current WPF Window/Silverlight UserControl, but nowhere else. This can be helpful if you have a complex layout system (using nested layout managers) and want all subcomponents to use a given object resource.
Resource Dictionary	This allows you to create a new XAML file, termed a *resource dictionary*, that contains nothing but object resources. This is a great choice when you are building resources to be used across projects, as new Blend projects can simply add the XAML file.

For this example, we will package up myBrush in a new resource dictionary named MyResources.xaml. Click the New button to generate this file. Figure 2–62 shows the final settings for the current resource extraction.

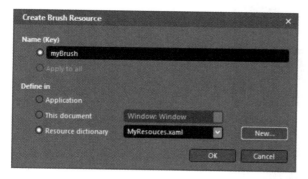

Figure 2–62. Creating a new resource dictionary with Blend

Once you are done, you'll see that your new XAML file has been added to the project, and that your App.xaml file has been modified to merge in the external file resources. Verify each of these points using the Projects panel. Also, if you examine the markup of the shape that used to contain the custom brush, you will now see that an XAML markup extension is used to refer to the resource by name. For example:[8]

```
<Path ... Fill="{DynamicResource myBrush}"/>
```

Managing Existing Resources

Once a resource has been extracted, you have a few ways to modify it after the fact. Because our resource happens to be a brush, you can go to the final tab of the Brushes editor (Brush Resources) to see all brush-based object resources in your project. If you click any resource icon, you will open a corresponding brush editor to change the resource at design time (see Figure 2–63).

---

[8] In WPF Blend projects, the {DynamicResource} markup extension is used by default. This ensures that if the resource changes in code, all UI elements using the resource are automatically updated. However, Silverlight projects use the {StaticResource} markup extension (which is also supported in WPF), which does not automatically reapply runtime changes.

Figure 2–63. *Modifying an existing resource*

The second way to view and modify resources in your application is to use the Resources panel, which you should find on the right side of the Blend IDE, next to the Properties panel. The usefulness of this panel is that you not only see each resource by name, but can also see the location in which it has been stored (in a `Window`, in a resource dictionary, and so forth). As before, you can select a resource for editing (see Figure 2–64).

Figure 2–64. The Resources panel

Applying Resources to New UI Elements

The last point to be made for now about object resources is that when you want to reuse a given item, you can simply pick the named resource using the appropriate editor. Again, since this example is using a brush-based resource, you can simply pick myBrush from the Brushes editor when setting a brush-centric property. If you were to add a new UI element to your artboard (for example, a Button control), you could switch to the Brush Resources tab of the Brushes editor. Figure 2–65 shows how to set the Background property of a Button control to use our custom brush object.

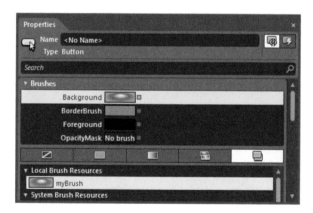

Figure 2–65. Applying an existing resource

That wraps up our exploration of how the Blend IDE can be used to work with vector graphics and object resources. You'll certainly see other tricks for manipulating graphical data in chapters to come, but you now should feel much more confident with the basics. Moreover, upcoming chapters will illustrate additional ways to capture object resources for further reuse; but at this point you are in good shape.

■ **Source Code** The **BlendResources** project can be found under the Chapter 2 subdirectory.

Summary

The point of this chapter was to examine a number of techniques supported by Expression Blend to help you create and manage vector-based graphics. We began by examining several core drawing tools (Pen, Pencil, etc.) as well as the Shapes section of the Assets library. As you have seen, the colors used to draw borders and interiors of these geometric shapes can be customized using the integrated Brushes editor and various visual effects. You also were shown how complex, vector-based art can be generated using Expression Design, exported as XAML, and imported into a Blend project.

We then examined a number of tools used to apply 2D and 3D transformations to UI elements. Both WPF and Silverlight projects use the same editors when applying 2D transformations such as flipping, rotating, and skewing data. However, 3D transformations differ quite a bit between these two APIs. WPF provides a comprehensive 3D programming model that enables you to manipulate cameras, lighting, and additional layers (which we did not directly examine here). Silverlight provides plane projections to provide a similar (but more lightweight) visual effect.

The chapter wrapped up with your first look at object resources. Remember that Blend provides a number of tools that allow you to easily reuse, modify, and apply graphical assets. You'll see additional examples of extracting graphical assets in chapters to come.

CHAPTER 3

■ ■ ■

The Animation Editor

In this chapter, you will learn about the animation tools of Expression Blend. If you have ever tried to author an animation sequence in XAML manually using Visual Studio, you know how cumbersome the process can be.[1] Thankfully, Blend ships with a very sophisticated animation editor that allows you to easily capture object state changes using a simple timeline metaphor. As you work through this chapter, you will see that animations are represented via *storyboards* that contain individual *keyframes*. Each keyframe is responsible for changing the value of a specified target property on a target object.

Once you understand how to use the core animation tools, you will then be exposed to the role of animation *easing effects*. In a nutshell, easing effects make it easy to integrate physics into an animation, including bouncing, snapping, and elastic effects. On a related note, Blend provides the KeySpline editor, which allows you more precision when changing interpolation values (a.k.a. speed effects) when a given keyframe is approached or exited.

You'll wrap up the chapter by previewing a topic explored in more detail in Chapter 4, specifically the role of *behaviors*. Here, you will learn about the `ControlStoryboardAction` behavior, which allows you to interact with a storyboard entirely in markup.

Defining the Role of Animation Services

In Chapter 2, I opened by commenting on the fact that understanding how to work with graphics is a key aspect of WPF and Silverlight development (even if you don't think this will be the case). In a similar manner, I'd like to point out the fact that animation services are also going to be very important when building real-world, production-level WPF/Silverlight applications. Despite what you may be thinking, use of animation services in no way ties you to the act of building a video game or rich multimedia application (although animation services obviously will be helpful in these cases).

In the world of WPF and Silverlight, an "animation" is nothing more than changing the value of an object property over a period of time. For example, if you wanted to have a control change its background color from bright green to dark green over five seconds, you could use a *brush animation*. Likewise, if you wanted to have a custom graphic orbit around a fixed geometric line, you could use a *path animation*. As you work through this chapter (and other chapters of the book), you will discover that just about any property you see in the Blend Properties panel can be the target of animation services.

---

[1] If you have ever attempted to build animations using other frameworks, you will be amazed at how simple building animations is via WPF and Silverlight. The need to manually create threads, erase and redraw images, create offscreen buffers, and calculate "dirty rectangles" no longer exists in a great number of cases.

The Scope of Animation Services

Animations, much like graphics, will pop up in some unexpected places. As you will see in Chapter 5, one of the most common uses of animations is to incorporate *visual cues* into a custom style or control template. For example, using animations, you can easily define how a custom control should look when the mouse enters, leaves, or clicks its surface. You could define additional animations that control how the control looks when it receives focus, loses focus, or whatnot.

Animations can also be used to cleanly and smoothly transition between values. By way of another example, you might be building a WPF Window, and use an animation to rotate a layout manager (with all contained controls) into a 3D plane. You could add a "page flip" animation to a Silverlight project to provide the illusion of turning pages of a book when viewing photos. And if you do happen to be building a video game, animations can be used to move walls of a maze, flash "Game Over" on the screen, and so forth. To be sure, the use of animation services is commonplace in WPF and Silverlight projects, and the Blend IDE makes capturing such visual effects very simple.

The Blend Animation Workspace

In Chapter 1, you learned about the Objects and Timeline panel, which allows you to select an object on the artboard for editing. As it turns out, this same panel is the entry point for the Blend animation editor. To begin learning how to create animations using the Blend IDE, let's create a new Silverlight application project[2] named **SimpleBlendAnimations**.

The first step in creating an animation with Blend is to pick the object (or objects) that will be the target of the animation logic. Currently, our new Silverlight application consists of only a Grid named LayoutRoot and the UserControl itself. While we could animate aspects of these objects, let's get a bit more granular and add a new object onto the artboard. You are free to add any type of object you wish (a Button, a Rectangle, a custom path created with the Pen or Pencil tool, etc.), but for this example, I'll assume you have created a simple Ellipse object (named myCircle) that has the Fill property set to a solid color of your choice (see Chapter 2 for details on working with the Blend Brushes editor).

When you are using the animation tools of Blend, you will most likely want to change to the Animation workspace layout, which you can activate via the Window ➤ Workspaces menu option or via the F6 key. Press the F6 key now. You should see that the IDE rearranges a number of panels such that the Objects and Timeline panel is now positioned along the bottom of the IDE (see Figure 3–1).

---

[2] The WPF API supports some additional animation features that Silverlight does not support. The techniques shown in this first example work identically regardless of which API you are using.

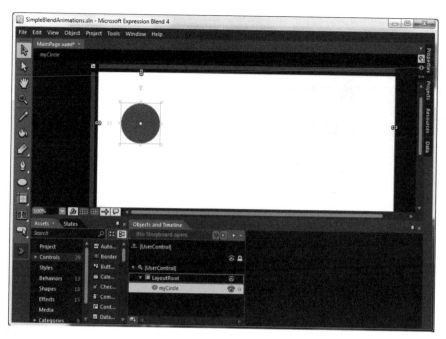

Figure 3–1. *The Animation workspace layout*

■ **Note** The F6 key allows you to toggle between the standard Design workspace and the Animation workspace.

Creating a New Storyboard

WPF and Silverlight animations are captured in XAML using a *storyboard*. Thus, when you wish to create a new animation sequence, you begin by creating a new storyboard using the Objects and Timeline panel. To do so, click the "New" button (which looks like a plus sign), as shown in Figure 3–2 (at this point, it does not matter which object is selected in the objects tree).

Figure 3–2. *Creating a new storyboard*

As soon as you click this button, you will be prompted to give your storyboard a unique name, which I will assume is `AnimateCircle` for this example (see Figure 3–3). Be aware that the name you give your storyboard is important, as you will use this name to control the animation in code, as well as via XAML.

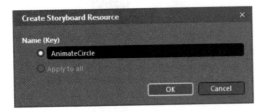

Figure 3–3. Naming a storyboard

Also be aware that Blend will store your new animation storyboard as a resource (see Chapter 2) within the current Silverlight `UserControl` or WPF `Window`. Thus, if you open the XAML viewer of the artboard, you will see the markup shown in Figure 3–4.

```
MainPage.xaml* ×
 1  <UserControl
 2      xmlns="http://schemas.microsoft.com/winfx/2006/xaml/presentation"
 3      xmlns:x="http://schemas.microsoft.com/winfx/2006/xaml"
 4      x:Class="SimpleBlendAnimations.MainPage"
 5      Width="640" Height="480">
 6      <UserControl.Resources>
 7          <Storyboard x:Name="AnimateCircle"/>
 8      </UserControl.Resources>
 9
10      <Grid x:Name="LayoutRoot" Background="White">
11          <Ellipse x:Name="myCircle" Fill="#FF1010F1" HorizontalAlignment="Left" Height="84" Margin="50,64,0,0" St
12      </Grid>
13  </UserControl>
```

Figure 3–4. Storyboards are stored as document-level resources.

■ **Note** Unlike a typical object resource (see Chapter 2), storyboards are tightly coupled to the object they are animating. Therefore, it makes no sense to create an application-level storyboard. If you need to reuse an animation sequence, typically you will package up your storyboards in a dedicated custom style, template, or `UserControl`, and then reuse the contained animations. You'll learn about these topics in Chapter 5.

Managing Existing Storyboards

Once you create a new storyboard object (such as `AnimateCircle`), you will find it listed in the drop-down list mounted at the top of the Objects and Timeline panel. Given that it is not uncommon for a single `Window` or `UserControl` to have a good number of storyboards (each responsible for animating various objects), always remember that you can select a specific storyboard for editing by using this aspect of the Objects and Timeline panel.

On a related note, also know that you can search for a storyboard by name, using the Search option (just like you can do with the Assets library and Properties panel) of the same "open a storyboard" drop-down list box. See Figure 3–5.

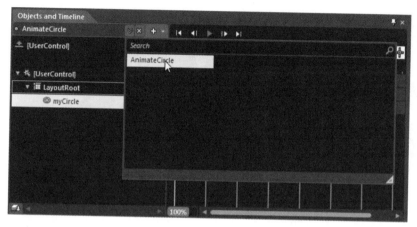

Figure 3–5. Individual storyboards can be selected via the drop-down list box.

On a final introductory note, you can easily rename, copy, or delete a storyboard by right-clicking the currently selected storyboard and using the resulting context menu, as shown in Figure 3–6 (note the Reverse option, which will flip-flop the keyframes in an animation—very useful!).

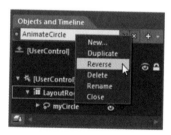

Figure 3–6. You can manage existing storyboards using the Objects and Timeline panel.

Adding Keyframes

Once you have created a new storyboard (or selected an existing storyboard for editing), you are ready to add any number of keyframes to the timeline editor. If you examine the current timeline editor, you will see a yellow line on the zero-second marker. This yellow line represents the current location of time within a given storyboard. Directly above this yellow line, you will see an icon which (at least to me) looks like a gray egg with a plus sign to its right. In reality, this is *not* an "Add an egg" button, but the Record Keyframe button, which, when clicked, adds a new keyframe to the current time location.

When you add a keyframe, you will want to be mindful of the object currently selected in the Objects and Timeline panel. The reason is that it is possible for a single storyboard to control animations for a set of objects on the artboard, and therefore you can have multiple keyframes on the same unit of time. For this example, make sure you select your `Ellipse`, and click the Record Keyframe button to add a new keyframe at the zero-second marker. Figure 3–7 shows the end result.

Figure 3–7. Adding keyframes to your timeline

Once you have added a keyframe, you'll notice that the artboard is now surrounded by a red border. At the upper left of the artboard, you'll also notice a small control has appeared that allows you to toggle on or off the recording of an animation sequence (see Figure 3–8).

Figure 3–8. You can toggle animation recordings on or off using the artboard.

■ **Note** Individual keyframes can be relocated on the timeline editor using standard mouse drag operations. Thus, if you added a keyframe at the three-second marker, but would rather it be at the six-second marker, you can easily move the keyframe. Also note you can delete (or copy) a keyframe via a standard right-click mouse operation.

Capturing Object Property Changes

Once you have added the first keyframe (which, by the way, does *not* need to be at time slice zero; the first keyframe could be at any position of time based on what you are attempting to do), you will then need to add at least one additional keyframe that collectively captures a segment of time in which a given animation will take place. To advance the timeline, you can either click the little triangular "hat" at the top of the yellow timeline marker and drag it via the mouse, or click directly on the timeline editor at a given location of time using the mouse. Using whichever technique you wish, add a second keyframe at the two-second marker (i.e., click that gray egg icon again), as shown in Figure 3–9.

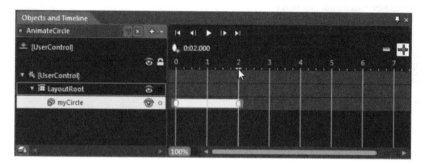

Figure 3–9. Defining a two-second time slice

Now for the interesting part. Ensure that you have selected your `Ellipse` on the artboard, and use the Properties panel and artboard to make a few state changes. By way of a few suggestions, you might want to select the `Ellipse` and move it to a new location on the artboard (you'll see a small dashed line appear showing you the distance of the object movement). You might also want to change the `Fill` property of the `Ellipse` to a new color via the Brushes editor or change the `Height` and `Width` properties via the Layout section of the Properties panel. Go ahead and make three or four changes to your `Ellipse`. Figure 3–10 shows how my circle looks once the two-second marker has been reached.

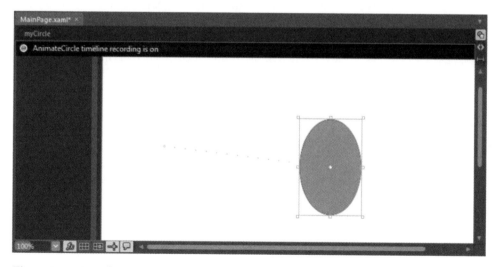

Figure 3–10. My Ellipse at the two-second marker (your circle will likely differ!)

Testing Your Animation

At this point, you can test your animation by clicking the Play button of the timeline tool area (see Figure 3–11). You will see that your circle changes from its first state to its final state in a smooth manner over the course of two seconds.

Figure 3–11. *Use the Play button to test your storyboard.*

Much like a digital media player, these tools allow you to step between the previous and next frames on the animation and advance to the first or last frame of the storyboard. Take a minute to play with these options, and be aware that you can also move to unique positions in the storyboard by moving the yellow timeline via its "hat" or simply by clicking directly on the timeline editor.

Viewing the Animation Markup

Before moving on, be sure to take a moment to view the underlying XAML that was generated by the Blend IDE. As you can see, your `<Storyboard>` element has been populated with a number of new subelements that control how the `Ellipse` object will be animated. I won't dive into all the particulars, but you can see that a given animation object (such as `ColorAnimationUsingKeyFrames`) knows which property on which object to change via the `TargetProperty` and `TargetName` properties, and knows at which time to apply the changes via the `KeyTime` property:

```
<ColorAnimationUsingKeyFrames
  Storyboard.TargetProperty="(Shape.Fill).(SolidColorBrush.Color)"
  Storyboard.TargetName="myCircle">
  <EasingColorKeyFrame KeyTime="0" Value="#FF1010F1"/>
  <EasingColorKeyFrame KeyTime="0:0:2" Value="#FFF110DE"/>
</ColorAnimationUsingKeyFrames>
```

Configuring Storyboard Properties

If you select a storyboard object from the Objects and Timeline panel, via the drop-down list box (see Figure 3–5 for a reminder of where this is located), you will be able to configure the storyboard itself via the Properties panel.[3] In Figure 3–12, you'll notice that a storyboard can be

---

[3] It is also possible to configure individual keyframes. You'll learn how to do so later in this chapter when we examine the role of animation easing effects.

configured with auto-reverse behaviors. If you were to check this AutoReverse check box, your total animation would now take four seconds, which is two seconds in each direction.

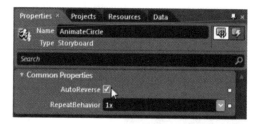

Figure 3–12. Enabling auto-reverse behaviors on a storyboard

Also note that you can configure a repeat behavior, the setting for which provides four preset options (1x, 2x, 3x, and Forever, where "x" stand for "times"). You are free to enter any possible number of iterations, however! Simply type in the number of times you would like the animation to repeat followed by the letter *x*. Thus, if you wanted to perform the animation five times, you would enter **5x** into the RepeatBehavior property text area.

You can also enter into the RepeatBehavior property text area a numerical value that specifies an *amount of time* the animation should perform, rather than the number of full iterations. If you want to specify a unit of time, you enter a value that breaks down to the following general format (note the use of dot *and* colon separators):

```
days.hours:minutes:seconds.fractionalSeconds
```

Specifying a value for days or fractionalSeconds is optional. In many cases, you will typically create a value that uses the following general template:

```
hours:minutes:seconds
```

For example, if you wanted your animation to run for 15 seconds and then stop completely (regardless of whether the animation has cycled through all keyframes), you would enter the value 00:00:15 into the RepeatBehavior property text area, as shown in Figure 3–13.

Figure 3–13. Specifying a unit of time for an animation to cycle

Zooming the Timeline Editor

Before we look at some ways to interact with our storyboards in code, I should point out one other detail of the Blend animation editor. On the extreme lower left of the animation editor, you will see a timeline zoom editor (set to 100% by default). By default, the timeline editor shows you values that correspond to individual seconds. If you need to get more granular and place keyframes on a smaller unit of measurement (fractions of a second) or a more granular amount of time, you can change this value as required. In Figure 3–14, I've set my timeline zoom scale to 750%, where I can break things down to fractions of a second.

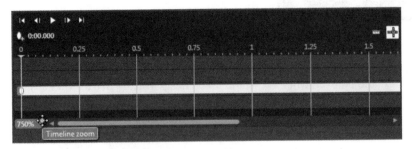

Figure 3–14. Zooming in on the units of time

■ **Note** Reenter the value **100%** into the timeline zoom editor to return to the default view (one second at a time).

Interacting with Storyboards in Code

When you use Blend to build an animation *and* you do so within a Silverlight application, the IDE will not automatically add any logic to start your storyboard when your application runs. In stark contrast, a WPF application will automatically run storyboard animations when the main window loads into memory (this, of course, can be changed after the fact). You'll examine how to change this default WPF behavior a bit later in this chapter; for the current example, let's see how we can start our animation via code (you'll see how to control a storyboard in markup later in the chapter when we examine the `ControlStoryboardAction` behavior object).

First of all, we need to decide what user action will start the animation. This action could be clicking a button, accessing a menu option, clicking the circle itself, pressing a keyboard key, or entering any other sort of input you specify. For our purposes, let's assume that the animation will start if the user clicks a `Button` control. Using the Tools panel, locate the `Button` control object (don't forget, you can also search for controls in the Assets library/Assets panel).

■ **Note** You can change the text of a selected `Button` by setting the `Content` property located in the Common Properties section of the Properties panel.

Once you have added a `Button` to your artboard, name your UI element `btnStartAnimation` using the Properties panel. Next, also using the Properties panel, click the Events button[4] and locate the `Click` event for the selected `Button`. Once you do, double-click the text area to the right of the `Click` event name. At this point, you will find the following empty event handler:

```
private void btnStartAnimation_Click(object sender,
  System.Windows.RoutedEventArgs e)
{
  // TODO: Add event handler implementation here.
}
```

Recall that the Blend IDE will automatically store storyboard elements as an object resource, located in the resource dictionary of the related WPF `Window` or Silverlight `UserControl`. Given this point, your first coding task is to find your storyboard object from your resource collection (via the key name you defined when you first created your storyboard; `AnimateCircle` if you were following my suggestion). Once you find this object, simply call the `Begin()` method. Here is the completed code[5]:

```
private void btnStartAnimation_Click(object sender,
  System.Windows.RoutedEventArgs e)
{
  Storyboard animCircle;
  animCircle = (Storyboard)this.Resources["AnimateCircle"];
  animCircle.Begin();
}
```

With this, you can run your application, click the `Button`, and see your animation execute!

Further Details of the Storyboard Class

As you would guess, the `Storyboard` class defines much more functionality than a single `Begin()` method. For example, this class provides `Pause()` and `Stop()` methods, as well as a number of properties to control the same sort of repeating and auto-reverse settings we examined via the Properties panel. If you are interested in seeing the full details of the `Storyboard` class, consult the .NET Framework 4.0 SDK/Silverlight SDK documentation.

■ **Note** The solution code for this example includes a few additional button objects that further control the storyboard. I'm sure you'll find that the code is very straightforward.

Sweet! This wraps up our first look at working with animations in the Blend IDE. There are still a number of interesting topics yet to explore, so once you feel comfortable with the basic tools you have examined thus far, move on to the next part of the chapter.

---

[4] Chapter 2 illustrated the process of handing events for a given object using the Properties panel (recall the "lightning bolt" button?).

[5] The code file that uses the `Storyboard` class will need to import the `System.Windows.Media.Animation` namespace (which will typically already be added by the IDE).

■ **Source Code** The **SimpleBlendAnimations** project can be found under the Chapter 3 subdirectory.

WPF-Specific Animation Techniques

The Windows Presentation Foundation API supports a few useful animation techniques that the current version of Silverlight (unfortunately) does not support. The first of these techniques is the use of *motion paths*, which allow you to easily move UI elements around a `Path` object created with the Pen or Pencil tool. While it is certainly possible to achieve the same end result in a Silverlight application, it does require a bit more elbow grease.

The second WPF-specific animation technique is the use of *triggers* to interact with a storyboard. In WPF, a trigger represents once possible way to respond to an event condition in XAML. For example, using triggers, it is possible to author markup that is on the lookout for various mouse events (mouse over, mouse down, mouse up, etc.), focus events, keyboard events, and so on. You can author additional markup that will start a particular storyboard when these events occur. As you may know, WPF's trigger framework was the original way in which a developer could incorporate visual cues into custom templates (to redefine the UI for controls and shapes).

While Silverlight has very limited support for triggers, the same general spirit comes through via use of the Visual State Manager (VSM). In fact, the VSM was so well received by the programming community that WPF has incorporated its own VSM into the API as of .NET 4.0. Given this, a WPF developer now has two choices when incorporating visual cues into custom templates (triggers or the VSM). You will learn about how to use triggers and the VSM to build custom templates in Chapter 5. Until then, we will focus on triggers as a way to control independent storyboard objects, but first, let's check out the role of WPF motion paths.

■ **Note** As shown at the conclusion of this chapter, the `ControlStoryboardAction` behavior object also makes it possible to manipulate animations in markup using WPF or Silverlight.

Working with WPF Motion Paths

Blend provides the very useful ability to automatically generate a WPF storyboard that will move a selected object around a predefined path. You could use motion paths to easily move a custom graphic along the peaks of a line chart (showing company profits, hopefully, rather than losses), or perhaps move an `Image` control containing an automobile icon that moves along the calculated path for a GPS software application.

Creating a motion path is very easy when using Blend. To illustrate, create a new WPF application project named **WPFMotionPathApp**. Now, just like when you are building a custom storyboard object, your first task is to establish the objects you wish to travel across the path. Any object can be used to move across a motion path, so I suggest creating a few different UI elements, such as one `Ellipse`, one `Button`, and one `Rectangle`. Go ahead and create three UI elements of your choice and place them anywhere on the artboard. Also, make sure to give each of your objects a fitting name using the `Name` property text area of the Properties panel (I've called my objects `circleOne`, `btnClickMe`, and `myRect`).

Once you have defined a set of objects that will be the target of the path animations, you next need to make the paths. You can use any of the Shape controls of the Assets library, or make some arbitrary geometric paths using the Pen and Pencil tools. Create three unique geometric shapes on your artboard (again, be creative…location, size, and dimension really do not matter). To keep your artboard orderly, however, be sure you give each path a fitting name (I've picked the names `myStar`, `myPolygon`, and `myArc`).

For each of your geometric shapes (which would be the star, polygon, and arc in my example), I also recommend that you set the `Fill` property to the No Brush setting of the Brushes editor, and change the `StrokeThickness` property (in the Appearance section) to be somewhere in the ballpark of 2 or 3 (these settings will help you see the path). Figure 3–15 shows my current WPF `Window`.

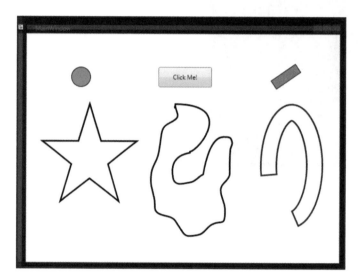

Figure 3–15. Three UI objects to animate, and three paths to define the animation path

Using your Objects and Timeline panel, select the first path you wish to convert into a motion path (I'll be picking the "star path"). Right-click this tree node and select Path ➤ Convert to Motion Path (see Figure 3–16).

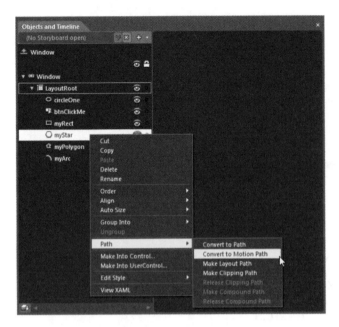

Figure 3–16. *Converting a path to a motion path*

Once you select this option, you will be presented with a dialog box in which you can select the object, or objects, that will move along the path you are converting. For this example, pick one of your target objects, such as the circle (see Figure 3–17).

Figure 3–17. *Selecting an object to move along the motion path*

As soon as you have selected the target object, a new storyboard object is created, named Storyboard1 (you can see it directly at the top of the Objects and Timeline panel). Use the rename operation, explained earlier in this chapter, to change this to the name MoveShapes. Notice that once the storyboard has been created, you can use any of the tricks shown earlier in this chapter to tweak the storyboard properties (auto-reverse, duration, etc.). As well, you can change the starting and ending points for each keyframe time slice. To do so, simply drag a given keyframe to a new unit of time. Tweak your animation sequence so that it begins at the zero-second marker and ends at the five-second marker (thus, it will take approximately five seconds for the circle to orbit around the path of the star object).

Repeat this general pattern to move the second and third target objects (the Button and Rectangle in my example) around the circumference of your other remaining paths. Feel free to change the starting and ending times for each of your animations. Figure 3–18 shows that the entire amount of time taken for this animation is eight seconds, but that each target object (the circle, button, and rectangle) starts and stops at different moments.

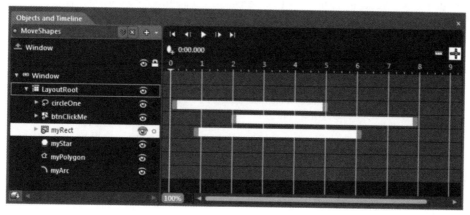

Figure 3–18. Animating each target object on the paths

Just to make this example a tad more interesting, use the Properties panel to handle the Click event of the Button object. In your implementation, display an informative message box:

```
private void btnClickMe_Click(object sender,
  System.Windows.RoutedEventArgs e)
{
  MessageBox.Show("You clicked me!");
}
```

Run your program by pressing F5 (or Ctrl+F5). You will see your three objects automatically follow the predefined paths (see if you are quick enough to click the Button object while it is moving). Note that unlike our Silverlight example, the animation starts as soon as the main Window loads into memory. The reason for this behavior is that, by default, any storyboard created within the scope of a WPF application will automatically start when the Window is loaded, thanks to the following XAML in MainWindow.xaml:

```
<Window.Triggers>
  <EventTrigger RoutedEvent="FrameworkElement.Loaded">
    <BeginStoryboard x:Name="MoveShapes_BeginStoryboard"
                     Storyboard="{StaticResource MoveShapes}"/>
  </EventTrigger>
</Window.Triggers>
```

Locate this markup using the XAML editor of your artboard. As you can see, this markup describes a WPF trigger, which, as you may recall, is a way to intercept an event condition without needing to author C# or VB code. Here, the trigger is testing to see when the Loaded event fires for the Window object[6]. When this occurs, the <BeginStoryboard> element will be processed, which will then execute the MoveShapes animation.

While this default WPF animation trigger is useful when you want to quickly see how an animation will behave at runtime, it should be clear that not all animations should occur upon the loading of a window. You might rather start an animation only when the user selects a given menu option, clicks a given button, or what have you. While you could certainly manually handle events and then start a storyboard in code, the WPF trigger framework provides a "code free" alternative. Next up, let's examine the WPF trigger-centric tools of the Blend IDE.

■ **Source Code** The **WPFMotionPathApp** project can be found under the Chapter 3 subdirectory.

Controlling WPF Animations Using Triggers

I've already defined the role of a WPF trigger (a way to respond to event conditions in markup), and you have already seen an example of a simple trigger. To see further details of the WPF trigger framework, let's make a fresh WPF application project, appropriately called **WPFAnimationTriggerApp**.

For this example, we will create a new storyboard that will spin a Button object in a full rotation. First, add a new Button named btnMyButton to your artboard and change the Content property to a fitting value. Next, create a new storyboard named SpinButtonAnimation (remember, you do this by clicking the + icon in the Objects and Timeline panel). Define a one-second time slice (beginning at the zero-second marker) by adding two keyframes that affect the selected control (see Figure 3–19).

Figure 3–19. The initial storyboard

Now, select the Button on your artboard, and rotate this object in a 360-degree rotation using the mouse. Recall that you can apply a number of transformations directly on the artboard; in this case, place your mouse cursor just outside one of the corners and move the control while pressing and holding the left mouse button (see Figure 3–20).

---

[6] The Window class extends the FrameworkElement parent class.

Figure 3–20. *Spinning the Button control*

Once again, if you run the application, you should see the `Button` control spin in a full circle when the application starts, given the autogenerated trigger. Before we investigate how to change this default behavior, take a moment to view the full XAML the IDE has generated thus far. Here is an edited, and annotated, version of what you should be seeing in the XAML editor:

```
<Window ... >
  <!-- Recall! Storyboard objects are
        bundled as object resources -->
  <Window.Resources>
    <Storyboard x:Key="SpinButtonAnimation">
      ...
    </Storyboard>
  </Window.Resources>

  <!-- This trigger will start the SpinButtonAnimation
        when the Window loads into memory -->
  <Window.Triggers>
    <EventTrigger RoutedEvent="FrameworkElement.Loaded">
      <BeginStoryboard x:Name="SpinButtonAnimation_BeginStoryboard"
          Storyboard="{StaticResource SpinButtonAnimation}"/>
    </EventTrigger>
  </Window.Triggers>

  <Grid x:Name="LayoutRoot">
    <!-- This button is the target of the animation -->
    <Button x:Name="btnMyButton" ... >
      ...
    <Button/>
  </Grid>
</Window>
```

Adding a Trigger with the Triggers Panel

Switch back to Design view (if you have not done so already, by pressing the F6 key), and locate the Triggers panel of the Blend IDE, which will be located close to the Assets panel (the Blend Windows menu provides a way to show or hide any panel of the IDE). As you can see in Figure 3-21, the Triggers panel shows you the one and only trigger for this `Window`, specifically a trigger that will start the `SpinButtonAnimation` storyboard when the window is loaded.

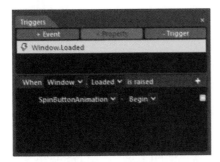

Figure 3–21. The Triggers panel allows you to start storyboards when event conditions occur.

The upper area of the Triggers panel provides three selectable buttons that allow you to interact with the following two types of WPF triggers:

- *Event trigger*: This type of trigger is used to interact with an animation timeline when a given event (such as a mouse Click event) occurs. Event triggers can be set on any object on an artboard.

- *Property trigger*: This type of trigger is useful when creating a custom style or template (see Chapter 5). Basically, this mechanism allows you to change a property value based on the change of another property value.

The +Event button allows you to add a new event trigger, the +Property button allows you to start a storyboard when a property on the selected object changes, and the –Trigger button deletes the currently selected trigger from the editor and markup. This chapter will not examine the role of property triggers, so we will ignore the +Property button for the time being (more information on triggers is provided in Chapter 5).

If you look at the current trigger configuration in Figure 3–21, you can see that the trigger is monitoring the Window.Loaded event (note the lightning bolt symbol next to the event name). Below the list of current triggers, you can see a handful of drop-down list boxes, which can be used to construct a simple, human-readable sentence that corresponds to what will happen when the trigger fires. The general template of this sentence breaks down as so:

```
When objectName.eventOnObject is raised storyboardName.storyboardAction
```

Currently, the sentence essentially reads "When Window.Loaded is raised, begin the SpinButtonAnimation storyboard." Let's delete this current trigger completely by selecting the Window.Loaded trigger and then clicking the –Trigger button.

Now, let's add a new trigger that will begin the SpinButtonAnimation storyboard if the button itself is clicked. First, click the +Event button. Next, using the When drop-down list box (currently displaying Window), select your Button object by name. Then, select the Click event from the "is raised" drop-down list box, as shown in Figure 3–22.

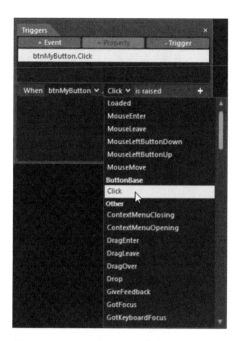

Figure 3–22. Defining a Click event trigger for the Button object

■ **Note** If you do not see the object you are looking to configure within the Triggers panel, make sure it is the selected node in the Objects and Timeline panel! By default, the Triggers panel shows you only options for the topmost `Window` and the currently selected item.

Once you have picked the object and event condition, click the + button at the very end of the trigger definition. This displays an additional part of the Triggers UI, where you can select any storyboard on the current document. Pick your `SpinButtonAnimation` storyboard, and then elect to start the animation sequence. (Note the additional options beyond starting the storyboard, as shown in Figure 3–23; they are the same core options as you would find if driving a storyboard in code.)

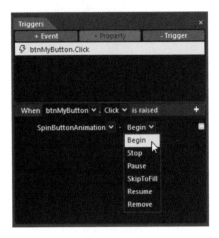

Figure 3–23. Starting a storyboard based on a trigger condition

If you run your program (press F5 or Ctrl+F5), you will find that the button will spin only after you click within it. As well, if you examine the generated XAML, you will find that the trigger now looks something like so:

```
<Window.Triggers>
  <EventTrigger RoutedEvent="ButtonBase.Click"
                SourceName="btnMyButton">
    <BeginStoryboard
      Storyboard="{StaticResource SpinButtonAnimation}"/>
  </EventTrigger>
</Window.Triggers>
```

Building a Menu System with Blend

To further illustrate how to use event triggers, we will now extend the current example to make use of a simple menu system to control the storyboard animation sequence. First of all, *delete* the current Button.Click trigger completely. Next, select your SpinButtonAnimation storyboard within the Objects and Timeline panel, and then use the Properties panel to set the RepeatBehavior property to Forever.

Now, use your Assets panel to locate a control named Menu, and double-click this item to add an instance to your artboard. Use the Properties panel to name your Menu control mainMenuSystem. Use the mouse to resize the Menu object so that it expands the full width of the window. Next, right-click the Menu control on the artboard and select the Add MenuItem option (see Figure 3–24).

Figure 3–24. Adding a MenuItem to a Menu control

Select your new `MenuItem` control, locate the `Header` property in the Properties panel (searching for an item is the fastest way to locate an item, but to give you a hint, you will find the `Header` property in the Common Properties section), and set its value to `File`. Also, name this item `mnuFile`.

■ **Note** The menu editor of Blend is similar to that of Visual Studio. You can right-click any `MenuItem` object on the artboard to add submenus and add separator bars (see the options shown in Figure 3–24). As well, when you select any `MenuItem` on the Objects and Timeline panel, you can configure any number of properties and handle any number of events.

Select the `mnuFile` object on the artboard once again, and right-click to add three submenu items. For purposes of this example, name the `Header` properties of these menu items `Play!`, `Stop!`, and `Pause!` (and name the menu items accordingly, `mnuPlay`, `mnuStop`, and `mnuPause`). Once you are done, your menu system should look like that shown in Figure 3–25.

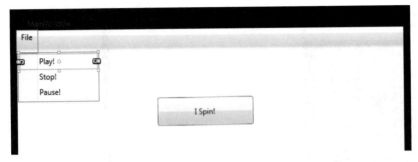

Figure 3–25. Building a menu system with Blend

Notice the nested nature of each menu component within the Objects and Timeline panel, a shown in Figure 3–26. Now that we have the basic menu system in place, we are ready to capture some event triggers.

Figure 3–26. The menu system as realized in the Objects and Timeline panel

Assigning Triggers to Menu Items

Select the mnuPlay object in your Objects and Timeline panel and then click the +Event button of the Triggers panel. Use the Triggers editor to start the SpinButtonAnimation storyboard when the Play menu is clicked. Replicate the previous steps to stop and pause the same storyboard when the user selects the File ➤ Stop! and File ➤ Pause! menu options. Figure 3–27 shows your final set of triggers.

Figure 3–27. Connecting an event trigger to a menu option

Now, run your application! You should find that you can use menu options to control your storyboard object. Take a moment to appreciate that all of this interactivity has been created without authoring a lick of C# (or VB) code (very cool indeed).

■ **Note** If you are interested, take a moment to view the generated XAML. You will find that the `<Window.Triggers>` collection now has multiple `<EventTrigger>` elements, which manipulate various options of the related storyboard.

You could certainly add additional menu items to capture the remaining event conditions of the storyboard object (such as Resume), or better yet, add additional UI elements to build brand new triggers for additional storyboards. I'll leave it to the interested reader to extend this example with some more triggers, target objects, and storyboards as they see fit.

■ **Source Code** The **WPFAnimationTriggerApp** project can be found under the Chapter 3 subdirectory.

Understanding Animation Easing Effects

At this point in the chapter, I hope you feel (more?) comfortable with the following core animation topics and techniques:

- The overall role of WPF and Silverlight animations (changing a property value over time)

- The role of a storyboard object (connecting objects, properties changes, and time segments)

- How to use the Objects and Timeline panel to create a new storyboard and set of keyframes

- How to use the artboard to change property values when in timeline animation edit mode

- How to control a storyboard in code

- How to control a storyboard using WPF triggers

While understanding these topics and techniques is a great step in the right direction, allow me to mention a few additional topics regarding creating animation sequences with Blend. Specifically, you will now examine how to use the animation editors to incorporate easing effects into an animation. Simply put, *easing effects* provide a way to configure various physical constraints as time moves between two adjacent keyframes. Using easing effects, you can inject effects that allow you to build storyboards that make objects bounce, spring effects, and so on.

Building the Initial Layout

To get started, create a new Silverlight application project named **AnimationEasingEffects**.[7] Much like the other examples thus far in this chapter, our initial goals are to define a set of objects to be animated and then define a set of storyboards to animate them. If you are following along, begin by drawing three UI elements on your artboard (anything will do; I'll be using a circle, triangle, and polygon shape created with the Pencil tool) and giving them fitting names using the Properties panel.

This time, be sure that each of these objects is located on the extreme upper portion of your artboard, as we will apply various easing effects to "drop" them to the bottom of the screen. Next, use the Pencil tool to draw a "landing zone" area on the bottom of the Silverlight application. Figure 3–28 shows my current layout system.

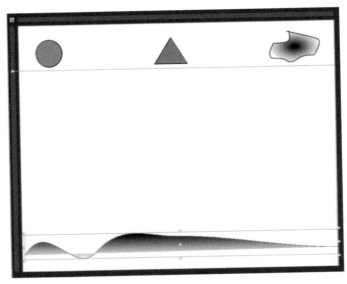

Figure 3–28. Objects…get ready to drop!

---

[7] WPF projects created with Blend also support animation easing tools, so the following techniques apply equally to desktop programs created with Windows Presentation Foundation.

Creating the Initial Storyboards

Your next task is to create three unique storyboards named DropAndBounceBall, RubberbandTriangle, and HoverAndCrashPoly. Begin with the DropAndBounceBall storyboard. This animation sequence will capture the movement of the Ellipse object as it moves from its starting point to the landing zone. Using the techniques shown over the course of this chapter, configure the DropAndBounceBall storyboard to capture this movement over the course of four seconds (simply move the Ellipse object to the new location when in recording mode).

Next, create and configure the RubberbandTriangle and HoverAndCrashPoly storyboards in a very similar manner. Over the course of approximately four seconds, move the remaining two objects from their starting location to the bottom part of the landing zone (again, while in recording mode).

Once you are done, test each of your animation sequences by first selecting the storyboard by name in the Objects and Timeline panel and then clicking the Play button. Once you are happy with the initial results, press on to the next section of this chapter, where we will apply a few easing effects.

Applying Animation Easing Effects

Select the DropAndBounceBall storyboard in the Objects and Timeline panel, and then click on the existing "egg" icon representing the final keyframe of the animation sequence. Much like an object to the artboard, when you click directly on a given keyframe in the animation editor, a number of configurable properties appear in the Properties panel.[8] Once you click a keyframe, you will see an Easing section appear, with the EasingFunction button selected by default. Currently, this keyframe has no easing effects applied, as shown in Figure 3–29.

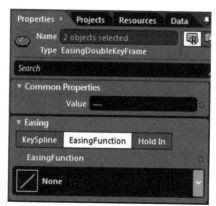

Figure 3–29. Configuring a keyframe for easing effects

Each keyframe can be configured using a variety of built-in animation easing effects, all of which can be selected using the EasingFunction drop-down list box. Each type of easing effect is partitioned into three categories (see Figure 3–30):

---

[8] Be aware that you can also give individual keyframes a name, via the Name property. This allows you to drive a keyframe and its features in code.

- The options in the In column will apply the chosen effect to the beginning part of the keyframe.

- The options in the Out column will apply the chosen effect to the ending part of the selected keyframe.

- The options in the InOut column will apply the effect to both the beginning and ending parts of the selected keyframe.

If you open the EasingFunction drop-down list box, you will see a great number of intrinsic easing functions. For the selected keyframe of the DropAndBounceBall storyboard, select the Bounce Out effect, as shown in Figure 3–30.

Figure 3–30. Various easing effects

Once you pick a given easing effect, you can further configure it using the Properties panel. Consider Figure 3–31, which shows how you can configure the number of, and aggressiveness ("Bounciness") of, each bounce.

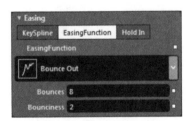

Figure 3–31. Configuring properties for an easing effect

After ensuring your `DropAndBounceBall` storyboard is selected in the Objects and Timeline panel, test this easing effect via the Play button. Continue to experiment with this Bounce Out effect (and, ideally, try a few additional effects for exploratory purposes).

Select your second storyboard (`RubberbandTriangle` in this example) and then click the final keyframe of the time slice. This time, try the Elastic In easing effect, which has some interesting values set for the `Oscillations` and `Springiness` properties (see Figure 3–32).

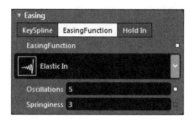

Figure 3–32. Configuring the Elastic In easing effect

Again, test your results using the Play button of the Objects and Timeline panel.

Working with the KeySpline Editor

The benefit of the built-in animation easing effects is that they provide a way to quickly incorporate common physical properties into an animation sequence. If you require a finer level of control, you can use the KeySpline editor. To illustrate, select your final storyboard object from the Objects and Timeline panel, and click its final keyframe. This time, click the KeySpline button. Here, you will find an editor that allows you to configure the speed ratio as a given keyframe is approached. Using this editor, you can change the x1, x2, y1, and y2 values using either the individual slider controls or by clicking and dragging a given yellow control point. In general:

- The steeper the line, the faster the change in value at that point.

- When the graph is a straight line from the lower-left corner to the upper-right corner, the interpolation is linear in time.

Figure 3–33 shows a spline configuration that will cause the final target object to hover at the midway point, then crash into the landing zone.

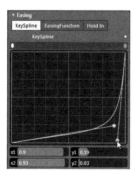

Figure 3–33. Using the KeySpline editor to capture a "crash" effect

Executing the Storyboard at Runtime

Recall that, unlike a WPF application, Silverlight storyboard objects are not automatically configured to start when the application launches.

Let's complete this project by handling the MouseLeftButtonDown event for each of the animated objects. To do so, select the objects one at a time in the Objects and Timeline panel, click the Events button of the Properties panel, and double-click the text area for the MouseLeftButtonDown event. Once you have created all three of the event handlers, start the correct storyboard; for example:

```
private void ellipse_MouseLeftButtonDown(object sender,
  System.Windows.Input.MouseButtonEventArgs e)
{
  Storyboard sb =
    (Storyboard)this.Resources["DropAndBounceBall"];
  sb.Begin();
}
```

When you run your Silverlight application now, you can click any of the three shapes (at any time) to start the animations. Remember, you do not have to wait for an animation to complete before starting another—you can run multiple animations at the same time.

■ **Source Code** The **AnimationEasingEffects** project can be found under the Chapter 3 subdirectory.

Learning More About Animation Easing Effects

Now, as I hope you agree, it would be tedious for me to attempt to describe with the written word how to configure each and every animation easing effect. Not only would the end result be impossible to show on a static printed page, but the number of configuration settings for each easing effect is quite expansive. At this point, I think you should be in good shape to examine on your own time further details of configuring an animation with various effects. If you are interested in more information, please look up the topic "Change animation interpolation between keyframes" within the Expression Blend User Guide (see Figure 3–34).

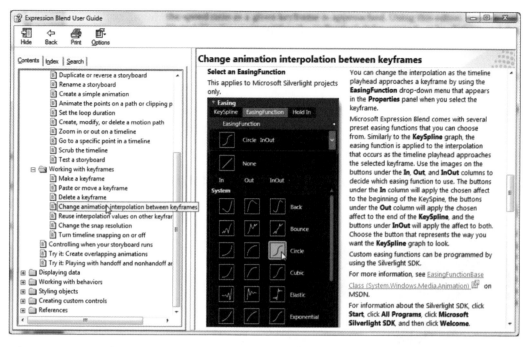

Figure 3–34. Consult the Expression Blend User Guide for more information on easing effects.

Controlling Storyboards in XAML via Behavior Objects

To conclude our study of Blend animations, I'd like to mention one final topic that will be more deeply examined in Chapter 4, specifically the role of *behaviors*. In a nutshell, a behavior object allows you to apply complex runtime logic to a UI element, without the need to author any procedural code.

As you will see in Chapter 4, numerous behavior objects exist that allow a UI element to be moved with the mouse, call methods on objects, and so forth. Here, I would like to point out that the `ControlStoryboardAction` behavior object provides a way to start, stop, and pause in XAML (in a way that does not tie you to the WPF trigger framework).

Modifying the SimpleBlendAnimations Example

To illustrate, reopen your **SimpleBlendAnimations** project in the Blend IDE (that was the first example of the chapter) and save a copy of the entire project using File ➤ Save Copy of Project (I named my copy **SimpleBlendAnimations_Behavior**). Once you have done so, make sure the new copy is currently open in the Blend IDE.

Now, open the XAML editor for your `MainPage.xaml` file and locate the definition of the "Start Animation!" button. You should see that it has a `Click` handler value, which looks something like so:

```
<Button x:Name="btnStartAnimation" Content="Start Animation!" ...
        Click="btnStartAnimation_Click"/>
```

Delete this `Click` handler value completely from the XAML definition, so that your markup looks like so (your exact properties may differ based on how you configured the object):

```
<Button x:Name="btnStartAnimation" Content="Start Animation!"
        HorizontalAlignment="Left" Margin="8,8,0,0"
        VerticalAlignment="Top" Width="124"/>
```

Next, open your C# code file and completely delete the `Click` handler logic that contains the code that programmatically started your storyboard (in other words, delete all traces of the `btnStartAnimation_Click()` method). For a sanity check, build and run your project and ensure you compile cleanly.

Adding the ControlStoryboardAction Behavior

Now, switch to the artboard designer for your `MainPage.xaml` file, open the Assets panel, select the Behaviors category, and locate the `ControlStoryboardAction` object, as shown in Figure 3–35.

Figure 3–35. The ControlStoryboardAction behavior

Drag this behavior object onto the `Button` on your artboard (see Figure 3–36). As an alternative, you could also drag the behavior object onto the correct node in the Objects and Timeline panel.

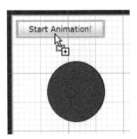

Figure 3–36. Behaviors can be dragged onto the artboard.

Select this new node in your Objects and Timeline panel (you will see it beneath the `Button` node), and examine the Trigger section of the Properties panel (see Figure 3–37). Notice that the `SourceObject` property is set to your `Button`, based on the previous drag-and-drop operation. This property specifies which object on the artboard will interact with the behavior. Also notice the `EventName` property is automatically set to `Click`, which you can change via the drop-down list box.

Figure 3–37. *SourceName and EventName are used to configure how the object triggers the behavior.*

All you need to do to finish configuring this particular behavior is to pick a storyboard object to manipulate, and then specify which action should occur when the event trigger occurs. In Figure 3–38, you can see that when my button is clicked, the `AnimateCircle` storyboard will play.

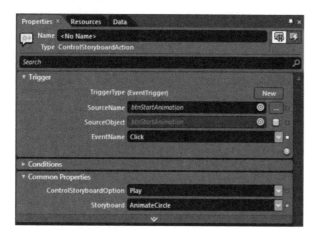

Figure 3–38. *The fully configured ControlStoryboardAction behavior*

Now, run your program! You should be able to start your animation without any C# code or custom event handlers. If you examine the generated markup, you will see the XAML that has been generated:

```xaml
<Button x:Name="btnStartAnimation" Content="Start Animation!"
        HorizontalAlignment="Left" Margin="8,8,0,0"
        VerticalAlignment="Top" Width="124">
  <i:Interaction.Triggers>
    <i:EventTrigger EventName="Click">
    <ei:ControlStoryboardAction
        Storyboard="{StaticResource AnimateCircle}"/>
```

```
      </i:EventTrigger>
    </i:Interaction.Triggers>
</Button>
```

If you'd like to, add some additional Button controls to your artboard and define new ControlStoryboardAction objects to pause, stop, or resume your animation cycle.

■ **Source Code** The **SimpleBlendAnimations_Behavior** project can be found under the Chapter 3 subdirectory.

Summary

This chapter illustrated how to use the Blend animation editor, which allows you to create WPF and Silverlight storyboard objects. Recall that a storyboard contains a set of keyframes, which collectively change the values of an object's properties over time. After examining the various aspects of the Animation workspace, you then learned how to interact with storyboards in code. Here you learned that once you obtain the correct resource, you are able to control the animation using the Storyboard class.

Next, you learned about some WPF-specific animation topics, beginning with the role of motion paths, which allow you to move a target object around a predefined path. You then took your first look at the WPF trigger architecture. As you saw, triggers provide a way to interact with property changes and events in markup, oftentimes for the purpose of controlling a storyboard (you'll see more information about triggers in upcoming chapters).

The chapter wrapped up with a tour of animation easing effects and a brief introduction to behavior objects. Using the built-in easing effect objects, you can very easily (and very quickly) apply various physical properties to your animations such as bounce effects, spring effects, and so on. If you require a finer level of control, you can also tweak keyframe timing using the Blend KeySpline editor. As well, using the ControlStoryboardAction object, you can manipulate animations entirely in markup, without being tied to the WPF trigger framework.

CHAPTER 4

Controls, Layouts, and Behaviors

Unless you intend to build a UI entirely composed of interactive geometries, the chances are very good that your WPF or Silverlight applications will require the use of various controls. As expected, the WPF and Silverlight APIs both ship with a set of intrinsic controls that allows you to gather user input and respond to user actions. In this chapter, you will learn how to use the Expression Blend IDE to configure UIs consisting of controls arranged in various *layout managers*. As you will see, the WPF and Silverlight frameworks both ship with a collection of layout objects, including `Grid`, `StackPanel`, and `Canvas` (among others), all of which can be configured via the Blend artboard.

Once you feel comfortable using Blend to lay out graphical user interfaces (GUIs), you will then be introduced to the role of behaviors. As introduced in Chapter 4, you learned that *behaviors* allow you to incorporate a number of advanced features into an application, without the need to author procedural code. For example, there are behavior objects that enable items to be moved via the mouse, control animation storyboards (as you saw in the previous chapter), change property values (or call methods) based on defined conditions, and so on.

■ **Note** This chapter will expose you to a "sane subset" of controls and behaviors. However, you will see additional examples throughout the remainder of this book.

A First Look at GUI Controls

If you have created GUIs using any sort of graphical designer in the past (such as a Java Swing editor, web page designer, or Visual Studio's GUI creation tools), you won't be surprised when I tell you that Blend allows you to configure common controls such as `Button`, `ListBox`, `ComboBox`, `MenuItem`, `DataGrid`, `ProgressBar`, and so forth to build a UI for your projects.

WPF and Silverlight both ship with a control library, but the WPF API provides a greater number of options. By way of one example, WPF ships with a set of controls that comprises the

Document API. As shown later in this chapter, this API enables a WPF application to incorporate PDF-style text formatting using the XML Paper Specification (XPS).[1]

Although each API ships with an independent set of controls, by and large, a given control can be configured in a similar (if not identical) manner when you are using the Blend IDE. Therefore, regardless of whether you are using the WPF `Button` or the Silverlight `Button`, the Blend Properties panel will show you the same general set of configuration options even though the controls are from different classes in different libraries.

■ **Note** The Blend Tools panel and Assets library always show you the "correct" components based on your selected project type (WPF or Silverlight [or Windows Phone 7; see Chapter 7]).

Locating Controls Within the IDE

When you want to add a GUI control to the artboard, you could hunt for a given item on your Tools panel. However, remember that the Tools panel shows you only a selection of commonly used UI controls, grouped by category. If you take a moment to examine your options, you'll see that the Tools panel has groups for layout managers, text controls (`Label`, `TextBox`, etc.), and basic user input controls (`Button`, `Slider`, `ListBox`, and so on). See Figure 4–1.

Figure 4–1. The Tools panel provides quick access to common UI controls.

■ **Note** Remember, you can interact with items in a Blend panel only when the artboard is in design or split mode (i.e., not in the full-screen XAML editor).

---

[1] In a nutshell, XPS is a Microsoft alternative to the Adobe PDF file format.

When you want to see the full set of UI controls, access the Assets panel (or the Assets library, located on your Tools panel). Here you can see all possible controls by looking under the All section of the Controls category. Figure 4–2 shows some of the options you will find for a WPF application project.

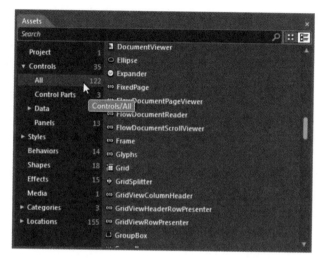

Figure 4–2. The Controls category of the Assets library shows all controls based on your API of choice.

Configuring Controls via the Properties Panel

Regardless of how you locate and select a UI control, you can then draw an instance of the component on your artboard, just like you would draw a geometric shape (see Chapter 2). Once you perform a selection operation on the component (recall that V is the shortcut key), you can configure the item using the Properties panel, handle events (via the Events button of the Properties panel), and so on. Since you've already worked with these aspects of the Properties panel, I won't bother to re-describe the basics; however, this chapter will show you a few more exotic (and not as intuitive) aspects of working with the Properties panel.

Learning About Control Details

Given the nature of this book, the goal of this chapter is *not* to talk about the functionality of every single WPF or Silverlight control, but rather to help you understand how to use the Blend IDE to configure the look and feel of controls generally. If you are a programmer by trade, you are certainly aware of the role of the .NET Framework 4.0 SDK documentation and Silverlight SDK documentation. Both of these guides are available online, and can be installed on your local machine via the Visual Studio 2010 Help Library Manager.[2]

---

[2] Launch this tool by navigating to Windows Start ➤ All Programs ➤ Microsoft Visual Studio 2010 ➤ Visual Studio Tools ➤ Manage Help Settings. Here, you can download and install documentation for a number of APIs (including Silverlight and Windows Phone 7).

If you want to see full details of WPF controls but do not have a local installation of the help system, the Expression Blend User Guide provides a section named "Controls, properties, and events reference," which contains links to the WPF and Silverlight online documentation. Assuming you have the Blend User Guide open, you will find this topic under the References folder, as shown in Figure 4–3.

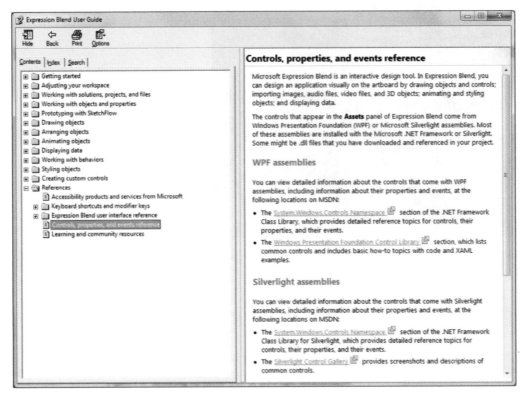

Figure 4–3. *The Blend User Guide provides links to WPF and Silverlight control documentation.*

From here, you can click the provided links to navigate to the documentation system for your controls of choice. Figure 4–4 shows the web page that opens if you click the `Silverlight System.Windows.Controls Namespace` link.

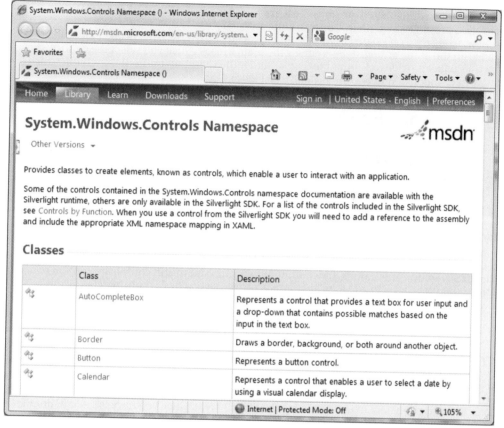

Figure 4-4. *Accessing the online Silverlight control documentation*

In this chapter (and the chapters to come), you will see details of various controls, but you should make sure to consult the documentation for full details.

Understanding the Control Content Model

The first project of this chapter focuses on one particular aspect of WPF and Silverlight controls that deserves special mention, specifically the *control content model*. Under the APIs in this model, the term "content" refers to what is used to fill the interior of a GUI control. For example, a typical Button control has a blurb of text data as content (such as OK, Cancel, Submit, or whatnot).

While some GUI controls might need nothing more than a simple blob of text, WPF and Silverlight allow you to define much more complex content.[3] For example, you could define a Button control that defines an animated arrow *and* a blob of text as content. When you wish to define complex internal content, the Blend IDE provides the tools to do so; however, how you

---

[3] A control that supports the control content model must derive from the ContentControl base class.

do so may not be immediately obvious. To learn the ropes, begin by creating a new WPF application project named **BlendControlContent**.[4]

Now, using the Tools panel or Assets library, locate the Button control and place one instance on top of the artboard designer for the main Window. Once you select the control, the Properties panel provides a Content text area (under the Common Properties section), which allows you to supply a simple textual value (see Figure 4–5).

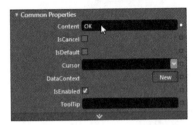

Figure 4–5. *Simple control content can be set via the Properties panel.*

Clearly, this simple input area cannot be used to define more complex content such as embedded graphics, animations, or whatnot. When you want to add composite content to a control, your first step is to add a *layout manager* to the selected GUI control. This layout manger, in turn, will contain the set of individual elements that represents the content as a whole.

Creating Composite Content

You will learn about the details of working with layout managers a bit later in this chapter, but for the time being, locate the StackPanel control in the Assets library (remember, you can quickly locate a given item of interest using the Search area). Once you have located it, double-click this layout manger to add it to the Window. Drag this StackPanel over the Button control and press the Alt key (see Figure 4–6). This will place the StackPanel within the scope of the Button control and will be used to hold the new, composite content.

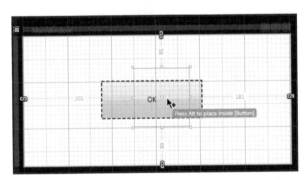

Figure 4–6. *Composite content is contained within a layout manager*

---

[4] The techniques shown in this example would be identical for a Silverlight project.

> ■ **Note** When you are building composite content, you may find it helpful to zoom into the control you are editing using the Blend artboard controls or your mouse wheel (see Chapter 1).

At this point, you will likely want to resize the embedded layout manger to take up the interior of the control (via a Selection operation; the black arrow on the Tools panel or the V shortcut key). Also, for this example, we want the StackPanel to position its data in a horizontal position rather than in the default, vertical position. Change the Orientation property for your StackPanel to Horizontal using the Properties panel.

If you now examine the Objects and Timeline panel, you can select the Button control's layout manager (i.e., the StackPanel) and then add any number of additional components. Go ahead and add a geometry of your choosing (such as an ellipse, star, or arrow) and a Label control to your layout manager. Figure 4–7 shows one possibility.

Figure 4–7. *A Button control with a StackPanel (and its children) as content*

You can now select each component for editing. As shown in Figure 4–8, I used the Properties panel to change some basic settings of the Label (font sizes via the Text section, text positioning via the Layout section, and assigning the value "OK!" to the Content property). As well, I've configured some custom brushes for the border and interior colors of the star shape.

More interestingly, I've defined an animation that will change the color of the star over a one-second interval as long as the Button object is in memory (in other words, the AutoReverse property has been selected, and the RepeatBehavior property has been set to Forever). I won't reiterate every aspect of working with the Blend animation editor here (see Chapter 3 for full details); however, recall the basic steps of creating a new animation storyboard:

- Create a new storyboard using the Objects and Timeline panel.

- Add keyframes to the storyboard using the Record Keyframe button (the "gray egg" icon).

- Change property settings on a selected UI element to record state changes.

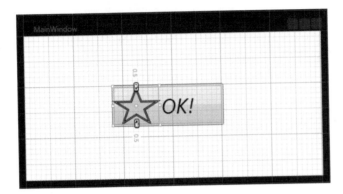

Figure 4–8. A fancy button

Handling Events for Controls with Composite Content

Be aware that when you build a control with composite content, you can handle events for any of the subcomponents if you wish. For example, you could handle the MouseDown event on the star component (which is a RegularPolygon object) and the Click event for the Button itself. In this way, you can capture not only the act of "clicking the button," but also the acts of clicking (or what have you) the individual pieces of composite content. Here are some event handlers for the situation just presented that will change the caption of the Window based on where the user clicks:[5]

```
private void regularPolygon_MouseDown(object sender,
   System.Windows.Input.MouseButtonEventArgs e)
{
   this.Title = "You clicked on the star!"

   // Stop the mouse event from bubbling to the button.
   e.Handled = true;
}

private void Button_Click(object sender, System.Windows.RoutedEventArgs e)
{
   this.Title = "You clicked on the Button!";
}
```

Notice that when the user clicks the star shape, I am preventing the event from "bubbling" through the tree of XAML by setting the Handled property of the incoming event arguments to true. If this were not done, the mouse event would first be handled by the star and then the button. In any case, run your application (via the F5 key) and verify your control can receive mouse input as expected.

---

[5] Recall from Chapter 2 that the Events button of the Properties panel (the button with the lightning bolt icon) allows you to generate event handlers for the currently selected item on the artboard.

Reusing Composite Content

If you view the generated XAML, you will find that the Button has been defined as expected; the StackPanel is the direct content, and the StackPanel contains two items. For example:

```
<Button Height="65" Margin="147,73,153,0" VerticalAlignment="Top"
        Click="Button_Click">
  <StackPanel Height="57" Width="174" Orientation="Horizontal">
    <ed:RegularPolygon x:Name="regularPolygon" Fill="#FFE3EF0D" Height="56"
        InnerRadius="0.47211" PointCount="5" Stretch="Fill" Stroke="Black"
        HorizontalAlignment="Left" Width="71" StrokeThickness="3"
        MouseDown="regularPolygon_MouseDown"/>
    <Label Content="OK!" HorizontalAlignment="Center"
        VerticalAlignment="Center"
        FontSize="32" FontStyle="Italic"/>
  </StackPanel>
</Button>
```

However, as you recall from Chapter 3, when you create an animation, the Blend IDE adds the storyboard as a named resource of the Window or UserControl. If you examine the animation markup, you'll see that the objects of your custom button are mentioned directly by name, as in the case of my regularPolygon object that represents the star of the complex content:

```
<Window.Resources>
  <Storyboard x:Key="AnimateStar" AutoReverse="True" RepeatBehavior="Forever">
  <ColorAnimationUsingKeyFrames
      Storyboard.TargetProperty="(Shape.Fill).(SolidColorBrush.Color)"
      Storyboard.TargetName="regularPolygon">
      <EasingColorKeyFrame KeyTime="0" Value="#FFE3EF0D"/>
      <EasingColorKeyFrame KeyTime="0:0:1" Value="#FF2620F1"/>
    </ColorAnimationUsingKeyFrames>
  </Storyboard>
</Window.Resources>
```

In a similar way, the markup for our Window defines a trigger to start the animation sequence. In a nutshell, as things now stand, our custom button is rather disjointed. This brings up the question, what if you want *three* fancy star buttons?

Currently, this Button is tightly coupled to this specific Window and *cannot* be easily reused. While you could copy and paste the Button to reuse the complex content, the animation is forever connected to the star object of the original button.

In Chapter 5, you will learn about the process of building custom UserControl objects, custom templates, and custom styles. As you will see, it is more common (and more useful) to define a control with complex content as a unique style or UserControl, as this makes it possible to easily reuse your creation.

Until that point, just remember that a majority of WPF and Silverlight controls support composite content. Using Blend, you can generate such content by embedding a layout manager within its boundaries and populate the container with related components. Next up, let's examine a related concept, that of the items control model.

___

■ **Source Code** The **BlendControlContent** project can be found under the Chapter 4 subdirectory.

Understanding the Items Control Model

A number of WPF and Silverlight controls have the capability to contain a list of items within their interior (such as the ListBox or ComboBox). Similar to a true "content control," controls such as the ListBox can contain either a simple batch of string data or more complex, composite list items. In a very general sense, you can regard this list of custom items as the "content" of the control; however, more specifically, such controls use the *items control model.*[6]

To illustrate, let's make a fancy ListBox control within a brand new WPF application named (appropriately enough) **FancyListBox**. Begin by adding a ListBox to your artboard, and use the Properties panel to name this control customListBox. Next, add a Label control (named currentSelection) to your artboard, somewhere below the ListBox. This Label will be used to display the value of the currently selected item, and we will configure this UI element in just a bit.

Adding ListBoxItems

When you wish to add items to a ListBox control, one approach is to right-click the control on your artboard and select the Add ListBoxItem menu option (a ComboBox control would show an Add ComboBoxItem menu selection). If you take this approach, you add a new ListBoxItem that contains simple text (which can be configured after the fact). Using this approach, add a single ListBoxItem object to your ListBox control (see Figure 4–9).

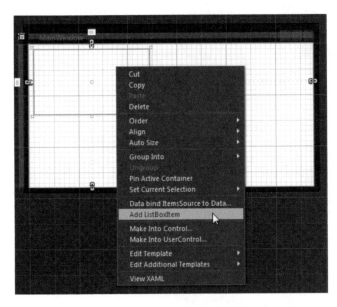

Figure 4–9. Adding new items to an items control

Now, using your mouse, select and stretch your new ListBoxItem to take up about one-half the height of the ListBox (see Figure 4–10).

---

[6] Such controls extend the ItemsControl parent class.

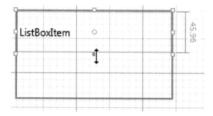

Figure 4–10. *Resizing a ListBoxItem*

Make sure that your ListBoxItem is currently selected in the Objects and Timeline panel, and add a StackPanel to this control, much like you added a StackPanel to the "fancy button" you created earlier. Once you have done so, select this StackPanel in the Objects and Timeline panel, locate the Orientation property in the Properties panel (via the Search area), and set this property to the value Horizontal. At this point, you will want to resize the new StackPanel so that it fits within the containing ListBoxItem. Take a moment to position things to your liking.

Now for the really interesting part. Select the StackPanel in your Objects and Timeline panel, and then add an Ellipse control and a Label control using standard Blend techniques (the Tools panel, the Assets library, etc.). Once you are done, the Objects and Timeline panel should look like Figure 4–11.

Figure 4–11. *A ListBoxItem with composite "content"*

Use your Properties panel and mouse to resize these new controls as you see fit. Likewise, set the Fill property of the Ellipse to the color red, and set the Content property of the Label to (you guessed it) the value **Red!**. Figure 4–12 shows the current layout.

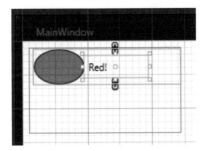

Figure 4–12. Our composite ListBoxItem

Now, select the ListBoxItem within the Objects and Timeline panel, right-click, and select the Copy menu option. Next, select the ListBox itself (again within the Objects and Timeline panel), right-click, and select Paste. Repeat these steps three times total, so that your ListBox has a set of four ListBoxItem objects. Use the Properties panel to set the Fill property of the new Ellipse controls to a unique set of colors and to set the Content property of the new Label controls to a unique set of corresponding names. Figure 4–13 shows my final design.

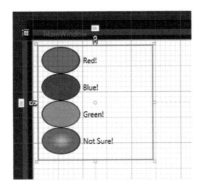

Figure 4–13. The final fancy ListBox

Viewing the XAML

If you switch to the XAML editor, you will find that your ListBox control does indeed contain four ListBoxItem objects. However, instead of having a simple text value, they contain composite UI elements. For example:

```
<ListBoxItem Height="41.96" Width="180">
  <StackPanel Height="41.96" Width="180" Orientation="Horizontal">
    <Ellipse Fill="#FF48D416" Stroke="Black" Width="62"/>
    <Label Content="Green!" Width="78.993" HorizontalAlignment="Center"
        VerticalAlignment="Center"/>
  </StackPanel>
</ListBoxItem>
```

Finding the Current Selection

Regardless of what a `ListBoxItem` contains (a simple text value or a `StackPanel` of elements), you can find which `ListBox` member has been selected by using the `SelectedIndex` property of the `ListBox`, which returns a zero-based value (0 is the first item, 1 is the second item, and so on).

Select your `ListBox` in the Objects and Timeline panel, and then click the Events button of the Properties panel to handle the `ListBox`'s `SelectionChanged` event, as shown in Figure 4–14 (remember, you can simply double-click the text area next to an event to autogenerate an event handler in your code file).

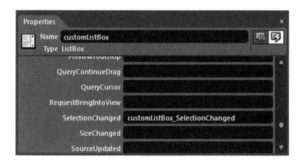

Figure 4–14. *Handling the SelectionChanged event of the ListBox*

Now, implement this handler to display the current selection on the `currentSelection` `Label` control:

```
private void customListBox_SelectionChanged(object sender,
  System.Windows.Controls.SelectionChangedEventArgs e)
{
  this.currentSelection.Content =
    string.Format("You Picked Item Number: {0}",
              this.customListBox.SelectedIndex);
}
```

Run your program, and notice that you can select any of your custom items as expected (see Figure 4–15).

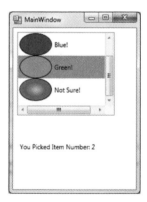

Figure 4–15. *The fancy ListBox in action*

Working with the Tag Property

At this point, you are able to discover the currently selected item as a numerical value. However, it might be interesting if you could somehow discover the related color (red, green, etc.) based on a selected item. As it turns out, you can, by using a *data template*, but that topic will not be examined until Chapter 6. As a simple (and handy) alternative, let's make use of the Tag property.

Select the ListBoxItem that contains the red Ellipse from the Objects and Timeline panel. Once you have done so, search the Properties panel for the Tag property (you'll find it under the advanced properties area of the Common Properties section). Set the Tag property for this ListBoxItem to the value **Red**. Repeat this process for the remaining ListBoxItem objects, setting the Tag property accordingly; for example:

```
<ListBoxItem Height="41.96" Width="180" Tag="Green">
  ...
</ListBoxItem>
```

You can now update your existing SelectionChanged event handler to extract the value of the Tag property of the selected ListBoxItem control, and then use that value to set the Content property of the Label control:

```
private void customListBox_SelectionChanged(object sender,
  System.Windows.Controls.SelectionChangedEventArgs e)
{
  string selectedColor =
    ((ListBoxItem)this.customListBox.SelectedItem).Tag.ToString();

  this.currentSelection.Content = string.Format("You Picked the Color: {0}",
    selectedColor);
}
```

So, as you have seen, WPF and Silverlight both radically simplify the process of customizing the interiors of controls. Using just a few lines of markup, you can populate a control with just about any sort of custom, composite data. And, as you have also seen, composite data needs to be arranged within a layout system. Given this point, let's switch gears a bit and examine some details of the various layout managers we have at our disposal.

■ **Source Code** The **FancyListBox** project can be found under the Chapter 4 subdirectory.

Working with Layout Managers

As you have seen over the initial chapters of this book, when you create a new WPF or Silverlight project using Expression Blend, you are automatically given a Grid object as your default layout manager. Recall that this Grid object is named LayoutRoot (although you are free to change this if you so choose, by changing the value of the Name property). For example, if you create a new WPF application, Blend generates the following XAML by default:

```
<Window
  xmlns="http://schemas.microsoft.com/winfx/2006/xaml/presentation"
  xmlns:x="http://schemas.microsoft.com/winfx/2006/xaml"
  x:Class="WPFLayoutManagers.MainWindow"
  x:Name="Window"
  Title="MainWindow"
  Width="640" Height="480">
```

```
  <Grid x:Name="LayoutRoot"/>
</Window>
```

While the `Grid` is a reasonable default for a number of WPF (or Silverlight) applications, other layout options exist. As it turns out, the WPF API provides more choices than the Silverlight API insofar as layout managers are concerned. However, in practice, this should seldom be an issue. Remember that a Silverlight application typically is deployed as a smaller part of a larger web page, and typically does not change its default size within the hosting browser. Given this, Silverlight does not ship with layout managers that dynamically reposition UI elements based on size.

In contrast, WPF applications are most often designed such that the `Window` objects can be maximized, minimized, and resized at the whim of the user. For this reason, the WPF API provides a number of additional options that allow for dynamic layouts. Table 4–1 lists and describes the core layout managers and identifies which APIs support them.

Table 4–1. *The Core WPF and Silverlight Layout Managers*

Layout Manager	WPF Support?	Silverlight Support?	Meaning in Life
Canvas	X	X	Allows you to arrange child objects using absolute X, Y positioning. This layout manager is ideal for holding complex graphical data.
DockPanel	X	X	Allows you to dock child objects to a specified edge of the container (top, left, bottom, or right).
Grid	X	X	Allows you to define a set of cells (based on rows and columns) to position child objects.
ScrollViewer	X		Allows you to enable scrolling of the elements that it contains. This layout manager can wrap only a single UI element, which will almost always be another layout manager.
StackPanel	X	X	Allows you to arrange child objects in a single vertical or horizontal line.
UniformGrid	X		Arranges child elements within equal (uniform) grid regions (for example, imagine a Tic-Tac-Toe playing board, with symmetrical cells).
ViewBox	X		Scales all its child elements much like a zoom control. Like the `ScrollViewer`, the `ViewBox` will almost always wrap a secondary layout manager.
WrapPanel	X		Allows you to arrange child objects in a sequential position from left to right. If it runs out of room at the far-right edge of the panel, the remaining controls wrap to the next line, and so on from left to right, top to bottom.

Additional Layout Types

Beyond the core layout mangers identified in Table 4–1, both WPF and Silverlight ship with a Border class and a TabControl class. As their names imply, Border allows you to define a visual outline (and optional background) around a related child layout system, while TabControl allows you to arrange a set of UI elements into independent tabbed panels. You will work with the TabControl and Border classes later in this chapter.

In addition, the WPF API provides the BulletDecorator control, which allows you to "connect" two related UI elements (typically a graphic and a blurb of text) to quickly create a customized bulleted list. The benefit of grouping this related content into a BulletDecorator (rather than directly into a bare-bones stand-alone StackPanel) is that the BulletDecorator supplies properties to independently (and easily) interact with the bullet image (via the Bullet property). Here is a simple example of connecting *.jpg image data to textual data in a TextBlock:

```
<BulletDecorator Background="#FF001BFF" Height="53">
  <BulletDecorator.Bullet>
    <Image Source="apple.jpg" Height="60" Width="60"/>
  </BulletDecorator.Bullet>
  <TextBlock Width="257" TextWrapping="Wrap"
    HorizontalAlignment="Center"
    Foreground ="#FF849DB8"
    FontSize="35"
    VerticalAlignment="Center">
      <Run Text="Yum! Apples!"/>
  </TextBlock>
</BulletDecorator>
```

In any case, when working with any sort of layout manager (including a simple BulletDecorator), be aware that you can typically create a suitable layout system using a wide variety of techniques. For example, you can enable "canvas mode" on a Grid object to gain absolute positioning of content, based on the size and margin settings of contained UI elements. In contrast, the same layout could be created using a collection of nested StackPanel objects arranged in different orientations.

To be sure, you should take time to experiment with each container and test the final results by resizing (and possibly repositioning) the containers at runtime. In just a few pages, you will work with a number of these layout managers in the context of a larger Blend application; until then, allow me to point out a few basic tricks of the trade.

Changing the Layout Type

Once you have created a new WPF or Silverlight project using Blend, you can change the type of any layout manager simply by right-clicking the node within the Objects and Timeline panel and selecting Change Layout Type.

■ **Note** If you change layout managers that currently contain controls, be aware that the controls will follow the rules of the container! For example, if you have items positioned in a Grid and then switch to a StackPanel, all your items will be stacked on top of each other.

Figure 4–16 shows the layout options for a WPF application (a corresponding Silverlight project would show slightly fewer options).

Figure 4–16. *Changing the layout manager via the Objects and Timeline panel*

Designing Nested Layouts

Be aware that it is very common for a WPF or Silverlight application to use a nested layout system. For example, you could split your initial `Grid` object into two columns, mount a vertical `StackPanel` within the leftmost column, and mount a `Canvas` in the rightmost column (to create a layout system for a simple painting program, perhaps).

When you wish to add child layout mangers under a parent layout manager, select the parent node within the Objects and Timeline panel, select the child to add via the Layout section of the Tools panel, and then double-click the item. You have no need to do so right now, but Figure 4–17 illustrates the process.

Figure 4–17. *The Tools panel allows you to select and add child layout objects.*

Grouping and Ungrouping Selected UI Elements

Blend makes it very simple to select a set of UI elements on the artboard and group those elements into a new, nested layout manager that is positioned in the parent. For example, assume you have a Grid object that contains three Button objects, which you have arranged within the Grid to sit side by side of each other. Once you select each object on the artboard (via a Shift+click), you can right-click your selection and select the Group Into menu option, as shown in Figure 4–18.

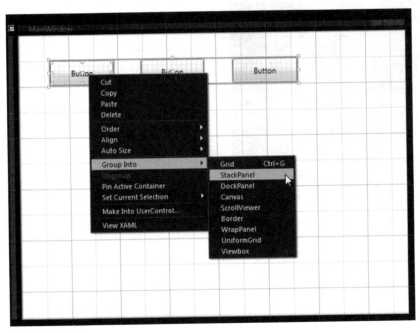

Figure 4–18. Grouping selected objects into a layout manager

■ **Note** You can also select multiple UI elements in the Objects and Timeline panel and activate the Group Into menu option.

Assuming you grouped three Button objects into a StackPanel, you will find the configuration shown in Figure 4–19 in the Objects and Timeline panel (note that the new StackPanel can be independently selected for configuration within the Properties panel).

Figure 4–19. *A simple nested layout system*

Also be aware that you can select a layout manager on the artboard (or via the Objects and Timeline panel) and activate the Ungroup menu option via a standard right-click. This operation will remove the child layout manager from the tree of XAML and place the orphaned UI elements into the immediate parent container.

Repositioning a UI Element into a Layout Manager

When you have a nested layout system for a given WPF `Window` or Silverlight `UserControl`, you will occasionally need to relocate an item. For the current example, assume that after you grouped the `Button` controls into a new `StackPanel`, you decide that the rightmost `Button` really should be positioned in the parent `Grid`. One way to make this change is to select said `Button` on the artboard, drag it outside of the current container to the desired outermost container, and then press Alt (similar to what you did when creating composite content earlier in this chapter; see Figure 4–20).

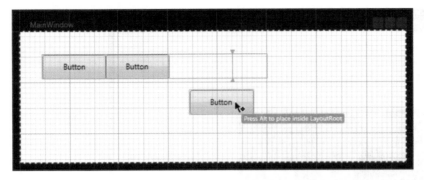

Figure 4–20. *Relocating a UI element into a parent container*

It is also possible to drag and drop UI elements into (and from) a layout manager directly via the Objects and Timeline panel. This is always useful to remember, given that when you add a new item from the Tools panel to the artboard, it will be contained in the currently selected layout manager. Thus, if you accidentally selected the incorrect layout manager before adding a child, you can simply drag the node to the correct home (see Figure 4–21).

Figure 4–21. *You can also relocate UI elements via the Objects and Timeline panel.*

Building a User Interface with Blend

Now that you have a better understanding of the role of layout managers and the control content model and items control model, let's build a new example program that illustrates various aspects of the Blend IDE. Here, I will be choosing a WPF application; however, many of the techniques shown here would work in a similar (if not identical) manner for Silverlight projects. If you are following along, create a new WPF application project named **WpfControlsApp**.

Creating a Tabbed Layout System

In this project, you will create a tabbed layout system, where each tab will illustrate the use of a particular set of controls, layout managers, and APIs. The first step, therefore, is to locate the TabControl component within the Assets library via the Search function (see Figure 4–22).

Figure 4–22. *Locating the TabControl*

■ **Note** For the remainder of this chapter, I assume that you use the Search area to locate a given UI control, and therefore I do not show you additional screenshots of a control in the Assets library.

Once you have located the `TabControl` component, select it from your Tools panel and draw an instance of this control so that it takes up a majority of the initial `Grid`. You'll notice that, by default, the `TabControl` defines two initial `TabItem` objects, each of which represents a specific tab on the control. You'll also notice that these `TabItem` objects are mounted on the upper portion of the owning `TabControl`. If you wish to change the placement of the tabs, you may do so by setting the `TabStripPlacement` property, which you will find in the Common Properties section of the Properties panel for the selected `TabControl` (not the individual `TabItem` objects; see Figure 4–23).

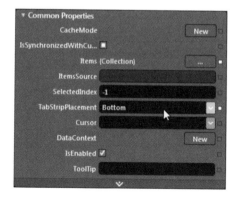

Figure 4–23. *Defining the location of your TabItem objects*

■ **Note** For the remainder of this chapter, I also assume that you use the Search area of the Properties panel to quickly locate a property under examination. I'll still show a few relevant screenshots where necessary, but by and large, I'll leave it in your capable hands to locate a property (or event) by name via a search.

Now, locate your Objects and Timeline panel. Notice that each TabItem is a child of the owning TabControl object. More interesting, notice that each TabItem has its own dedicated layout manager, specifically a Grid object.[7] Furthermore, each TabItem has a Header element that allows you to set the text (or complex content) for a given tab. Figure 4–24 shows the unmodified layout thus far.

Figure 4–24. Each TabItem has a dedicated layout manager.

For this example, we will add one additional tab to the TabControl. To do so, simply right-click the TabControl node of the Objects and Timeline panel and select the Add TabItem menu option. At this point, change the Header property for each of the TabItem objects to the following textual values:

- Fun with Ink
- Documents API
- Behaviors!

---

[7] This is an example of the *headered control model*, which is similar to the content and items control models introduced earlier in this chapter.

■ **Note** When attempting to change the text of a header, you won't get too far if you try to select the Header item in the Objects and Timeline panel, as Header is a property of TabItem, not a selectable item. Thus, use the Properties panel to change the text.

Be very aware that when you select any TabItem object on the artboard, you have activated that tab for editing, and can begin dragging and dropping controls to the root layout manager (of course, you can get to the same end result by selecting a TabItem on the Objects and Timeline panel as well). Finally, set the Name property of your TabControl to myTabControl, and set the Name property for each TabItem object to tabInk, tabDocs, and tabBehaviors, respectively.

Working with the Grid

Our first tab will display a UI that will capture user input using the Ink API, which is supported by both WPF and Silverlight (although their programming model is a bit different). This particular API is very useful if you are building programs that will run on a touch-screen computing device and you want to capture input via a stylus or finger. As it turns out, this same API can capture graphical strokes via standard mouse input, which we will do here. The Grid layout manager will be used to contain each of the UI elements for this tab. The Grid object can be configured to work in two modes:

- *Grid layout mode*: This is the default mode. In this mode, you can create a set of rows and columns, and place components within the cells. If you resize cells using the column and row dividers, the contained objects change in size to preserve the values set on the Margin properties (described in just a moment).

- *Canvas layout mode*: This option provides an editing experience that is just like editing inside a Canvas panel, where items are positioned exactly where you place them, regardless of where they are positioned in the grid cells.

If you are using the default, Grid layout mode, you can place child objects in a cell and then set (directly or indirectly) the Margin property on the object in the Grid. Every UI element in a Grid can set four margin values, which control its top, left, bottom, and right position in a cell. Each of these margin values can be edited via the Layout section of the Properties panel. This default behavior can be very useful when you place a UI element into a grid cell such that it fills the entire space of the cell *and* you want to make sure this UI element grows (or shrinks) when you resize the cell.

Canvas layout mode is very different in that child objects of the grid are positioned based on *absolute positioning*. If you resize any rows or columns, the child objects do not automatically change size (but the Margin properties are still updated). I'd guess most of the time you will be happy with the default, Grid layout mode, but you can easily switch between the modes by clicking the toggle in the extreme upper left of the selected grid editor (see Figure 4–25).

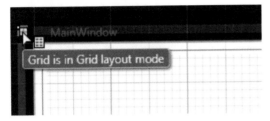

Figure 4–25. You can toggle between Grid layout mode and Canvas layout mode.

Defining Grid Rows and Columns

The Blend IDE makes it simple to add rows and columns to a selected Grid object. To begin, activate the Grid object within the "Fun with Ink" tab using the Objects and Timeline panel. Next, using your artboard, divide this Grid into two rows, where the top row takes up about one-fourth of the UI. To do so, simply position your mouse cursor on an outer edge of the Grid and click the mouse button (see Figure 4–26; note the mouse cursor on the left side of the grid editor).

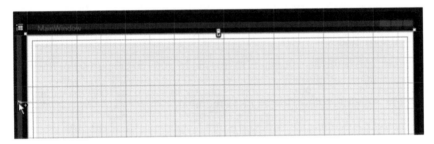

Figure 4–26. Carving the grid into two rows

You can add any number of rows or columns using this technique, and once you have done so, you can reposition them by dragging a given separator with the mouse. Add a few additional rows and columns now, and experiment with how you can change the size of each cell. Once you have done so, undo your operations (via Ctrl+Z) until you are once again back to a Grid with two rows.

■ **Note** You can also populate a grid with columns and rows via the ColumnDefinitions and RowDefinitions properties, which are located under the advanced properties area of the Layout section.

Adding Items to Grid Cells

After you have defined the rows and columns for a given grid, you can then place UI elements (including any geometric shapes) into the cells. Remember, when you are in Grid layout mode (the default operation for a Grid), the child items will be placed in a cell based in part on the

`Margin` settings. More specifically, the child's position within a grid is based on the following settings:

- *Alignment Settings*: Determine what position an object takes in relation to the parent object.

- *Margin Settings*: Determine the amount of empty space around the control, between the outside of the child object and the boundaries of the grid cell.

- *Width and Height*: Fixed values measured in pixels (device-independent units that are approximately 1/96 inch). You can set these properties to Auto so that child objects will automatically resize depending on the sizing of the parent panel.

The printed page really does not do justice to viewing how these settings configure child items, so let's add an `InkCanvas` control (named `myInkArea`) to the bottom row of the `Grid`. Locate this component in the Assets library and double-click it. By default, any item added to a grid via a double-click will be added to the first row and column. Select this object and drag it into the second row, and stretch it out so that it takes up the entire row (see Figure 4–27).

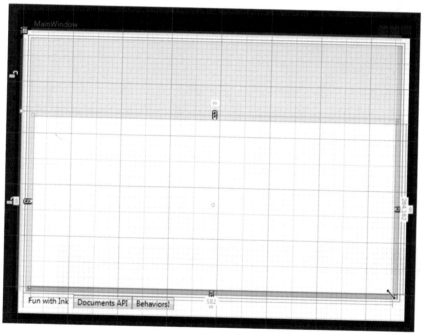

Figure 4–27. Adding an item to a grid row

Recall from Chapter 1 that the artboard displays red "snaplines" to allow you to easily see when an item takes up the real estate of its container. Because the `InkCanvas` has been snapped to each side of this row, you will see that if you resize the row (or the entire `Grid`), the `InkCanvas` will grow or shrink accordingly (give it a try now). This would be true for any item added to a grid cell in this manner.

Before you add components to the upper row of the grid layout, take a look at the Layout section of the Properties panel for the selected `InkCanvas`, as shown in Figure 4–28. Notice that the Layout section allows you to control margins, height, and width (which are now set to `Auto`, as we have snapped to our parent), and also allows you to manually specify in which row and column to place the item (assuming the item is indeed in a `Grid`). Take a few minutes to tinker with these settings, and notice how the `InkCanvas`'s layout changes (and then press Ctrl+Z so that you are back to the original design).

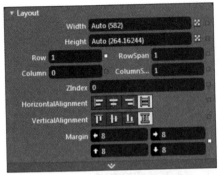

Figure 4–28. The Layout section allows you to position an item in the parent layout manager.

Creating a Grid Splitter

Many `Grid` objects are designed to be invisible at runtime, meaning the user will never see the sets of rows and columns (however, if you *do* want to show these gridlines, you can set the `ShowGridLines` property to `true`). Even if the end user cannot see every row and column of a `Grid` layout manager, it is very common for a grid to supply visible *splitters* that allow the user to resize rows and columns.

To illustrate how to add this functionality to the current layout, locate the `GridSplitter` control within the Assets library and then select it for use. Now, the trick here is that when you draw an instance of the `GridSplitter` on your artboard, you want to snap it on to the row or column you wish to make resizable. In Figure 4–29, notice that I have made a slightly thicker `GridSplitter` with a blue background (and that I also set the `Background` color of the `InkCanvas` to a light shade of orange).

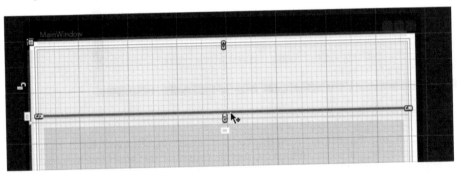

Figure 4–29. Adding a GridSplitter to the Grid object

If you were to run the application right now, you would find that you can draw on top of the ink area with the mouse, and also resize the rows of the grid using your grid splitter. When you do so, the InkCanvas object will grow in height (not bad for a few lines of markup; see Figure 4–30).

Figure 4–30. *The resizable InkCanvas area*

Adding a Nested StackPanel

To complete this first tab, we will add a few controls to the upper area of the Grid that will allow the user to change the color of ink and the size of the ink pen. Add a StackPanel to the upper row of the Grid and, once again, snap it to all four sides so that it fills the entire area. Set the Orientation property of this StackPanel to Horizontal, and then add three Button controls (named btnRed, btnGreen, and btnBlue) and one TextBox control (named txtPenSize) with a Label control holding some descriptive text. Figure 4–31 shows a possible layout (I added some spacing between each control by changing the Margin property values for each item in the StackPanel).

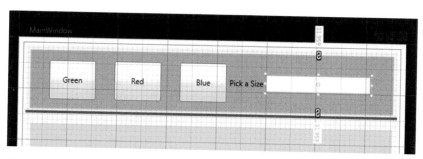

Figure 4–31. *A nested StackPanel of controls*

To simplify how we will change colors, make sure that the Content property for each Button is a textual value representing a known solid color (here, Red, Green, and Blue). Handle the Click event for each Button control, using the Properties panel, and specify a method named ChangeColor each time. Implement this method as so:

```
private void ChangeColor(object sender, System.Windows.RoutedEventArgs e)
{
  // Get the string value in the Button which was clicked.
  string colorToUse = ((Button)sender).Content.ToString();

  // Now set the color by converting the string to
  // solid color.
  this.myInkArea.DefaultDrawingAttributes.Color =
    (Color)ColorConverter.ConvertFromString(colorToUse);
}
```

To complete this first tab, handle the LostFocus event of your TextBox. Within the implementation of this method, use the value in the TextBox to set the height and width of the pen:

```
private void txtPenSize_LostFocus(object sender,
  System.Windows.RoutedEventArgs e)
{
  try
  {
    // Change the height and width of the pen
    // based on the data in the text box.
    this.myInkArea.DefaultDrawingAttributes.Height =
      int.Parse(txtPenSize.Text);
    this.myInkArea.DefaultDrawingAttributes.Width =
      int.Parse(txtPenSize.Text);
  }
  catch
  {
    this.Title = "Bad Pen Size Value!";
  }
}
```

Now, run your program! You should be able to set the pen's size and color to render out strokes (see Figure 4–32).

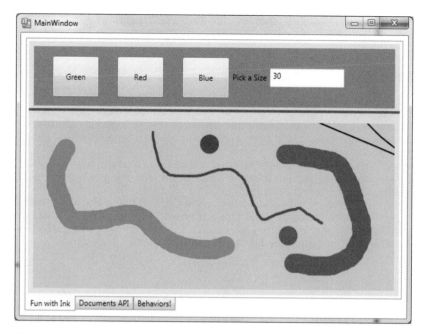

Figure 4–32. Rendering data on the InkCanvas

That wraps up the first of our three tabs. At this point, hopefully, you feel more comfortable configuring `Grid` objects and `StackPanel` objects and populating containers with controls. At the same time, you learned a bit about the WPF Ink programming model.[8] Next up, let's examine some more-elaborate editing tools you may encounter.

Introducing the WPF Document API[9]

The first tab of this example uses controls that are simple to configure. Even if you were to add custom content, the Blend IDE makes things fairly straightforward. However, there are a number of controls that require much more sophisticated editors, as they expose internal collections of other objects. It would be quite impractical to attempt to show *every* editor of *every* control, so the next tab will work with the WPF Document API, which will serve as a good example.

When you need to display simple blurbs of text, the WPF `Label`, `TextBox`, `TextBlock`, and `PasswordBox` controls fit the bill. While they are certainly useful, some WPF applications require the use of sophisticated, highly formatted text data, similar to what one might find in an Adobe PDF file. The WPF Document API provides such functionality; however, it does not use the PDF file format, but rather uses the XML Paper Specification (XPS) format.

Using the Document API, you can construct a print-ready document using a number of classes from the `System.Windows.Documents` namespace. Here you will find a number of types

---

[8] The Ink API is much more feature rich than shown in this simple example. If you are interested in exploring this topic in greater detail, consult the .NET Framework/Silverlight documentation.

[9] Remember, the Silverlight API does not support a similar "documents" API.

that represent pieces of a rich XPS document, such as List, Paragraph, Section, Table, LineBreak, Figure, Floater, and Span.

Block Elements and Inline Elements

Formally speaking, the items you add to an XPS document belong to one of two broad categories. First we have *block elements*. Examples of block elements include List, Paragraph, BlockUIContainer, Section, and Table. Classes from this category are used to group together other content (e.g., a list containing paragraph data, a paragraph containing subparagraphs for different text formatting, and so on).

The second category, *inline elements*, includes elements that are nested within another block item (or possibly another inline element inside of a block element). Some common inline elements include Run, Span, LineBreak, Figure, and Floater.

As you can tell, these classes have been named using terms that you might encounter when building a rich document with a professional editor. Like any other WPF control, these classes can be configured in XAML or via code. Therefore, you could declare an empty <Paragraph> element that is populated at runtime (you'll see how to do such tasks in this example).

Document Layout Managers

Unlike what you might be thinking, you do not simply place inline and block elements directly into a panel container such as a Grid. Rather, you need to wrap them in a <FlowDocument> element or a <FixedDocument> element.

Items in a FlowDocument are ideal when you wish to have your end user change the way the data is presented on the computer screen, by zooming text or changing how it is presented (a single long page, a pair of columns, etc.). FixedDocument is better used for true print-ready (WYSIWYG), unchangeable document data.

For our example, we will concern ourselves only with the FlowDocument container. Once you have inserted inline and block items into your FlowDocument, it is placed in one of four specialized XPS-aware layout managers, listed in Table 4–2.

Table 4–2. XPS Control Layout Managers

Panel Control	Meaning in Life
FlowDocumentReader	Displays data in a FlowDocument and adds support for zooming, searching, and layout of content in various forms.
FlowDocumentScrollViewer	Displays data in a FlowDocument, but the data is presented as a single document viewed with scrollbars. This container does not support zooming, searching, or alternative layout modes.
RichTextBox	Displays data in a FlowDocument, and adds support for user editing.
FlowDocumentPageViewer	Displays a document page by page, only one page at a time. Data can also be zoomed, but not searched.

The most feature-rich way to display a FlowDocument is to wrap it within a FlowDocumentReader manager. When you do, the user can alter the layout, search for words in the document, and zoom the data using the provided zoom UI. The one limitation of this container (as well as `FlowDocumentScrollViewer` and `FlowDocumentPageViewer`) is that the data they display is read-only. However, if you do want to allow the end user to enter new information into the `FlowDocument`, you can wrap it in a `RichTextBox` control.

Creating a ToolBar Control

Click the Documents API tab of your `TabItem` via the Blend artboard to activate this tab for editing. You should already have a default `Grid` control as the direct child of the `TabItem` control; however, change it to a `StackPanel` using the Objects and Timeline panel (recall, you can right-click any layout manager node and select the Change Layout Type menu option).

The first item in this `StackPanel` will be a custom `ToolBar` control that has two `Button` controls. Locate the `ToolBar` control in the Assets library and add one instance to the selected `StackPanel`. The WPF `ToolBar` control can be configured to contain any number of controls. When you want to add a control via the Blend IDE, you may do so by locating the `Items` property and clicking the "…" button, as indicated in Figure 4–33.

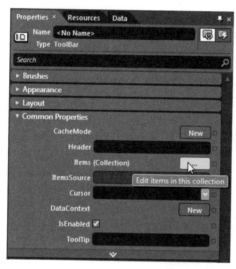

Figure 4–33. Populating a ToolBar

From the resulting dialog box, click the "Add another item" button (located at the bottom) to launch a second dialog box in which you can find a control by name. This same "Add another item" button has a drop-down list that shows some of the more common options (see Figure 4–34).

Figure 4–34. Adding objects to a control's Items collection

Use this editor to add two Button controls. Once you have done so, you will notice that each item can be selected and edited within this dialog box (see Figure 4–35).

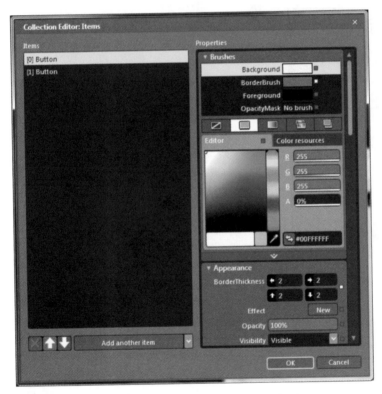

Figure 4–35. Editing objects in a control's Items collection

Feel free to tinker with the settings of each Button control, but for this example, set the Content properties to the values shown in the following XAML:

```
<Button BorderBrush="Green" Content="Save Doc"/>
<Button BorderBrush="Green" Content="Load Doc"/>
```

Switch back to the designer, open the Assets library, and locate the `FlowDocumentReader` control. Place it into your `StackPanel`, rename it to `myDocumentReader`, and stretch it out over the surface of your `StackPanel`. At this point, your layout should look similar to Figure 4–36.

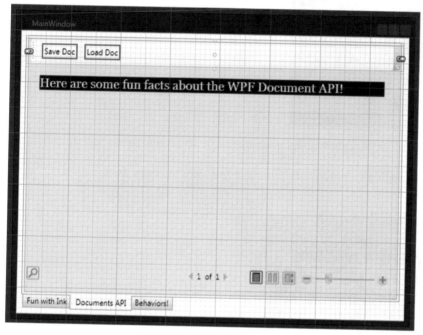

Figure 4–36. *The layout of the Documents API tab*

Select your `FlowDocumentReader` control in the Objects and Timeline panel and locate the Miscellaneous category of the Properties panel. Click the New button next to the `Document` property. Once you do, your XAML will be updated with an empty `<FlowDocument>`:

```
<FlowDocumentReader x:Name="myDocumentReader" Height="269.4">
  <FlowDocument/>
</FlowDocumentReader>
```

At this point, we can add document classes (again, such as `List`, `Paragraph`, `Section`, `Table`, `LineBreak`, `Figure`, `Floater`, and `Span`) to the element. Let's do this very thing next.

Populating a FlowDocument

As soon as you add a new document to a document container, the `Document` property in the Properties panel becomes expandable and displays a *ton* of new properties that allow you to build the design of your document. For our example, the only property we are concerned with is the `Blocks` (`Collection`) property (see Figure 4–37).

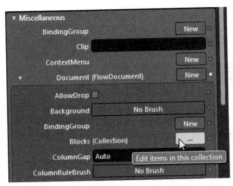

Figure 4–37. A FlowDocument can be populated using the Blocks (Collection) property.

Click its corresponding … button, and, using the "Add another item" button of the resulting dialog box, insert a List, Paragraph, and Section (see Figure 4–38).

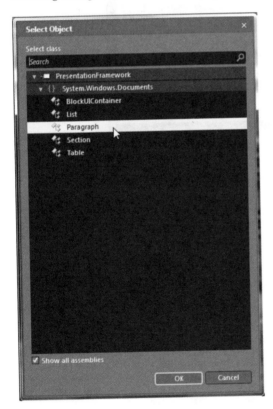

Figure 4–38. Adding blocks

You can edit each of these using the Blocks editor. Furthermore, a given block can contain related subblocks. For example, if you select your Section, you can add a Paragraph subblock. I configured my Section with a specific background color, foreground color, and font size, and inserted a sub Paragraph (see Figure 4–39).

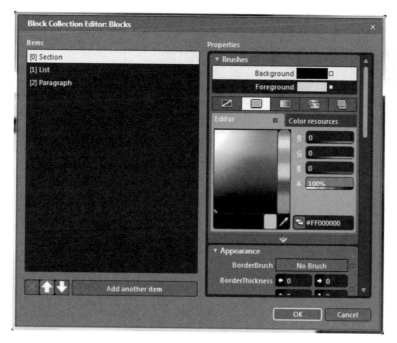

Figure 4–39. Configuring blocks

Go ahead and configure your Section as you wish, but leave the List and original Paragraph empty, as we will drive them through code. Here is one possible configuration of the FlowDocument within the FlowDocumentReader:

```
<FlowDocumentReader x:Name="myDocumentReader"
                    Height="339.4" Margin="0,0,8,0">
  <FlowDocument>
    <Section Foreground = "Yellow" Background = "Black">
      <Paragraph FontSize = "20">
        Here are some fun facts about the WPF Document API!
      </Paragraph>
    </Section>
    <List />
    <Paragraph />
  </FlowDocument>
</FlowDocumentReader>
```

If you run your program now (remember, just press the F5 key), you should already be able to zoom your document (using the lower-right slider bar), search for a keyword (using the lower-left Search editor), and display the data in one of three manners (using the layout buttons). In Figure 4–40, notice I searched for the text "WPF" and zoomed my document in a larger scale.

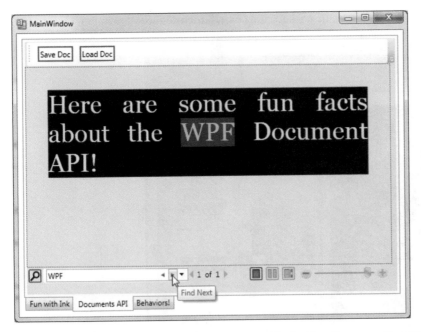

Figure 4–40. Manipulating our FlowDocument with the FlowDocumentReader

Before moving to the next step, you might want to edit your XAML to use a different
FlowDocument container, such as the FlowDocumentScrollViewer or a RichTextBox, rather than
the FlowDocumentReader. Once you have done so, run the application again and notice the
different ways the document data is handled. Be sure to roll back to the FlowDocumentReader
type when you are done.

Populating a FlowDocument Using Code

Although this book is focused on Blend as a tool, it is important to know that all document
elements can be driven through code. Now, let's build our List block and the remaining
Paragraph block in code. The ability to populate documents in code is certainly important, as
you may need to populate a FlowDocument based on user input, external files, database
information, or what have you. Before we do so, use the XAML editor of Blend to give the List
and Paragraph elements proper names, so we can access them in code:

```
<List x:Name="listOfFunFacts"/>
<Paragraph x:Name="paraBodyText"/>
```

In your code file, define a new method named PopulateDocument(). This method will first
add a set of new ListItems to the List, each of which will have a Paragraph with a single Run.
Then, this helper method will dynamically build a formatted paragraph, using three separate
Run objects. Here is the code (which you are free to copy and paste from the downloadable
solution):

```
private void PopulateDocument()
{
    // Add some data to the List item.
    this.listOfFunFacts.FontSize = 14;
```

```
    this.listOfFunFacts.MarkerStyle = TextMarkerStyle.Circle;
    this.listOfFunFacts.ListItems.Add(new ListItem(new
      Paragraph(new Run("Fixed documents are for WYSIWYG print ready docs!"))));
    this.listOfFunFacts.ListItems.Add(new ListItem(
      new Paragraph(new Run("The API supports tables and embedded figures!"))));
    this.listOfFunFacts.ListItems.Add(new ListItem(
      new Paragraph(new Run("By default Flow documents are read only!"))));
    this.listOfFunFacts.ListItems.Add(new ListItem(
      new Paragraph(new Run
        ("BlockUIContainer allows you to embed WPF controls"))));

    // Now add some data to the Paragraph.
    // First part of sentence.
    Run prefix = new Run("This paragraph was generated ");

    // Middle of paragraph.
    Bold b = new Bold();
    Run infix = new Run("dynamically");
    infix.Foreground = Brushes.Red;
    infix.FontSize = 30;
    b.Inlines.Add(infix);

    // Last part of paragraph.
    Run suffix = new Run(" at runtime!");

    // Now add each piece to the collection of inline elements
    // of the Paragraph.
    this.paraBodyText.Inlines.Add(prefix);
    this.paraBodyText.Inlines.Add(infix);
    this.paraBodyText.Inlines.Add(suffix);
}
```

Make sure you call this method from your window's constructor:

```
public MainWindow()
{
  this.InitializeComponent();

  // Insert code required on object creation below this point.
  PopulateDocument();
}
```

Once you add this code, you can run the application and see your new dynamically generated document content.

Saving and Loading Document Data

So far, so good. However, we still need to address the two buttons on our toolbar for the Documents API tab. Use the Properties panel to handle the Click event for each Button object, specifying a unique method name each time. In your Window's code file, import the following two .NET namespaces, which will give you access to the file I/O objects as well as the XamlReader and XamlWriter objects (which we will need to save and load the document data):

```
using System.IO;
using System.Windows.Markup;
```

Now, to save the document data, all you need to do is create an XAML file to store the document's contents. The `Document` property of the `FlowDocumentReader` gives you the markup that represents the data itself:

```
private void btnSaveDoc_Click(object sender,
  System.Windows.RoutedEventArgs e)
{
  using(FileStream fStream =
    File.Open("documentData.xaml", FileMode.Create))
  {
    XamlWriter.Save(this.myDocumentReader.Document, fStream);
  }
}
```

Loading document data is also very simple; just reverse the basic operation:

```
private void btnLoadDoc_Click(object sender, System.Windows.RoutedEventArgs e)
{
  using(FileStream fStream = File.Open("documentData.xaml", FileMode.Open))
  {
    try
    {
      FlowDocument doc = XamlReader.Load(fStream) as FlowDocument;
      this.myDocumentReader.Document = doc;
    }
    catch(Exception ex) {MessageBox.Show(ex.Message, "Error Loading Doc!");}
  }
}
```

If you run the application and click the Save button, the XAML document will be saved under the \bin\Debug directory of the project. If you click the Load button, the same data will be read and will be used to populate your document with the saved data.

Great! That wraps up tab two, and your introductory look at the WPF Document API. To wrap up the current chapter, our final tab will introduce you to the role of *behavior objects*.f *behavior objects*.

Introducing Blend Behavior Objects

Any Silverlight or WPF application will be a rich combination of XAML (look and feel) and code (application functionality). The exact sort of code you author will differ greatly based on the type of project under construction. You may need to author code to communicate with a remote WCF service,[10] read data from a relational database, generate dynamic content at runtime, or whatnot. While it is true that a core code base for an application is sure to be unique, there are a number of common situations that tend to be part of many graphically intensive applications.

For example, many WPF and Silverlight programs need to allow the user to relocate an item via a drag-and-drop operation, or maybe you need to play sound files based on various situations (menu item selection, clicking an element, etc.). Perhaps you are creating a UI that uses data binding operations (see Chapter 6) and you want different storyboard animations to execute when the data source is updated. While you could author custom C# or VB code to

---

[10] Windows Communication Foundation (WCF) is a .NET API that allows you to make remote method calls using a variety of different protocols (HTTP, TCP, named pipes, etc.).

account for such situations, the Blend SDK provides a variety of out-out-of-the-box *behavior objects* that take care of such commonplace coding tasks.

A behavior object is nothing more than a component that can be added to a tree of XAML and that manipulates another, related UI element. Internally, behaviors are true classes defined in a .NET library, and therefore any behavior can also be driven in code.[11]

A majority of these built-in behaviors are bundled in the `Microsoft.Expression.Interactivity.dll` library, and a reference to this library is automatically added to your Blend projects when you use them (if you wish to work with behavior objects within Visual Studio 2010, you will need to reference this library manually). Table 4–3 documents some (but not all) behaviors that ship with the Blend SDK, grouped by related functionality.

Table 4–3. *Sample of Behaviors Provided by the Blend SDK*

Behavior Object	Meaning in Life
FluidMoveBehavior	This behavior (which works in conjunction with a few related objects) allows you to control animations and transition effects (termed *fluid behaviors*) between UI objects.
ControlStoryboardAction	This behavior (shown in Chapter 3) allows you to start, stop, or pause a storyboard animation without the need to author procedural code.
CallMethodAction ChangePropertyAction InvokeCommandAction	These behaviors allow you to change an object's property, call a method on an object, or trigger a command[12] via XAML.
GoToStateAction	This behavior allows you to transition to a new state defined via the Visual State Manager. This is common when building custom templates (see Chapter 5).
PlaySoundAction	This behavior allows you to define a sound clip to play under various conditions.
DataStateBahavior SetDataStoreValueAction	These behaviors allow you to control how visual states are applied when a data binding operation occurs. You'll examine data binding techniques in Chapter 6.
MouseDragElementBehavior	This behavior allows the user to move an element within the containing layout manager.
ActivateStateAction NavigateToScreenAction NavigateBackAction NavigateForwardAction	These (and other) behaviors allow you to define a navigational structure when building a Blend SketchFlow prototype (see Chapter 8).

[11] It is also possible to create custom behavior classes; however, that topic is outside the scope of this text.

[12] Command objects are classes that implement the `ICommand` interface, and can be used to incorporate common user commands (such as copy, cut, paste) into an application without authoring a ton of code.

Remember that each of these behavior objects maps to a class type, and therefore each behavior supports a number of properties, methods, and events, many of which can be configured with the Properties panel just like a UI control. You will see various behaviors at work throughout the rest of this book; however, you should know that each behavior object is fully described within the Expression Blend SDK for WPF User Guide help system, which can be launched via the Expression Blend Help menu.

■ **Note** Remember, the Blend SDK for WPF User Guide help system is different from the Blend User Guide help system!

Once you have opened this help system, you will find details on each of the intrinsic behaviors, and examples on how to configure them (see Figure 4–41).

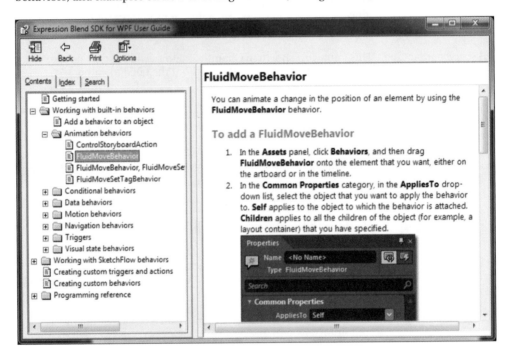

Figure 4–41. All behaviors are documented in the Blend SDK for WPF User Guide.

Like other components, you can locate behavior objects within the Blend IDE by using the Assets library. Figure 4–42 shows the Behaviors category of this panel.

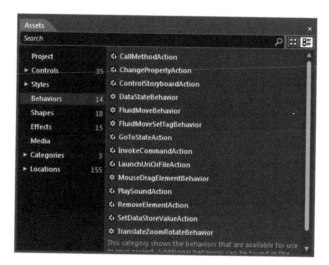

Figure 4–42. Behavior objects can be found within the Assets library.

The MouseDragElementBehavior Object

To complete our example application, and illustrate how useful behaviors can be, open the third tab on the Blend artboard for editing. Next, render on the designer a geometry of your choosing (I'll be using the hexagon shape, located in the Shapes category of the Assets library) and set up any basic property settings (colors, etc.). Next, select the `MouseDragElementBehavior` component in the Assets library and drag it onto your rendered shape.

■ **Note** As a friendly reminder, the Assets library icon (>>) on the Tools panel will disappear once you make a selection, and the selected item will appear at the bottom of the Tools panel. As mentioned earlier in this book, I prefer using the *Assets panel*, as it can be selected and will remain on the screen. The Assets panel makes working with behavior objects much easier (as you typically drag and drop behaviors on the artboard).

As the name implies, this behavior object can be used to easily enable drag-and-drop functionality for an element in your application *without* the need to handle a set of mouse events, calculate hit testing, or author complex code to reposition the item in the parent container. If you examine the Objects and Timeline panel, you should see that the `MouseDragElementBehavior` component is a child of the target geometry.

Select this behavior node, and then examine the Properties panel. This particular behavior object has a single setting, named `ConstrainToParentBounds`. When this property is checked, the behavior object will automatically make sure that the item cannot be dragged outside of the bounds of the parent layout manager (see Figure 4–43).

Figure 4–43. *Each behavior object supports its own unique configuration properties.*

Now, run your program, and verify you can move your shape around the grid. I am sure you can imagine how useful this behavior could be in a wide variety of projects. You might build a Silverlight shopping cart application and use this behavior to enable the user to drag items to a checkout graphic. You could also use it when building an interactive video game, multimedia application, or what have you.

There is one caveat with this particular behavior object: it cannot be applied to objects that support a `Click` event. Therefore, if you want to allow the user to drag and drop a UI control (such as a `Button`), you have a bit of extra work to do. Specifically, you need to wrap the UI control into a `Border` object, and then apply the `MouseDragElementBehavior` component *to the Border*, not the child control.

To test this first-hand, add a `Button` to your artboard, and then right-click the element to group it in a `Border` container (see Figure 4–44). Use the Properties panel to change the `BorderThickness` property to the value of 3 on all four sides, and pick a unique color for the `BorderBrush` property. Once you add a new `MouseDragElementBehavior` component to the `Border`, you will be able to move the `Button` around the grid at runtime (see Figure 4–45).

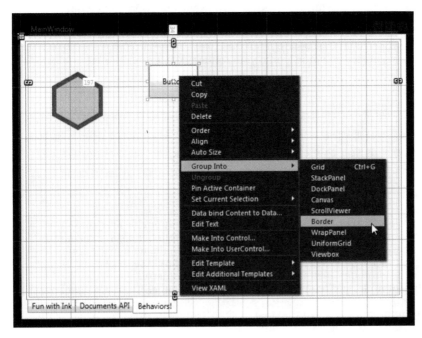

Figure 4–44. *Dragging "clickable" objects requires that you wrap them in a Border control.*

I also configured my `Border` control to use a hand icon when the mouse cursor is over the control, to give the user a clear signal that the contained `Button` control can be relocated (if you wish to do so, just set the `Cursor` property to one of the available options).

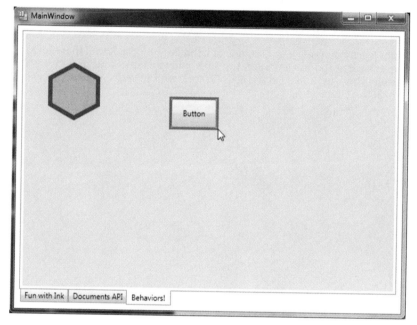

Figure 4–45. Relocating UI elements—no code required!

■ **Source Code** The **WpfControlsApp** project can be found under the Chapter 4 subdirectory.

That wraps up your examination of leveraging Blend to build control layout systems and incorporating controls and behavior objects into your applications. You will see other behavior objects (and controls) at work in the remaining chapters; at this point, I hope you feel more comfortable navigating the Expression Blend IDE when designing GUIs.

Summary

This chapter opened by examining two WPF and Silverlight programming models, specifically the control content model and the items control model. As you learned, both of these models allow you to create UI elements that have customized internal data.

During the first few examples, you were introduced to a few layout managers. The next part of the chapter took a deeper look at how the Blend IDE can facilitate the construction of complicated content layout using numerous layout tools. For example, recall that the artboard can be used to construct a `Grid` object with various rows and columns. As well, you learned various ways that Blend allows you to group selected items into new layout managers, learned how to change managers via the Objects and Timeline panel, and learned the role of the `GridSplitter` to boot.

The remainder of this chapter had you construct a WPF application that illustrated not only a number of new controls (`TabControl` and friends), but also a handful of useful APIs, including the Ink API, which allows you to capture mouse, stylus, or touch input, and the WPF Document API, which allows you to construct very sophisticated print-ready documents, similar to an Adobe PDF document.

Last but certainly not least, you took your first look at behavior objects. Recall that these elements allow you to quickly incorporate common runtime behaviors into your programs with little or no procedural code. Here, we looked at the `MouseDragElementBehavior` object; you will see additional behaviors in the chapters to come.

CHAPTER 5

■ ■ ■

Styles, Templates, and UserControls

In the previous chapter you learned how to create a user interface via Expression Blend and the WPF and/or Silverlight control libraries. The point of this chapter is to explore a collection of interconnected topics that allows you to deeply customize how these controls render their final visual output. The first part of this chapter will examine the WPF and Silverlight style mechanism. As you may know, styles serve the same general purpose as a web-centric cascading style sheet, in that both techniques provide a way to ensure that all instances of a given control (a Button, a TextBox, etc.) share the same property settings (fonts, colors, sizes, and so forth).

The next topic examined in this chapter is the role of control templates. As you will see, every WPF and Silverlight control contains a default set of rendering instructions (termed the *default template)* that will be used to render its out-of-the-box output. However, you are free to modify or completely replace this default template with a custom set of rendering instructions. Using templates, you can radically change the way a control is rendered, and you can do so without the need to author any procedural code. Along the way, you will learn how to use triggers and the Visual State Manager (VSM) to define how a template should change its appearance when various visual states occur (for example, when it gets focus, when the mouse is over its boundaries, when it is clicked, etc.).

The chapter wraps up by examining the role of custom UserControl classes, which allow you to build new custom WPF and Silverlight controls that are based on existing UI elements. Not too surprisingly, custom UserControl classes also typically use styles, templates, triggers, and the VSM to complete their implementation.

■ **Note** Building styles, templates, and UserControls requires that you are comfortable with a number of topics, including graphics, animations, and logical resources. See Chapters 2 and 3 for details on these topics.

The Role of Styles

When you are building the UI of a WPF or Silverlight application, commonly you'll want a family of controls to have a shared look and feel. For example, you may wish to ensure that all Button objects have the same height, width, background color, and font size for their textual content. If all UI elements are located on a single container (such as a `Window` or `UserControl`), you could quickly establish a common look and feel by selecting each control on the artboard (via a standard Ctrl+click operation) and then using the Properties panel to assign the various UI settings to all selected items.

While you *could* set each `Button`'s individual properties to identical values using this technique, this approach certainly makes it difficult to implement changes down the road, as you would need to reset the same batch of properties on multiple objects for every change.[1] The shortcomings of this approach are very evident when some properties have been set to complex objects (such as a custom brush). Consider for example how painful life would be if you needed to replicate the following settings for ten different `Button` controls in a multi-windowed WPF application:

```
<!-- Yuck. Too much markup to repeat! -->
<Button Content="OK" Width="100" Height="30"
        FontFamily="Arial Rounded MT Bold" FontSize="16">
  <Button.Background>
    <LinearGradientBrush EndPoint="0,1" StartPoint="0,0">
      <GradientStop Color="#FFF3F3F3" Offset="0"/>
      <GradientStop Color="#FFEBEBEB" Offset="0.5"/>
      <GradientStop Color="#FFDDDDDD" Offset="0.5"/>
      <GradientStop Color="#FF3620CE" Offset="1"/>
    </LinearGradientBrush>
  </Button.Background>
</Button>
```

Thankfully, WPF and Silverlight both offer a simple way to constrain the look and feel of related controls, by using *styles*. Simply put, a style is an object that maintains a collection of property/value pairs. Programmatically speaking, an individual style is represented using the `System.Windows.Style` class. This class has a property named `Setters`, which exposes a strongly typed collection of `Setter` objects. It is the `Setter` objects that allow you to define the property/value pairs.

In addition to the `Setters` collection, the `Style` class also defines a few other important members that allow you to restrict where a style can be applied and even create a new style based on an existing style (think of that as "style inheritance"). Now, as you would hope, the Blend IDE does provide a way to help automate the creation (and editing) of styles. However, before examining how to use these helpful shortcuts, let's briefly examine how a basic style could be constructed manually.

Creating a Simple Style by Hand

If you'd like to follow along, launch Expression Blend and create a new WPF application project named **WpfStyleByHand**.[2] While you could embed a style directly within a control, in almost every case, a `Style` object will be packaged as an object resource (see Chapter 2). Like any object resource, you can package it at the `Window` (or `UserControl`) level, the application level (in `App.xaml`), as well as within a dedicated resource dictionary (which is great because it makes the `Style` objects easily accessible throughout multiple projects).

---

[1] Additionally, this Blend IDE trick does little to help you when the controls you are trying to set are located in multiple locations (for example, five different WPF `Window` objects) within a project.

[2] The markup for this example would be similar, but not identical, for a Silverlight application. Be aware that XAML used for WPF and Silverlight styles is not 100 percent identical. Thankfully, when you are building styles using the Blend editors, the IDE will generate the proper XAML based on your API of choice.

Recall that the ultimate goal is to define a `Style` object that fills (at minimum) the `Setters` collection with a set of property/value pairs. Let's build a style that captures the basic font characteristics of a control in our application. Open your `App.xaml` file, and define the following style (identified by the key, `BasicControlStyle`) using the Blend XAML editor:[3]

```
<Application
  xmlns="http://schemas.microsoft.com/winfx/2006/xaml/presentation"
  xmlns:x="http://schemas.microsoft.com/winfx/2006/xaml"
  x:Class="WpfStyleByHand.App"
  StartupUri="MainWindow.xaml">

  <!-- This is a very simple style which can be applied
       to any control. -->
  <Application.Resources>
    <Style x:Key ="BasicControlStyle">
      <Setter Property = "Control.FontSize" Value ="14"/>
      <Setter Property = "Control.Height" Value = "40"/>
      <Setter Property = "Control.Cursor" Value = "Hand"/>
    </Style>
  </Application.Resources>
</Application>
```

Notice that this style adds three `Setter` objects to the internal `Setters` collection. Here, our style ensures that a control that adopts this look and feel will have a font size of 14, a height of 40, and display a hand icon if the mouse cursor is within the control's boundaries. Next, let's apply this style to a few controls on the artboard.

Assigning a Control's Style Property

First, open the artboard for your initial `Window` and place a `Label` control and a `Button` control anywhere within the `Grid` layout manager. Make sure you set the `Content` property of each control to a unique textual value, something such as the following:

```
<Grid x:Name="LayoutRoot">
  <Button Content="My Button" ... />
  <Label Content="Some Simple Text" ... />
</Grid>
```

Next, select both controls on the artboard via a Ctrl+click operation, and search the Properties panel for the `Style` property located under the Miscellaneous category (remember, you can always use the Search area of the Properties panel to quickly find a property or event). Once you have found the `Style` property, click the Advanced options button (the small square to the right of the property text area) and locate your application-level resource, specifically `BasicControlStyle` (see Figure 5–1).

---

[3] If you are creating this example with Silverlight, your opening `<Style>` declaration must add the `TargetType="Control"` attribute. See the section "Constraining a Style with TargetType" later in this chapter for more details.

Figure 5–1. The Style property is located under the Miscellaneous category of the Properties panel.

Once you have selected BasicControlStyle, you should see that both controls on the artboard are updated accordingly. If you run the application, you will also notice the mouse cursor will change to a Hand cursor when it is within the boundaries of either control. Furthermore, if you examine the generated markup, you will see that the Style property has been set to your custom style via the {DynamicResource}[4] markup extension (a Silverlight application would use {StaticResource}):

```
<Grid x:Name="LayoutRoot">
  <Button Content="My Button" ...
          Style="{DynamicResource BasicControlStyle}"/>
  <Label Content="Some Simple Text" ...
          Style="{DynamicResource BasicControlStyle}"/>
</Grid>
```

Also take a moment to view the Style property within the Properties panel. You'll notice this property is now surrounded with a green bounding box (see Figure 5–2). By convention, all properties that have been assigned to a named object resource (such as a custom style) will be marked in this manner, serving as a useful visual reminder during the development process.

---

[4] The {DynamicResource} markup extension ensures that if the resource changes at runtime, the objects using the resource are automatically updated. Also recall that {DynamicResource} is only supported under WPF.

Figure 5–2. *Properties bound to object resources are outlined by a green border.*

Overriding Style Settings

Currently, we have a `Button` and a `Label` that have both opted to use the constraints enforced by our style. Of course, if you want a control to apply a style and then change some of the defined settings, that is fine. For example, you can update your `Button` to use the `Help` cursor (rather than the `Hand` cursor defined in the style):

```
<Button Content="My Button" Cursor="Help" ...
        Style="{DynamicResource BasicControlStyle}"/>
```

The point to be aware of here is that styles are processed before the individual property settings of the control using the style, so controls can "override" settings on a case-by-case basis.

Constraining a Style with TargetType

Currently, our style is defined in such a way that *any* control can adopt it by setting the `Style` property. This is due to the fact that each property specified in a `<Style>` element has been qualified by the `Control` class;[5] for example:

```
<Setter Property = "Control.Height" Value = "40"/>
```

For a style that defines dozens of settings, this approach would entail a good amount of repeated markup. One way to clean up this style a bit is to use the `TargetType` attribute. When you add this attribute to the start tag of a `Style`'s element, you can mark exactly once where it can be applied. Consider the following reworking of `BasicControlStyle`:

```
<Style x:Key ="BasicControlStyle" TargetType="Control">
  <Setter Property = "FontSize" Value ="14"/>
  <Setter Property = "Height" Value = "40"/>
  <Setter Property = "Cursor" Value = "Hand"/>
</Style>
```

■ **Note** Silverlight styles must always be created using the `TargetType` attribute. Only WPF allows you to prefix the class name to the property being specified in a `<Setter>` element.

---

[5] The `Control` class is a common parent for all GUI controls. This is true for both WPF and Silverlight applications.

This is somewhat helpful, but we still have a style that can apply to *any* control. Use of the TargetType attribute is more useful when you truly wish to define a style that can be applied only to a particular type of control. To illustrate, add the following new style (named BigGreenButton) to the application's resource dictionary:

```
<!-- This style can only be applied to Button controls -->
<Style x:Key ="BigGreenButton" TargetType="Button">
  <Setter Property = "FontSize" Value ="20"/>
  <Setter Property = "Height" Value = "100"/>
  <Setter Property = "Width" Value = "100"/>
  <Setter Property = "Background" Value = "DarkGreen"/>
  <Setter Property = "Foreground" Value = "Yellow"/>
</Style>
```

This style will work only on Button controls (or a subclass of Button),[6] and if you apply it on an incompatible element, you will get markup and compiler errors. However, if the Button uses this new style as follows, we would see the output shown in Figure 5–3.

```
<Button Content="Button!" ...
        Style="{DynamicResource BigGreenButton}"/>
```

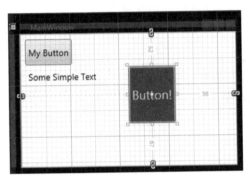

Figure 5–3. *A slightly more interesting style for Button controls*

■ **Note** When you are building a style for a specific target type, you needn't be concerned if you assign a value to a property that is not supported by the target. If the target type does not support a given property, it is ignored.

Subclassing Existing Styles

It is also possible to build new styles using an existing style as a starting point, via the BasedOn attribute. The style you are extending must have been given a proper x:Key in the dictionary, as the derived style will reference it by name using the {StaticResource} markup extension.

---

[6] If you want a style that applies to all kinds of buttons (i.e., Button, ToggleButton, RepeatButton, etc.), you can set TargetType to "ButtonBase".

■ **Note** The BasedOn property cannot be set using the {DynamicResource} markup extension. You must use {StaticResource} for both WPF and Silverlight projects when creating a derived style.

Here is a new style, TiltButton, based on BigGreenButton, that rotates the Button element by 20 degrees using a <RotateTransform> element:

```
<!-- This style is based on BigGreenButton -->
<Style x:Key ="TiltButton" TargetType="Button"
       BasedOn = "{StaticResource BigGreenButton}">
  <Setter Property = "Foreground" Value = "White"/>
  <Setter Property = "RenderTransform">
    <Setter.Value>
      <RotateTransform Angle = "20"/>
    </Setter.Value>
  </Setter>
</Style>
```

Assuming you had defined this new style in your App.xaml file, you would find the output shown in Figure 5–4 when a Button control uses this style.

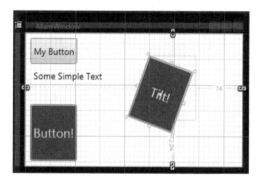

Figure 5–4. *An even more interesting style for Button controls*

Defining Default Styles

So far, so good. However, now assume you need to ensure that all TextBox controls within a given project must have the same look and feel. Also assume that you have defined a TextBox style as an application-level resource, so all windows in the program have access to it. While this is a step in the right direction, if you have numerous windows, with numerous TextBox controls, you will need to set the Style property numerous times!

WPF and Silverlight styles can be implicitly applied to all controls within a given XAML scope. To create such a style, you must use the TargetType property, but you *omit* assigning to the Style resource an x:Key value. This "unnamed style" will now apply to all controls that are of the correct type. Here is another application-level style that will apply automatically to all TextBox controls in the current application:

```
<!-- The default style for all text boxes -->
<Style TargetType="TextBox">
  <Setter Property = "FontSize" Value ="14"/>
  <Setter Property = "Width" Value = "100"/>
  <Setter Property = "Height" Value = "30"/>
  <Setter Property = "BorderThickness" Value = "5"/>
  <Setter Property = "BorderBrush" Value = "Red"/>
  <Setter Property = "FontStyle" Value = "Italic"/>
</Style>
```

Now, because we have defined this style *without* an x:Key value and have packaged it up in the application level, the Blend IDE automatically knows this is the default look and feel for any TextBox you add to the artboard. Give it a try. You'll see that the style is automatically applied with no effort on your part. In fact, if you take a minute to examine the generated markup, you'll see no trace of the Style property being set on the TextBox objects (after all, it is the *default style*).

■ **Note** If you want to define a control that does not receive the default style of the project, use the XAML editor to set the Style property to the string value "{x:Null}". This XAML markup extension basically informs the runtime to completely ignore any default style floating around your project, and to render the object as defined. As well, you can simply assign a different, keyed style to the control of interest.

As you might imagine, you could package up a full set of custom styles in a dedicated resource dictionary to define the default property settings for a large number of controls. If you make sure none of these resources has been named via the x:Key attribute, it becomes very easy to make sure new WPF or Silverlight projects automatically set controls to the desired styles. Just add the XAML file to your project, merge it into your application scope (see Chapter 2), and you are good to go!

Managing Existing Styles Using the Blend IDE

Before wrapping up this first example, open the Resources panel of the Blend IDE. You will notice that all of your styles are listed, just like any other custom object resource you happen to define. Figure 5–5 shows the application-level resources for the current example.

Figure 5–5. Styles are listed under the Resources panel.

If you click the Edit Resource button to the right of a given style, you will launch an integrated editor for the selected style. Once you have opened the editor for a given style, you are free to use the Properties panel to modify the style's property settings. Figure 5–6 shows the editor for the TiltButton style, which has been modified to use a purple background and a Width value of 200 via the Properties panel.

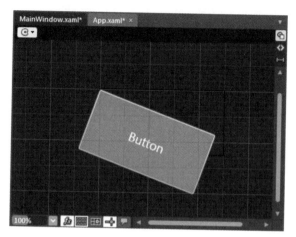

Figure 5–6. Existing styles can be opened for editing using the Blend IDE.

On a related note, if you view the Styles category of your Assets library, you'll see that your custom styles (minus any default styles defined in your project) are listed here as well (see Figure 5–7). If you drag one of these items onto your artboard, you'll automatically generate a control that has the Style property value set to the related resource.

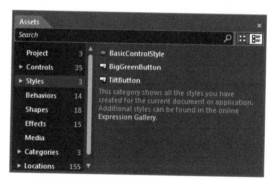

Figure 5–7. You can drag styles from the Assets library to quickly define a styled control.

Sweet! Now that you have a better idea of how styles operate, let's see how the Blend IDE can aid in the creation of styles.

■ **Source Code** The **WpfStyleByHand** project can be found under the Chapter 5 subdirectory.

Creating New Styles Using Blend

For the next example, we will create a few styles using the Blend IDE, and you will learn some more advanced style techniques to boot. Here, we will use a WPF application once again, only because the last part of this example (see the section "Working with WPF Simple Styles") will examine a few techniques *not* supported by Silverlight. If Silverlight is your primary API of interest, I still recommend you read over this section entirely, as you will find a number of IDE techniques common to both platforms.

In any case, create a new WPF application project named **WpfStylesWithBlend**. Building a custom style with Blend typically begins by placing an instance of the to-be-styled control on your artboard. You could pick from the Assets library any control you wish to tinker with, but for this example, I recommend you pick a simple control such as the Button. If you pick a more exotic control (such as the Calendar control or TreeView control), the generated style starter markup could be quite verbose.

Creating a New Empty Style

Select your control (which, again, I'll assume is a Button type for this example) on your artboard or, if you choose, via the Objects and Timeline panel. Next, choose Object ➤ Edit Style (see Figure 5–8).

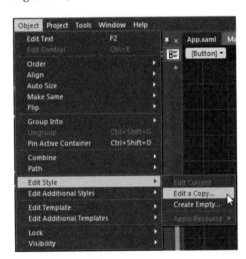

Figure 5–8. *The Object menu is your starting point to create styles with Blend.*

The Object ➤ Edit Style menu provides three primary options, which *may or may not* be enabled depending on how the control you are working with is currently defined in XAML. In a nutshell, your choices break down as so:

- *Edit Current*: If this option is enabled, you can edit the style currently applied to the selected item. This menu option is disabled if the selected control does not have the Style property currently set.

- *Edit a Copy*: This option allows you to get a copy of the currently applied style that captures the current properties of the selected item.

- *Create Empty*: This option creates a blank style, where `TargetType` is assigned based on the selected item.

■ **Note** You will also find the Apply Resource option enabled under the Object ➤ Edit Style menu if your project contains existing style resources. This is another way you can apply styles to selected items on the artboard.

Since the `Button` we are operating on does not have a custom style currently set, our only available options are Edit a Copy and Create Empty. For now, select Create Empty. Once you do so, you will be presented with a dialog box that allows you to give your style a name, or specify that you want to make a default, unkeyed style, by selecting the "Apply to all" option. As well, you are asked where you want to store your new object resource. For this example, create a custom style named `firstButtonStyle`, stored at the application level (see Figure 5–9).

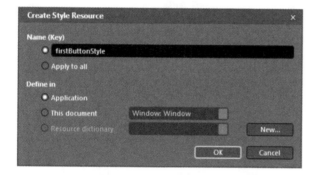

Figure 5–9. Creating a new named style based on a Button object

Once you click the OK button, a new designer appears for your style, which at this point looks exactly like an unstyled `Button` control (see Figure 5–10).

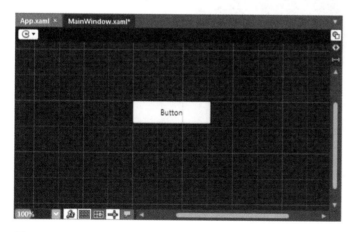

Figure 5–10. Styles can be edited via the Blend artboard and Properties panel.

■ **Note** Recall that you can always open a style for editing by locating it in your Resources panel and clicking the Edit resource button to the right of the style.

Your goal is to use the Properties panel to set various properties on the style, just like you would do if you were setting properties for a particular control instance on a Window or UserControl. For example, you can use the Brushes editor, the transformation tools, padding and margin editors, and so forth. Moreover, you could build a style that incorporates animations (which you will do a bit later in this chapter), uses data binding templates (see Chapter 6), and uses other items of interest.

■ **Note** You might recall from Chapter 1 that the content on the artboard can be zoomed in using the mouse wheel, as well as via the artboard controls. When you are building intricate styles and templates, this will be very handy.

While you are free to explore the options to your liking, I've opted to keep this example simple. Basically, I've edited the original starter markup, which looked like so (recall this was defined as an application-level resource, so the markup is placed in App.xaml):

```
<Style x:Key="firstButtonStyle" TargetType="{x:Type Button}"/>
```

Figure 5–11 shows how I have updated firstButtonStyle using various aspects of the Properties panel. Don't worry about making your style look exactly like the control you see here (for example, you might not have the same fonts installed on your machine). Just take some time and have a bit of fun, making changes to your style as you see fit.

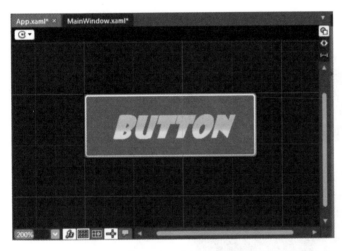

Figure 5–11. A custom button style created with the Blend style editor

Once you have finished creating your style, take a moment to view the generated XAML. Based on how complex your edits were, you could find a good deal of markup. Even my version of `firstButtonStyle` (which is not quite ready for mass commercial distribution) yielded the following XAML based on my settings:

```
<Style x:Key="firstButtonStyle" TargetType="{x:Type Button}">
  <Setter Property="Background" Value="#FF154BD0"/>
  <Setter Property="BorderBrush" Value="#FFE20C0C"/>
  <Setter Property="FontSize" Value="24"/>
  <Setter Property="FontFamily" Value="Showcard Gothic"/>
  <Setter Property="Foreground">
    <Setter.Value>
      <LinearGradientBrush EndPoint="0.5,1" StartPoint="0.5,0">
        <GradientStop Color="#FF26D096" Offset="0"/>
        <GradientStop Color="#FFEFE710" Offset="1"/>
      </LinearGradientBrush>
    </Setter.Value>
  </Setter>
  <Setter Property="BorderThickness" Value="5"/>
  <Setter Property="Height" Value="50"/>
  <Setter Property="Width" Value="140"/>
  <Setter Property="FontStyle" Value="Italic"/>
</Style>
```

At this point, you should find that the original control back on the initial `Window` has automatically taken on the updated look and feel (if this is not the case, make sure you have saved your edits). If you want to add more `Button` controls that have the same style, simply drag the style of interest onto your artboard from the Styles category of your Assets library (as shown earlier, in Figure 5–7). Figure 5–12 shows our main `Window` object, which now contains a series of `Button` objects all using `firstButtonStyle`.

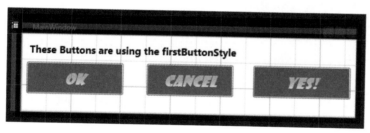

Figure 5–12. *Multiple Button objects with the same style*

Working with WPF Simple Styles

So far, you have learned how you can select a control on the artboard and generate an empty style (or a copy of a style) for editing. In some cases, this approach will be perfect; however, consider how you would proceed if you had a brand new WPF project and needed to define custom styles for 20 different controls. For example, maybe you want to make a "theme" for your application, where each control takes on the look of the current season (a winter theme, summer theme, etc.). As you might imagine, it would be tedious to drag each control onto the artboard to extract a style copy.

Thankfully, for WPF projects created with Expression Blend, you can use a full set of Simple Styles, which can be the starting point for your application's UI. When you insert Simple Styles into your WPF project, the IDE inserts a number of new object resources that you can edit to your heart's content. This approach can greatly simplify the construction of styles, as the generated markup includes numerous important settings that are required for the control to operate as expected.

To illustrate, open the Assets library (or Assets panel) and expand the Styles category. You'll notice a section named Simple Styles (see Figure 5–13).

Figure 5–13. WPF Simple Styles are located in the Assets library.

Select one of these Simple Styles (I'll be using SimpleSlider) and drag it to your artboard. Once you do, select the object and resize it so that it displays horizontally over a majority of the window. At this point, your SimpleSlider looks like any other Slider control (see Figure 5–14).

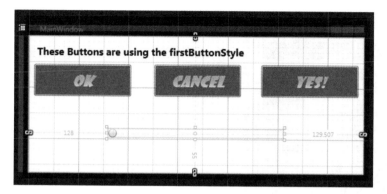

Figure 5–14. At first glance, a WPF Simple Style looks like a "normal" control.

However, if you examine the markup, you will see that the `Style` property has been set to use the `SimpleSlider` style:

```
<Slider Margin="128,0,129.507,55" Style="{DynamicResource SimpleSlider}"
        VerticalAlignment="Bottom"/>
```

Open the Resources panel of your project. The first thing you will notice is that your `App.xaml` resource section has a new `Linked To` node, which specifies a connection to a new XAML file named `Simple Styles.xaml` (see Figure 5–15).

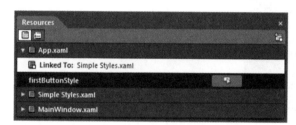

Figure 5–15. The Linked To node denotes that an external XAML file has been merged into an application.

In terms of XAML, this `Linked In` node is due to the merging of the external XAML file into the application's resource container. If you open the `App.xaml` file using the markup editor, you will find the following has been added:

```
<ResourceDictionary.MergedDictionaries>
  <ResourceDictionary Source="Simple Styles.xaml"/>
</ResourceDictionary.MergedDictionaries>
```

More importantly, if you return to the Resources panel (make sure your artboard is the active window in the IDE, or the Resources panel will be empty), you can expand the `Simple Styles.xaml` resource set and see that each of the core WPF controls has been replicated. As well, this file defines a number of additional resources, such as the default brushes used to paint aspects of the controls (backgrounds, foregrounds, etc.). Notice in Figure 5–16 that these default brushes can be edited using the integrated Brushes editor.

Figure 5–16. Simple Styles.xaml defines styles and related resources for each core WPF control.

Here I have changed `NormalBrush` to a shade of red, and lo and behold, the thumb of the `Slider` control is repainted accordingly, as shown in Figure 5–17.

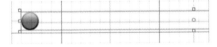

Figure 5–17. Changing the brushes of Simple Styles.xaml will alter the controls using the style.

And, of course, if you open a given style for editing using the Resources panel, you can modify the simple resource even further. Figure 5–18 shows the `SimpleSlider` opened for editing.

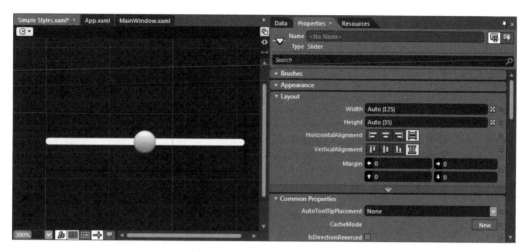

Figure 5–18. *Simple Styles can be edited like any other style.*

■ **Note** As you might guess, there are many online resources that allow developers and graphical artists to share WPF and Silverlight styles. One of my favorite web sites is www.wpfstyles.com. It provides access to dozens of free styles that you can download and use within your projects—very helpful for the artistically challenged (such as myself)!

Viewing Simple Style Markup

Open your `Simple Styles.xaml` file for viewing using the XAML editor, and take a moment to examine the markup. By way of an example, locate the `SimpleSliderThumb` style. Notice that it contains an embedded `<ControlTemplate>` element, which itself defines a number of other oddities, including a set of triggers. Here is some partial markup:

```
<Style x:Key="SimpleSliderThumb" d:IsControlPart="True"
       TargetType="{x:Type Thumb}">
...
  <ControlTemplate TargetType="{x:Type Thumb}">
    <Grid>
      <Ellipse x:Name="Ellipse" Fill="{DynamicResource NormalBrush}"
               Stroke="{DynamicResource NormalBorderBrush}"
               StrokeThickness="1"/>
    </Grid>
    <ControlTemplate.Triggers>
      <Trigger Property="IsMouseOver" Value="True">
        <Setter Property="Fill" Value="{DynamicResource MouseOverBrush}"
                TargetName="Ellipse"/>
      </Trigger>
...
    </ControlTemplate.Triggers>
...
```

```
</Style>
```

As you can see, these default Simple Styles are more complex than first meets the eye! To fully understand what is going on with this markup, we next need to examine the role of control templates. Before we do, however, let me point out that the Expression Blend User Guide provides an entire section discussing how to add common modifications to the WPF Simple Styles. Look up the topic "Styling tips for WPF Simple Styles." As you can see in Figure 5–19, the help system describes how you could (for example) customize the thumb of the SimpleSlider style.

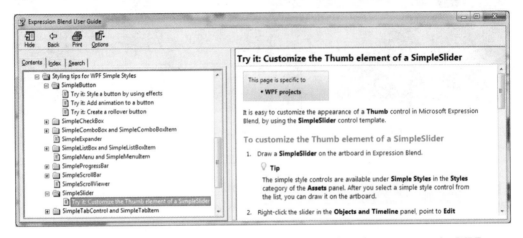

Figure 5–19. The Blend User Guide provides numerous tutorials on how to customize WPF Simple Styles.

■ **Source Code** The **WpfStylesWithBlend** project can be found under the Chapter 5 subdirectory.

The Role of Control Templates in Styles

A very basic style is really just a container for common settings for a given control type. While styles can be useful when you want the style to simply tweak a handful of properties (colors, font sizes, etc.) of the target control type, the overall rendering of the control remains as is. Thus, no matter how you stylize a Button, it still looks like a basic rectangle (or maybe a square if you resize it correctly).

Sometimes, you might want to build a style that not only changes a few common settings of the target control, but also redefines the shape of the control itself. For example, what if you wanted a round button style? Or perhaps you have used the Pen or Pencil tool to render an arbitrary polygon, and wish to use this as the starting point for a new style for a particular control type?

When you want to create a style that has the power to reshape how the control renders its defining geometry, you must define a style that contains an embedded *control template*, which is represented in XAML using the <ControlTemplate> element. Within this element, you can define the new control's look and feel, use layout managers for content, and perform other common operations.

■ **Note** While a template is most often part of a larger style, it is possible to define a `<ControlTemplate>` as a stand-alone object resource. You can make controls adopt a given template by setting their `Template` property. You'll see this approach in action in the next example.

By default, every WPF and Silverlight control renders its look and feel using its associated *default template*. For example, the default template for a `Button` contains instructions used to render the default rectangular display we all know and love (the same general idea holds true for any WPF or Silverlight control). These default templates are packaged up as embedded XAML resources within the WPF and Silverlight libraries, and therefore cannot be *directly* changed. However, as you will see, Blend provides several mechanisms to extract a copy of a default template for editing.

In addition to defining various instructions regarding how a control should render its overall appearance, a template also contains instructions regarding how a control should respond to user interactions and other state changes. By way of a few examples, the default template of a `Button` control describes how it should look when it receives focus, when the mouse clicks within its boundaries, when it is disabled, and so on.

When you define a new template (or modify an existing template), you typically will be required to supply custom XAML elements that describe how your control will respond to these same state changes. As you will see over the next several pages, a WPF template can define visual cues using either of two approaches: triggers or the Visual State Manager (VSM). Silverlight templates, however, are restricted to the use of the VSM. As you will also see, Expression Blend has built-in editors to work with each approach.

■ **Note** The VSM was first introduced with the Silverlight API and is used to incorporate visual cues for a Silverlight template. Historically, WPF programmers use a similar approach, via triggers. However, with the release of .NET 4.0, WPF has been updated to support the VSM as well, thereby giving WPF programmers *two* ways to add visual cues. You'll see examples of each approach in the pages to come.

Building a Custom Control Template by Hand

Before we examine the various ways Blend can facilitate the construction of custom templates, I'd like to show you how to build a simple template by hand. I really can't think of a better approach to understanding the nuts and bolts of template creation. Once you have completed the next example, you'll create additional templates using the tools of the Blend IDE.

Create a new WPF application project named **WpfTemplatesByHand**. Once you have done so, add a single `Button` to the artboard of your initial `Window`. Currently, this `Button` is rendered using the associated default template, which, as you'll recall, is an embedded resource within a given WPF (or Silverlight) library. When you define your own template, you are essentially replacing this default set of instructions with your own creation.

To begin creating your template, open the XAML editor of your initial `Window` and update the definition of the `<Button>` element to specify a new, embedded template,[7] which we will

---

[7] Over the course of this example, we will move the template into the application's resource dictionary.

modify and improve upon as we proceed. Note that I've assigned to the Height and Width properties the value 100 and deleted the Content property of the Button. The remaining attributes in the opening <Button> definition can remain as is:

```
<Button Width="100" Height="100" ... >
  <Button.Template>
    <ControlTemplate>
      <Grid x:Name="controlLayout">
        <Ellipse x:Name="buttonSurface" Fill = "LightBlue"/>
        <Label x:Name="buttonCaption" VerticalAlignment = "Center"
               HorizontalAlignment = "Center"
               FontWeight = "Bold" FontSize = "20" Content = "OK!"/>
      </Grid>
    </ControlTemplate>
  </Button.Template>
</Button>
```

Here, we have defined a template that consists of a named Grid control containing a named Ellipse and a Label. Because our Grid has no defined rows or columns, each child stacks on top of the previous control, allowing us to easily center the content using the VerticalAlignment and HorizontalAlignment properties. Also notice that the entire <ControlTemplate> is assigned to the Template property of the Button, via the <Button.Template> scope.

To further test our template, handle the Click event for the Button using the Properties panel (remember, the lightening bolt icon is used to select the events for a selected item). In the generated event handler, add some code to display a simple message box:

```
private void Button_Click(object sender, System.Windows.RoutedEventArgs e)
{
  MessageBox.Show("You clicked the button!");
}
```

If you run your application, you will notice that the Click event fires *only* when the mouse cursor is within the bounds of the Ellipse (i.e., not in the corners around the edges of the Ellipse). This is a great feature of the WPF and Silverlight template architecture, because we do not need to recalculate hit testing, bounds checking, or any other low-level detail. So, if your template uses a Path object to render some oddball geometry, you can rest assured that the mouse hit-testing details are relative to the shape of the control, not the larger bounding rectangle.

Storing Templates as Resources

Currently, our template is embedded within a specific Button control, which limits our reuse options. Ideally, we would place our template into a resource dictionary so that we can reuse our "round button template" between projects or, at minimum, move it into the application resource container for reuse within this project. Let's move the local Button resource to the application level. First, locate the Template property for your Button in the Blend Properties panel. Next, open the advanced settings menu (by clicking the white square to the right of the property text area) and select Convert to New Resource, as shown in Figure 5–20.

Figure 5-20. Extracting a local resource

In the resulting dialog box, define a new template named RoundButtonTemplate that is stored as an application resource. At this point, you will find the following data in your App.xaml file:

```
<Application
  xmlns="http://schemas.microsoft.com/winfx/2006/xaml/presentation"
  xmlns:x="http://schemas.microsoft.com/winfx/2006/xaml"
  x:Class="WpfButtonTemplate.App"
  StartupUri="MainWindow.xaml">
  <Application.Resources>
    <ControlTemplate x:Key="RoundButtonTemplate"
                     TargetType="Button">
      <Grid x:Name="controlLayout">
        <Ellipse  x:Name="buttonSurface" Fill = "LightBlue"/>
        <Label x:Name="buttonCaption" VerticalAlignment = "Center"
            HorizontalAlignment = "Center"
            FontWeight = "Bold" FontSize = "20" Content = "OK!"/>
      </Grid>
    </ControlTemplate>
  </Application.Resources>
</Application>
```

Also note that the original Button has been modified by setting the Template property to your custom named resource:

```
<Button HorizontalAlignment="Left" Margin="44,30,0,0"
      VerticalAlignment="Top" Width="100" Height="100"
      Click="Button_Click"
      Template="{DynamicResource RoundButtonTemplate}"/>
```

Because this resource is now available for the entire application, we can define any number of round buttons. Go ahead and add two additional `Button` controls to your `Window`'s artboard. Then, using the Properties panel, set the `Template` property of each to the `RoundButtonTemplate` resource (see Figure 5–21).

Figure 5–21. Setting the Template property

Figure 5–22 shows the end result.

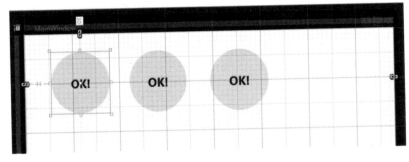

Figure 5–22. Three Button objects using the same template

Incorporating Visual Cues Using WPF Triggers

When you define a custom template, all the visual cues of the default template are removed as well. Recall that a default template contains markup instructions that inform the control how to look when certain UI events occur, such as when it receives focus, when it is clicked with the mouse, when it is enabled (or disabled), and so on. Users are quite accustomed to these sorts of visual cues, as they give the control somewhat of a tactile response.

Our RoundButtonTemplate does not define any such markup, so the look of the control is identical regardless of the mouse activity, focusing, and so forth. Ideally, our control should look slightly different when clicked (maybe via a color change or reduction in size) to let the user know the visual state has changed.

When WPF was first released, the way to add such visual cues was to add to the template any number of triggers that typically would change values of object properties or start a storyboard animation (or both) when the trigger condition was true.

To illustrate this approach, update your RoundButtonTemplate as shown here, which will change the background color of the control to blue and the foreground color to yellow when the mouse cursor is over the surface:

```
<ControlTemplate x:Key="RoundButtonTemplate" TargetType="Button" >
  <Grid x:Name="controlLayout">
    <Ellipse x:Name="buttonSurface" Fill="LightBlue" />
    <Label x:Name="buttonCaption" Content="OK!" FontSize="20"
           FontWeight="Bold" HorizontalAlignment="Center"
           VerticalAlignment="Center" />
  </Grid>

  <ControlTemplate.Triggers>
    <Trigger Property = "IsMouseOver" Value = "True">
      <Setter TargetName = "buttonSurface"
              Property = "Fill" Value = "Blue"/>
      <Setter TargetName = "buttonCaption" Property = "Foreground"
              Value = "Yellow"/>
    </Trigger>
  </ControlTemplate.Triggers>

</ControlTemplate>
```

If you run the program yet again, you should find that the color does toggle based on whether or not the mouse cursor is within the control's boundary. Notice that this particular <Trigger> element is defined such that when the IsMouseOver property is set to True, two target elements (buttonSurface and buttonCaption) are specified (via TargetName) and changed accordingly. Don't stress out too much over this XAML. Most WPF programmers are in agreement that manually authoring triggers is no fun at all. I'll show you in just a bit how Blend can generate trigger logic using the Triggers panel.

Here is another trigger, which will shrink the size of the Grid (and therefore all child elements) when the control is clicked via the mouse. Add this to your <ControlTemplate.Triggers> collection, and then run your application to test it.

```
<Trigger Property = "IsPressed" Value="True">
  <Setter TargetName="controlLayout"
          Property="RenderTransformOrigin" Value="0.5,0.5"/>
  <Setter TargetName="controlLayout" Property="RenderTransform">
    <Setter.Value>
      <ScaleTransform ScaleX="0.8" ScaleY="0.8"/>
    </Setter.Value>
  </Setter>
</Trigger>
```

So at this point, we have a custom template with a few visual cues incorporated using WPF triggers. In an upcoming example, you will learn about an alternative way to incorporate visual cues, using the Visual State Manager. Before we get to that point, however, let's talk about the role of the {TemplateBinding} markup extension and the <ContentPresenter> element.

Understanding the Role of {TemplateBinding}

Because our template can be applied only to `Button` controls, it stands to reason that we could set properties on the `<Button>` element that will cause the template to render itself in a unique manner. For example, the `Fill` property of the `Ellipse` currently is hard-coded to be blue, while the `Content` property of the `Label` is always set to the string value `"OK!"`. Of course, we might want buttons of different colors and textual values, so we might try to define the following buttons in our main `Window`:

```
<Grid x:Name="LayoutRoot">
  <Button Background="Red" Content="Howdy!" ...
          Template="{DynamicResource RoundButtonTemplate}"/>
  <Button Background="LightGreen" Content="Cancel!" ...
          Template="{DynamicResource RoundButtonTemplate}" />
  <Button Background="Yellow" Content="Format" ...
          Template="{DynamicResource RoundButtonTemplate}"/>
</Grid>
```

However, regardless of the fact that each `Button` is defined to use unique `Background` and `Content` values, we still end up with three blue buttons that contain the text `OK!`. The problem is that the properties of the control *using* the template (the `Button` objects) have properties that do not match identically the properties *on the template* (such as the `Fill` property of the `Ellipse`). As well, although the `Label` does have a `Content` property, the value defined in the `<Button>` scope is not automatically routed to the internal child of the template.

We can solve these issues by using the `{TemplateBinding}` markup extension when we build our template. This allows us to capture property settings defined by the control using our template, and use them to set values in the template itself. Here is a reworked version of `RoundButtonTemplate`, which now uses this markup extension to map the `Background` property of the `Button` to the `Fill` property of the `Ellipse`, as well as to make sure the `Content` property of the `Button` is indeed passed to the `Content` property of the `Label`:

```
<ControlTemplate x:Key="RoundButtonTemplate" TargetType="Button" >
  <Grid x:Name="controlLayout">
    <Ellipse x:Name="buttonSurface"
             Fill="{TemplateBinding Background}"/>
    <Label x:Name="buttonCaption"
           Content="{TemplateBinding Content}"
           FontSize="20" FontWeight="Bold"
           HorizontalAlignment="Center"
           VerticalAlignment="Center" />
  </Grid>
  ...
</ControlTemplate>
```

With this update, we can now create buttons of various colors and textual values (see Figure 5–23).

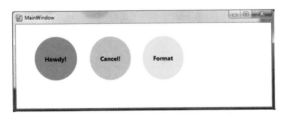

Figure 5–23. *Template bindings allow values to pass through to the internal controls.*

Understanding the Role of <ContentPresenter>

When we designed our template, we used a `Label` to display the textual value of the control. Like the `Button`, the `Label` supports a `Content` property. Therefore, given our use of `{TemplateBinding}`, we could define a `Button` that contains complex content, beyond that of a simple string. For example, the following markup results in the control shown in Figure 5–24:

```
<Button Width="100" Height="100" Background="Yellow"
        Template="{StaticResource RoundButtonTemplate}"
        HorizontalAlignment="Left" ...
>
   <ListBox Height="50" Width="75">
     <ListBoxItem Content="Hello"/>
     <ListBoxItem Content="Hello"/>
     <ListBoxItem Content="Hello"/>
   </ListBox>
</Button>
```

Figure 5–24. *A Button with composite content, used by the current template*

For this particular control, things work just as hoped. However, what if you need to pass in complex content to a template member that does *not* have a `Content` property? When you wish to define a generalized "content display area" in a template, you can use the `<ContentPresenter>` class as opposed to a specific type of control (`Label` or `TextBlock`).

Although we have no need to do so for this example, here is some markup that illustrates how we could build a custom template that uses `<ContentPresenter>` to show the value of the `Content` property of the control using the template:

```
<!-- This button template will display whatever is set
       to the Content of the hosting button -->
<ControlTemplate x:Key="NewRoundButton" TargetType="Button">
  <Grid>
    <Ellipse Fill="{TemplateBinding Background}"/>
    <ContentPresenter HorizontalAlignment="Center"
                      VerticalAlignment="Center"/>
  </Grid>
</ControlTemplate>
```

Incorporating Templates into Styles

Currently, our template simply defines a custom look and feel that a `Button` control could adopt. However, the process of establishing the basic properties of the control (content, font size, font weight, etc.) is the responsibility of the `Button` itself:

```
<!-- Currently the Button must set basic property values,
     not the template -->
<Button Content="Yo!" Foreground ="Black" FontSize ="20"
```

```
     FontWeight ="Bold"
     Template ="{StaticResource RoundButtonTemplate}"
     Height="100" Width="100"/>
```

If you wish to, you can embed your template within a larger style. By doing so, you can assign values to various properties of the target type, as well as define a custom look and feel. Here is the final version of our template, which is now embedded within a style. Note that we have removed the x:Key attribute in the <ControlTemplate> element but have added (and renamed) our style to RoundButtonStyle in the <Style> scope:

```
<!-- A style containing a template -->
<Style x:Key ="RoundButtonStyle" TargetType ="Button">
  <Setter Property ="Foreground" Value ="Black"/>
  <Setter Property ="FontSize" Value ="14"/>
  <Setter Property ="FontWeight" Value ="Bold"/>
  <Setter Property="Width" Value="100"/>
  <Setter Property="Height" Value="100"/>
  <!-- Here is our template! -->
  <Setter Property ="Template">
    <Setter.Value>
      <ControlTemplate TargetType ="Button">
        <Grid x:Name="controlLayout">
          <Ellipse x:Name="buttonSurface"
                   Fill="{TemplateBinding Background}"/>
          <Label x:Name="buttonCaption"
                 Content ="{TemplateBinding Content}"
                 HorizontalAlignment="Center"
                 VerticalAlignment="Center" />
        </Grid>
        <ControlTemplate.Triggers>
          <Trigger Property = "IsMouseOver" Value = "True">
            <Setter TargetName = "buttonSurface" Property = "Fill"
                    Value = "Blue"/>
            <Setter TargetName = "buttonCaption"
                    Property = "Foreground" Value = "Yellow"/>
          </Trigger>
          <Trigger Property = "IsPressed" Value="True">
            <Setter TargetName="controlLayout"
                    Property="RenderTransformOrigin" Value="0.5,0.5"/>
            <Setter TargetName="controlLayout"
                    Property="RenderTransform">
              <Setter.Value>
                <ScaleTransform ScaleX="0.8" ScaleY="0.8"/>
              </Setter.Value>
            </Setter>
          </Trigger>
        </ControlTemplate.Triggers>
      </ControlTemplate>
    </Setter.Value>
  </Setter>
</Style>
```

With this update, we can now create Button controls by setting the Style property as before:

```
<Button Background="Red" Content="Howdy!"
        Style="{StaticResource RoundButtonStyle}"/>
```

While the rendering and behavior of the button is identical before this update, the benefit of nesting templates within styles is that you are able to provide a canned set of values for common properties. That wraps up our look at how to build a template from the ground up. Next, let's turn our attention to building templates via the tools of Expression Blend.

■ **Source Code** The **WpfTemplatesByHand** project can be found under the Chapter 5 subdirectory.

Creating Control Templates Using Expression Blend

Even though our "round button template" is quite simple, it did require a healthy dose of XAML. To be sure, if you were to create large-scale templates that contain complex brushes, animations, and so forth, you would be sure to experience cramps in your fingers due to the copious amounts of typing. Thankfully, Expression Blend has a number of features that simplify the process of working with the control templates.

Creating a Copy of a Default Template

The first way you can use Blend to ease the construction of custom templates is to extract a copy of the default template and modify its appearance as you see fit. While this approach does provide the greatest level of customization, it is also the most complex, as all the low-level details of a template are directly in view. Before I show you some very useful (and easier) alternative approaches, let's examine the basics of modifying a default template.

■ **Note** I do not recommend taking this approach to template construction unless you are well versed in WPF and Silverlight template internals. If you are not careful, you can very easily delete parts of the template copy that are required for the control to work properly!

Create a new WPF application project called **WpfTemplatesWithBlend**, and place a single `Button` control (to keep things somewhat simple) on the artboard of the initial `Window`.

■ **Note** This example assumes you are using WPF. If you are using Silverlight, the generated XAML will be quite different, but the basic template editing techniques will be the same.

Right-click this UI element and select Edit Template ➤ Edit a Copy, as shown in Figure 5–25.

Figure 5–25. *Making a copy of a control's default template*

Once you select this menu option, you will be presented with the Create Template Resource dialog box, which is similar to the Create Style Resource dialog box shown in Figure 5–9 earlier in the chapter. Name your new style `rawButtonTemplate` and save it as an application-level resource.

Examining Style Properties of a Default Template

Open the XAML editor for your `App.xaml` file and notice that your `<Style>` element establishes a number of default values for common UI properties such as `Background`, `BorderBrush`, `Padding`, and so forth. However, the values assigned to these properties are not hard-coded values, but rather are discovered at runtime based on a number of predefined resources, some of which have also been defined in your application's resource container, others of which are based on system settings. Consider the following partial definition of the `rawButtonTemplate` style:

```
<Style x:Key="rawButtonTemplate" TargetType="{x:Type Button}">
  <Setter Property="FocusVisualStyle"
          Value="{StaticResource ButtonFocusVisual}"/>
  <Setter Property="Background"
          Value="{StaticResource ButtonNormalBackground}"/>
  <Setter Property="BorderBrush"
          Value="{StaticResource ButtonNormalBorder}"/>
  <Setter Property="BorderThickness" Value="1"/>
  <Setter Property="Foreground"
          Value="{DynamicResource
                 {x:Static SystemColors.ControlTextBrushKey}}"/>
  <Setter Property="HorizontalContentAlignment" Value="Center"/>
```

```
<Setter Property="VerticalContentAlignment" Value="Center"/>
<Setter Property="Padding" Value="1"/>
...
</Style>
```

If you want to change any of these basic property settings, you can do so by using the Blend artboard. After ensuring that you have switched back to design mode for your template, use the breadcrumbs navigation area on the upper left to select the "Style" aspect of the template being edited, as shown in Figure 5–26.

Figure 5–26. *Selecting the style properties of a default template for editing*

Once you have done so, you can use the Properties panel as expected to change values of the selected properties, just like you would when modifying a simple style that does not contain any control template aspects.

Examining the Template Itself

In addition to the simple property settings just discussed, your style also contains a `<ControlTemplate>` element, which defines a number of subelements. First, you will find an element that associates the default template to the official "Microsoft Button Theme," named `ButtonChrome`:

```
<ControlTemplate TargetType="{x:Type Button}">
  <Microsoft_Windows_Themes:ButtonChrome x:Name="Chrome"
    BorderBrush="{TemplateBinding BorderBrush}"
    Background="{TemplateBinding Background}"
    RenderMouseOver="{TemplateBinding IsMouseOver}"
    RenderPressed="{TemplateBinding IsPressed}"
    RenderDefaulted="{TemplateBinding IsDefaulted}"
    SnapsToDevicePixels="true">
    <ContentPresenter
      HorizontalAlignment="{TemplateBinding HorizontalContentAlignment}"
      Margin="{TemplateBinding Padding}"
      RecognizesAccessKey="True"
      SnapsToDevicePixels="{TemplateBinding SnapsToDevicePixels}"
      VerticalAlignment="{TemplateBinding VerticalContentAlignment}"/>
  </Microsoft_Windows_Themes:ButtonChrome>
...
</ControlTemplate>
```

Notice that a number of these property values are assigned to a value returned from the {TemplateBinding} markup extension. As shown in the previous example, this particular XAML token is very useful when building templates because it provides a way for you to map property values that have been set on the control using the style to properties used within the style itself. Also note that the template is once again using <ContentPresenter> to allow the style to use arbitrary content.

The default button template also defines a set of WPF triggers. At first glance, the triggers in the following template don't appear to do much, but in fact they map back to additional embedded resources within the WPF libraries to obtain their full details:

```
<ControlTemplate.Triggers>
    <Trigger Property="IsKeyboardFocused" Value="true">
        <Setter Property="RenderDefaulted" TargetName="Chrome" Value="true"/>
    </Trigger>
    <Trigger Property="ToggleButton.IsChecked" Value="true">
        <Setter Property="RenderPressed" TargetName="Chrome" Value="true"/>
    </Trigger>
    <Trigger Property="IsEnabled" Value="false">
        <Setter Property="Foreground" Value="#ADADAD"/>
    </Trigger>
</ControlTemplate.Triggers>
```

■ **Note** You will also see that this template copy has some empty markup for the .NET 4.0 Visual State Manager. You'll come to know the role of this aspect of template building later in the chapter.

Using Tools to Edit a Template Copy

Now that you better understand the structure of a default template, let's look at how to use Blend to edit various aspects of it. You've already learned that you can click the Style area of the style breadcrumbs navigation area to change basic style properties. However, when you want to drill into the template details (including <ContentPresenter>), you will need to select an item via the Objects and Timeline panel (or by directly selecting an item on the artboard). In Figure 5–27, you can see that each individual aspect of the <ControlTemplate> can be selected for editing.

Figure 5–27. The Objects and Timeline panel allows you to select a template part for editing.

For this example, don't bother to change settings for this copy of the `Button` template. The reason is that this template has too many hard-coded settings that tether the control to the default Microsoft look and feel. While you *could* charge ahead and modify each aspect of the Microsoft default, it would be a fairly complex undertaking (don't worry, a simpler alternative will be shown in just a moment).

On a related note, the Triggers panel of the Blend IDE can be used to add, remove, or modify a given WPF trigger. Figure 5–28 shows the current trigger settings for our copy of the button template. Again, don't be too concerned with all of the details at this point, as the next example will show you a much simpler way to craft a custom template via Blend.

Figure 5–28. *The Triggers panel allows you to change triggers for a template copy.*

■ **Source Code** The **WpfTemplatesWithBlend** project can be found under the Chapter 5 subdirectory.

Creating a Stylized Template from a Graphic

As I am sure you picked up in the preceding discussion, it is my opinion that attempting to modify a copy of an existing control template is a tedious process (even when you are using Expression Blend). Thankfully, there is a much simpler alternative, using the Tools ➤ Make Into Control menu option. The idea behind this menu option is premised on the fact that a majority of custom templates are based on an existing graphic.

For example, let's say that you have used the tools of Blend to create a "perfect" graphic (or have imported a graphic from Expression Design; see Chapter 2). You may wish to use this graphic as a starting point for a new template for a WPF (or Silverlight) control. Once you have done so, you can then add unique triggers to your style to incorporate visual cues. The benefit of this approach (as opposed to editing a copy of an existing template) is that you have a "clean slate" and will not bump into the numerous default settings of the Microsoft look and feel. Let's see how we could do this very thing.

Creating the Initial Graphic

First up, create a new WPF application project named **StyleTemplateFromGraphic**. Next, create a custom geometry using either the Expression Blend drawing tools (the Pen or Pencil) or one of the predefined geometries found in the Shapes category of the Assets library. In Figure 5–29, you can see I've opted to use the Star shape, with a `PointCount` property value of 8.

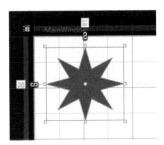

Figure 5–29. *The initial graphic, which will be transformed into a control template*

Before moving on, take a moment to examine the generated XAML. Depending on which type of geometry you constructed (and which approach you took to construct it), you will find a particular blob of markup. My geometry ended up being defined as so:

```
<ed:RegularPolygon Fill="#FF5050B4" HorizontalAlignment="Left"
    Height="113" InnerRadius="0.47211" Margin="20,18,0,0" PointCount="8"
    Stretch="Fill" Stroke="Black" VerticalAlignment="Top" Width="126"/>
```

Extracting the Stylized Template

Select your geometry on the artboard and choose Tools ➤ Make Into Control.[8] Alternatively, you can right-click the geometry and choose Make Into Control, as shown in Figure 5–30.

---

[8] Make sure you don't select Tools ➤ Make Into UserControl, as this is for a very different operation, discussed in the section "Generating UserControls Using Blend" later in this chapter.

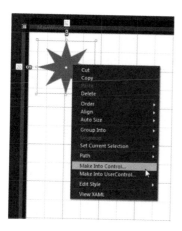

Figure 5–30. Activating the Make Into Control option of the Blend IDE

At this point you will be presented with a dialog box that allows you to select a name for your new stylized template, the location for your new resource, and, most importantly, the control target. For this example, let's define a new application-level resource named starButtonStyle that targets the Button type (see Figure 5–31).

Figure 5–31. Creating a new Button template based on the Star geometry

When you click the OK button, Blend responds by opening the new style for editing (see Figure 5–32).

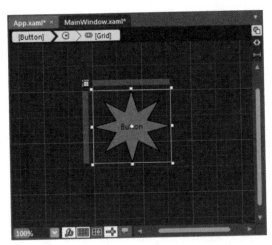

Figure 5–32. The extracted stylized template

If you examine the generated XAML, it should look quite familiar, given your work earlier in this chapter where you created a control template by hand. Here is the XAML generated based on my geometry (stored in `App.xaml`):

```
<Style x:Key="starButtonStyle" TargetType="{x:Type Button}">
  <Setter Property="Template">
    <Setter.Value>
      <ControlTemplate TargetType="{x:Type Button}">
        <Grid>
          <ed:RegularPolygon Fill="#FF5050B4" InnerRadius="0.47211"
              PointCount="8" Stretch="Fill" Stroke="Black"/>
          <ContentPresenter HorizontalAlignment=
            "{TemplateBinding HorizontalContentAlignment}"
            RecognizesAccessKey="True"
            SnapsToDevicePixels=
            "{TemplateBinding SnapsToDevicePixels}"
            VerticalAlignment=
            "{TemplateBinding VerticalContentAlignment}"/>
        </Grid>
         <ControlTemplate.Triggers>
            <Trigger Property="IsFocused" Value="True"/>
            <Trigger Property="IsDefaulted" Value="True"/>
            <Trigger Property="IsMouseOver" Value="True"/>
            <Trigger Property="IsPressed" Value="True"/>
            <Trigger Property="IsEnabled" Value="False"/>
         </ControlTemplate.Triggers>
      </ControlTemplate>
    </Setter.Value>
  </Setter>
</Style>
```

Notice that your new style has the `TargetType` property set to the selected target control (`Button`). As you can also see, a `<ControlTemplate>` has been generated that uses the `<ContentPresenter>` element, as well as a set of empty WPF triggers (which we will populate in just a moment). Also take a moment to examine how the XAML of the original geometry has been updated to (surprise, surprise) a new `<Button>` element that uses your new style! Upon examining your `MainWindow.xaml` file, you should see markup such as the following:

```
<Button Content="Button" HorizontalAlignment="Left" Height="113"
        Margin="20,18,0,0" Style="{DynamicResource starButtonStyle}"
        VerticalAlignment="Top" Width="126"/>
```

Not bad for a few mouse clicks, eh? At this point, you can handle any event you wish on the `Button`, edit additional properties, and so forth.

Building a ListBox Stylized Template

Before we add some interactivity to our template, let's define one additional template for a second geometry. Open the artboard for your initial `Window`, and draw a secondary shape of your choosing. In Figure 5–33, you can see I've used the Pencil tool to define a slightly "wiggly" rectangle.

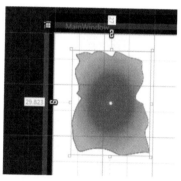

Figure 5–33. A second geometry, created via the Pencil tool

Select this new item, and activate the Make Into Control menu option once again. This time, however, define an application-level style named `wigglyListBoxStyle` that targets the `ListBox` control (see Figure 5–34).

Figure 5–34. *Targeting the ListBox control*

This template uses the `<ItemsPresenter>` element, rather than `<ContentPresenter>`, given the fact that `ListBox` controls (typically) have a set of individual items that can be viewed via scrollbars. Here is a partial snapshot of the generated XAML:

```
<Style x:Key="wigglyListBoxStyle" TargetType="{x:Type ListBox}">
  <Setter Property="Template">
    <Setter.Value>
      <ControlTemplate TargetType="{x:Type ListBox}">
        ...
        <ScrollViewer>
          <ItemsPresenter/>
        </ScrollViewer>
        ...
      </ControlTemplate>
    </Setter.Value>
  </Setter>
</Style>
```

Before we add items to the newly defined `ListBox` control back on the artboard of the main window, let's update the `<ItemsPresenter>` element to ensure that each `ListItem` will be aligned to the center. To do so, ensure you have opened the designer for your new `wigglyListBoxStyle`, and then select `<ItemsPresenter>` within your Objects and Timeline panel (see Figure 5–35).

Figure 5–35. *Selecting the ItemsPresenter for editing*

Next, use your Properties panel to set the `HorizontalAlignment` and `VerticalAlignment` properties to `Center` (see Figure 5–36).

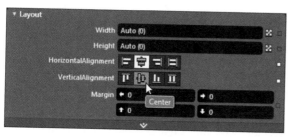

Figure 5–36. *Centering items in the ItemsPresenter*

At this point, save your changes, and then populate the `ListBox` control on the artboard of the initial `Window` with a few `ListBoxItem` objects. Recall from Chapter 4 that you can use the `Items` editor (by clicking the "..." button) in the Common Properties section of the Properties panel, or simply type in XAML such as the following (I've added a few additional settings to the `ListBox` itself to increase the font size of each `ListBoxItem`):

```
<ListBox HorizontalAlignment="Left" Height="162.101"
        Margin="29.823,27,0,0"
        Style="{DynamicResource wigglyListBoxStyle}"
        VerticalAlignment="Top" Width="125.177"
        FontSize="16" FontStyle="Italic">
  <ListBoxItem Content="Item One"/>
  <ListBoxItem Content="Item Two"/>
  <ListBoxItem Content="Item Three"/>
</ListBox>
```

Now, run your application. Sure enough, you have just defined a unique template for the `ListBox` control! In Figure 5–37, notice that you can select each individual `ListBoxItem` as expected.

Figure 5–37. Our custom templates in action

You can (and should) take some time to experiment with other graphic-to-control transformations. Using the techniques demonstrated here, you can quickly generate custom templates for any number of controls. Furthermore, you can edit and enhance the extracted template (and the containing style) in numerous ways to define some very unique UI elements.

I'll allow you to tinker with your templates (and create new, additional templates) as you see fit. Once you are done, move on to the next section to learn how to add some interactivity to a control template via WPF triggers.

Adding Interactivity via WPF Property Triggers

Currently, our templates are static images that do not change appearance when the user interacts with them (e.g., places the mouse cursor within the geometry, clicks the template, and so on). Earlier in this chapter, you manually added a handful of WPF triggers to a template to account for such interactivity. Now let's see how Blend can simplify the process. Using the Resources tab, open your starButtonStyle for editing, as shown in Figure 5–38.

Figure 5–38. Selecting a style for editing

Next, use the breadcrumbs editor on the upper left of the style editor to select the current internal control template (see Figure 5–39).

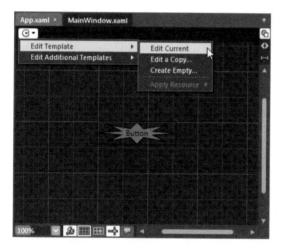

Figure 5–39. Using the breadcrumbs editor to select the internal style template

With the template selected, you can now activate the Triggers panel of the Blend IDE (remember, if you can't find a given panel, you can use the Window menu of the IDE to show or hide the given panel). As you can see in Figure 5–40, the starButtonStyle has empty triggers for five WPF properties, specifically IsFocused, IsDefaulted, IsMouseOver, IsPressed, and IsEnabled.

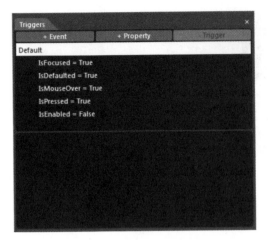

Figure 5–40. Empty template triggers, begging for interactivity

Your goal is to use the Triggers panel to define how your template should look when each property is `True` (recall, these properties are set internally by the control when the corresponding event fires). Select the `IsMouseOver` property. As soon as you do so, you will notice that your template artboard is in recording mode, just as if you were using the animation editor (see Chapter 3).

Now, use the Properties panel to make a few changes to your template that will occur when the mouse cursor is over the control. By way of a suggestion, select the geometry object within the Objects and Timeline panel and change the `Fill` property to a different color. Once you are done, you can exit recording mode by clicking the red stop button located on the upper left of the artboard or via the red stop button by the trigger you are modifying in the Triggers panel. In any case, when you are done, your Triggers panel will look something like Figure 5–41.

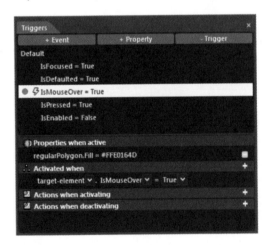

Figure 5–41. Changing the Fill color of the geometry when IsMouseOver is True

If you examine the generated XAML, you will find the template's triggers collection is updated as so:

```xml
<ControlTemplate.Triggers>
  <Trigger Property="IsFocused" Value="True"/>
  <Trigger Property="IsDefaulted" Value="True"/>
  <Trigger Property="IsMouseOver" Value="True">
    <Setter Property="Fill" TargetName="regularPolygon"
            Value="#FFFDFF11"/>
  </Trigger>
  <Trigger Property="IsPressed" Value="True"/>
  <Trigger Property="IsEnabled" Value="False"/>
</ControlTemplate.Triggers>
```

Now, use this same general technique to change some aspect of the defining geometry when the IsPressed property is True. I've updated my template in such a way that when IsPressed is True, the size of the control will be reduced by a small amount (I used the Scale tab of the Transform section of the Properties panel to do so). Here is the resulting XAML:

```xml
<ControlTemplate.Triggers>
...
  <Trigger Property="IsPressed" Value="True">
    <Setter Property="RenderTransform" TargetName="regularPolygon">
      <Setter.Value>
        <TransformGroup>
          <ScaleTransform ScaleX="0.9" ScaleY="0.9"/>
          <SkewTransform/>
          <RotateTransform/>
          <TranslateTransform/>
        </TransformGroup>
      </Setter.Value>
    </Setter>
  </Trigger>
  <Trigger Property="IsEnabled" Value="False"/>
</ControlTemplate.Triggers>
```

You could use the Triggers panel to add some additional state changes to the remaining properties (IsDefaulted, IsEnabled, and IsFocused), but I think you get the general idea. At this point, run your program, move your mouse cursor over your star button, and click the control. You should see that your state changes take effect!

WPF Triggers: Further Resources

Over the course of this chapter, you have been given a taste of how to use the integrated Triggers panel of Expression Blend to incorporate visual cues into a custom template. To be sure, many of your custom WPF control templates will make liberal use of this editor. However, it is time to switch gears and introduce the role of the Visual State Manager, which is positioned to be the preferred way to account for visual cues via markup (and is your only choice under the Silverlight API), so if you are interested in learning more about WPF triggers or simply wish to work through some additional template tutorials, look up the topic "Styling a control that supports templates" in the Expression Blend User Guide (see Figure 5–42). There you will find more details on the WPF trigger framework.

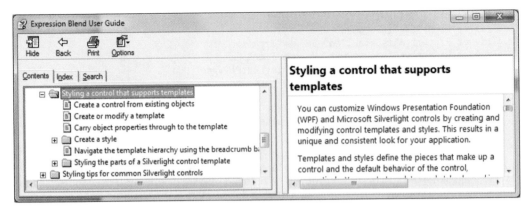

Figure 5–42. *The Expression Blend User Guide provides numerous tutorials regarding WPF triggers.*

■ **Source Code** The **StyleTemplateFromGraphic** project can be found under the Chapter 5 subdirectory.

Building Templates Using the Silverlight API

As mentioned a few times already in this chapter, the Silverlight API has very limited support for traditional WPF-style triggers, but it can achieve the same end result using the Visual State Manager (VSM). As well, recall that as of .NET 4.0 the WPF API has incorporated its own version of the Silverlight VSM, and therefore both APIs now support a unified manner to add visual cues to custom templates and styles. Given this, for the next example, let's create a custom template using the Silverlight API (but keep in mind that WPF projects can use the same techniques shown next).

We will basically re-create the "round button template" example shown earlier, but this time we will use the VSM rather than WPF triggers. To start, create a new Silverlight application project named **SLControlTemplate**. Next, draw a custom shape on your artboard using the Pen or Pencil tool or add a shape from the Shapes category of the Assets library (again, I'll be using a simple Ellipse component, specifically an Ellipse with a green background). Right-click this geometry and, once again, select the Make Into Control menu option (see Figure 5–43).

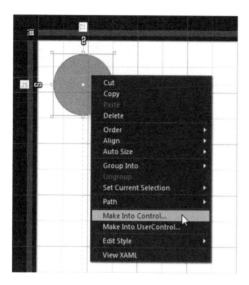

Figure 5–43. Silverlight projects also support the Make Into Control option.

In the resulting dialog box, define a new application-level resource named
SilverlightRoundButtonTemplate that targets the Button control. Once you click OK, you will
once again find a designer for a new stylized template for a round button, which you can
modify using the Properties panel, breadcrumbs editor, and the Objects and Timeline panel
(just like the other examples in this chapter; see Figure 5–44 for a reminder).

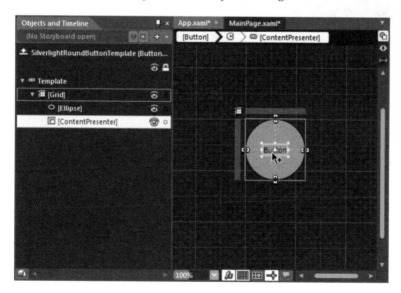

Figure 5–44. The new Silverlight template, ready for editing

However, if you take a look at the generated XAML, you will not see any set of default triggers. When you want to add visual cues to a Silverlight template, you need to do so using the States panel.

Working with the VSM via the States Panel

Like the WPF Triggers panel, the States panel can be used to add visual state changes to a given template, but, for better or worse, it requires you to use a completely different approach. Assuming the artboard for your Silverlight template is the active Blend window, open the States panel and notice the default settings, shown in Figure 5–45.

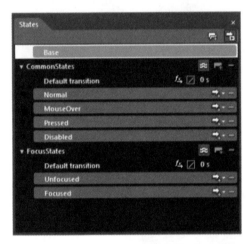

Figure 5–45. *The States panel of Expression Blend*

By default, an empty template is devoid of any visual states. However, once you open the States panel, Blend suggests a handful of common "visual states" (Normal, MouseOver, Pressed, Disabled, Unfocused, and Focused) arranged into two "visual state groups," named CommonStates and FocusStates.[9] As you will see later, it is possible to add additional groups with custom states as well.

Consider these default states and groups "freebees," in that the WPF and Silverlight controls automatically know how to transition into these states when the underlying action occurs. In other words, if the user literally clicks the control, it will transition into the Pressed state with no effort on your part. When the control is not focused, and has no mouse activity, it will automatically transition to the Normal state, and so on.

Let's add some animation markup that will occur when the control transitions to the MouseOver state. To begin, select the MouseOver state within the States panel. You'll notice that you are automatically placed into recording mode. Thus, just like when you are building an animation (see Chapter 3), you are free to make any sort of property changes using the Properties panel, and the IDE will capture your changes. For the MouseOver state, simply change the Fill value of the Ellipse to a darker shade (see Figure 5–46).

---

[9] WPF and Silverlight controls have been written to support a number of common states arranged in common groups. This is a good thing, as you can rest assured that a majority of controls support identically named states you can edit.

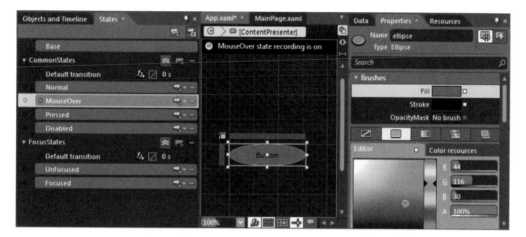

Figure 5–46. Recording changes that will happen when the mouse cursor is over the ellipse

Now, select the `Pressed` state within the States editor. Apply a graphical transformation to the `Ellipse` so that the size of the control shrinks by some amount. Use the Transform section of the Properties panel to do so (recall, the Scale tab allows you to apply scaling transformations; see Figure 5–47).

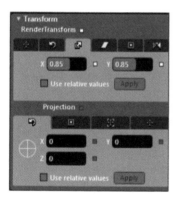

Figure 5–47. Applying a transformation to the ellipse when it has been pressed

Once you are done, exit recording mode by clicking the red animation button on the upper left of your artboard (see Chapter 3 for details of working with the animation editor). Now, run your application and test your changes. You should see that the control transitions to new visual states when you interact with the `Button` using the mouse! However, what exactly took place? We'll look at that next.

Viewing the Generated XAML

If you open your `App.xaml` file for viewing within the XAML editor, you will see that your `<Style>` has been updated with a number of new instructions that establish the various visual state changes you have made. Notice in the following markup that the entirety of the VSM logic is wrapped within a `<VisualStateManager.VisualStateGroups>` scope. Within this scope, we find that each of the default groups and states is present and accounted for, many of which are empty. If a given state has no rendering instructions, the control renders its appearance using the current settings of the control.

```xml
<VisualStateManager.VisualStateGroups>
  <VisualStateGroup x:Name="CommonStates">
    <VisualState x:Name="Normal"/>
    <VisualState x:Name="MouseOver">
      <Storyboard>
        <ColorAnimation Duration="0" To="#FF2C741E"
          Storyboard.TargetProperty="(Shape.Fill).(SolidColorBrush.Color)"
          Storyboard.TargetName="ellipse" d:IsOptimized="True"/>
      </Storyboard>
    </VisualState>
    <VisualState x:Name="Pressed">
      <Storyboard>
        <DoubleAnimation Duration="0" To="0.85"
          Storyboard.TargetProperty=
          "(UIElement.RenderTransform).(CompositeTransform.ScaleX)"
          Storyboard.TargetName="ellipse" d:IsOptimized="True"/>
        <DoubleAnimation Duration="0" To="0.85"
          Storyboard.TargetProperty=
          "(UIElement.RenderTransform).(CompositeTransform.ScaleY)"
          Storyboard.TargetName="ellipse" d:IsOptimized="True"/>
      </Storyboard>
    </VisualState>
    <VisualState x:Name="Disabled"/>
  </VisualStateGroup>
</VisualStateManager.VisualStateGroups>
```

Establishing State Group Transition Timing

By default, when a state is encountered, the associated `<Storyboard>` executes immediately. If you like, you can define a new transition time value for *all* states in a given group by changing the default transition time value. Again, by default, the default transition time value is zero seconds. In Figure 5–48, you can see I've changed the default transition time for states in the CommonStates group to two seconds.

Figure 5–48. *Changing the default transition time for a state group*

If you run and test your program once again, you'll see the that state transitions happen at a much slower rate (as you might agree, too slow!). Feel free to change this value as you see fit.

Defining Transition Effects

In the States panel, notice that each state group has a small button with the letters *fx* and a small arrow beneath *fx*. This option allows you to define a graphical effect that will be applied when a given transition occurs. Click this button for the `CommonStates` default transition and notice the options for the `CommonStates` group. As you can see in Figure 5–49, I've added a Smooth Swirl Grid effect.

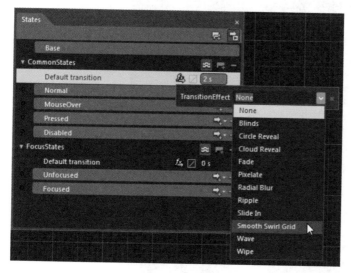

Figure 5–49. Adding a transition effect

■ **Note** If your transition time is set to 0, you will not see the transition effect animate. You must have a transition time of at least 1 to see the result of any transition effect.

Also be aware that once you select a given transition effect, you can edit its individual settings by clicking the *fx* button once again (see Figure 5–50).

Figure 5–50. Editing a transition effect

It is also worth pointing out that a given group can be configured to use the same animation easing effects examined in Chapter 3. Simply use the choices exposed by clicking the easing function icon (a box with a line through it) next to the *fx* button, as shown in Figure 5–51.

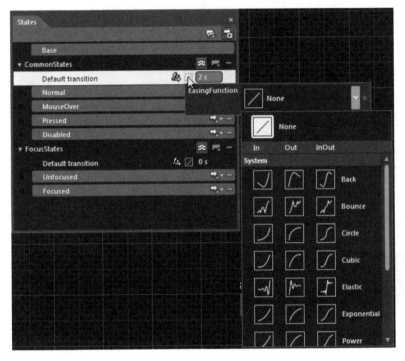

Figure 5–51. *Adding animation easing effects*

I certainly encourage you to take a few minutes to play around with how your states transition based on various settings, as the printed page really can't do this justice.[10]

Configuring Individual Transitions

When you are changing transition times and effects for a given group of states, the assumption is that these settings will be applied to *all* states within the group. Thus, if you set up a bounce effect for a group, this "bounce" will occur regardless of which state you are currently in and which state you are about to transition to. In many cases, this is just what you require. However, the States panel provides you some ways to get much more granular.

Select the Focused state from the FocusedStates group for editing. Notice that this state (or any state for that matter) has an icon that looks like an arrow pointing to the right (with a little + sign next to it). If you click this option, which is formally called the Add Transition button, a set of state transition editors appears. In Figure 5–52, you can see that (if you choose) you can control unique transition effects when you move from the current state to the Focused state, the

---

[10] I must say, I've spent more time than I would like to admit tinkering with these settings.

Focused state to an Unfocused state, and the Focused state back to any other state (don't bother to set any transitions just yet).

■ **Note** The star-shaped icon in the Add Transition editor symbolizes "any state."

Figure 5–52. *The Add Transition option allows you to define unique storyboards for specific state transitions.*

As soon as you specify a unique state-to-state transition, a separate editor appears for that *specific* transition, offering the same basic options as you find when configuring a state group. As you can see in Figure 5–53, a unique transition from the MouseOver state to the Normal state has been specified. Here, I've added an Elastic Out effect that will happen when the mouse cursor is over my control and then leaves.

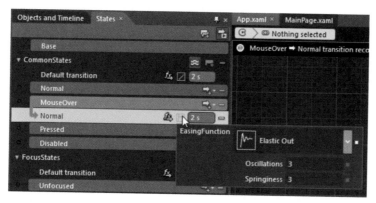

Figure 5–53. *A bounce effect added to a unique transition*

A Brief Word Regarding Custom States

In addition to the default "freebee" states we have been examining, it is certainly possible to define a unique set of control-specific states. You might wish to do so when you want your templates to behave in various ways based on custom events you have written, or based on arbitrary input events *not* captured by the default groups.

For example, assume that you want your template to appear a specific way when the user Shift+clicks the control. You could achieve this by using some "custom" state groups. To illustrate how we can work with the VSM in this manner, we will move on to the final major topic of this chapter, that of creating custom UserControls.

■ **Source Code** The **SLControlTemplate** project can be found under the Chapter 5 subdirectory.

Generating UserControls Using Blend

To wrap up this chapter, I'll explain how the Blend IDE can simplify the construction of full-blown UserControl classes. As you may know, WPF and Silverlight both support the concept of a *user control*, which is a class that encapsulates a collection of related UI elements. In contrast to a control template, which is applied to a given control to make it look and behave a certain way, a custom UserControl is a brand new UI element that you create by aggregating existing controls.

If this were a book focused on building feature-rich custom WPF or Silverlight controls, I'd be launching into a discussion of some fairly dense topics, such as dependency properties and the routed event architecture. However, given that this book is focused squarely on the use of the Blend IDE, I will *not* go down that road here. Rather, I'll show you how the Blend IDE can facilitate the creation of a new UserControl class that supports some unique visual states.

Much like the Make Into Control menu option, Blend supplies a Make Into UserControl menu option, which you can select once you have selected an item on the artboard. Again, in many cases, a custom UserControl begins life from a custom graphic. So, for the final example of this chapter, begin by creating a new WPF (or Silverlight, if you wish) application project named **BlendUserControl**.

■ **Note** I am selecting WPF at this point to give you an example of working with the VSM from within that context.

Draw a graphic on your artboard, and then right-click the item to activate the Make Into UserControl menu option (see Figure 5–54).

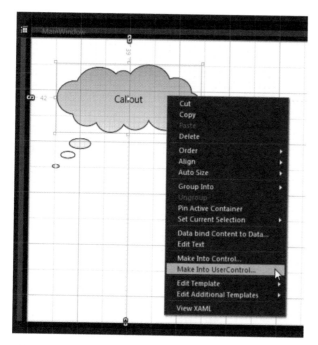

Figure 5–54. *Creating a new UserControl*

Using the resulting dialog box, give your control a fitting name (I called mine
`BubbleThoughtsControl`; see Figure 5–55).

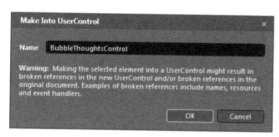

Figure 5–55. *Naming your new UserControl*

Click the OK button, and locate your Projects panel. You can see that the Blend IDE
automatically added a new XAML file, and a related code file, for the new `UserControl` (see
Figure 5–56).

Figure 5–56. The new XAML and code files for your UserControl

---

■ **Note** Here, we generated a new UserControl based on a single graphic. However, many UserControls are based on a collection of existing objects. If you select multiple UI elements on your artboard and select the Make Into UserControl menu option, the IDE will group all selected items into a new layout manager and place them in a UserControl class.

If you examine the markup of the original main Window, you will see that your graphic has been replaced with an instance of the new UserControl:[11]

```xml
<Window
  xmlns="http://schemas.microsoft.com/winfx/2006/xaml/presentation"
  xmlns:x="http://schemas.microsoft.com/winfx/2006/xaml"
  xmlns:local="clr-namespace:BlendUserControl"
  x:Class="BlendUserControl.MainWindow"
  x:Name="Window"
  Title="MainWindow"
  Width="640" Height="480">

  <Grid x:Name="LayoutRoot">
    <local:BubbleThoughtsControl HorizontalAlignment="Left" Height="107"
          Margin="42,39,0,0" VerticalAlignment="Top" Width="233"/>
  </Grid>
</Window>
```

■ **Note** If you notice a slightly transparent yellow warning sign over the window's copy of the UserControl, don't worry. This is just Blend's way of letting you know you should rebuild your project.

---

[11] If you have previously created UserControls by hand, also note that Blend was kind enough to pick a custom xmlns that maps to your new class!

Adding Visual States

Given the fact that this is a brand new control, we do not have any "freebee" visual states that are granted to us by default. Therefore, if you want to use the VSM, you need to define custom groups, define custom states, and then determine when the transitions will occur.

■ **Note** Of course, if you wanted to, you could use the WPF trigger framework if you are building a WPF UserControl; however, here I'll focus on the VSM.

Ensure that the artboard for your new UserControl is active in the IDE (i.e., open BubbleThoughtsControl.xaml, or whatever you named your control, in the designer) and open the States panel, which should currently be empty. Click the "Add state group" button (see Figure 5–57).

Figure 5–57. *Adding a new state group to your custom UserControl*

Once you have done so, name the group MyMouseStates by selecting the default name and typing in your unique name. Notice that, just like the CommonStates and FocusedStates groups described earlier, your custom state group can be assigned default transition times and effects. Click the Add state button (see Figure 5–58).

Figure 5–58. *Adding a state to your group*

Name this new state MouseOverState. You will notice that you are automatically placed into recording mode for this state, so go ahead and make some sort of changes to the UI using the Properties panel (and don't forget to leverage the Objects and Timeline panel if you need to quickly select aspects of the control). To keep it simple, I'd again suggest simply changing the color of the UI in some way.

Add a second (and final) state to your MyMouseStates group named MouseDownState. Once you have done so, make some sort of custom changes to the UI via the Properties panel (apply a transformation, for example). Figure 5–59 shows my final set of states, where I changed the default transition time to one second for my custom group.

Figure 5–59. *The final group of custom states*

Transitioning States in Code

If you were to run your project now, you might be surprised to find that none of your states seem to activate, regardless of how you interact with the control with your mouse. Again, this is because you have not yet told the control *when* to transition! To do so, you can take either of two approaches, the first of which is to programmatically force a state transition using the static GoToState() method of the VisualStateManager class (the other will be examined in the next section).

Ensure that the editor for your UserControl is open in the Blend IDE, and click the Events button of the Properties panel (the lightening bolt button). Handle the MouseDown event as normal, and then add the following code to the generated event handler:

```
private void callout_MouseDown(object sender,
    System.Windows.Input.MouseButtonEventArgs e)
{
    // Move to a new state!
    VisualStateManager.GoToState(this, "MouseDownState", true);
}
```

The first argument of the GoToState() method represents which control has the state groups, and typically is the UserControl itself. The second argument is the name of the state to transition to, while the final Boolean value is used to specify whether you wish to use any defined state transition timing values. Now, run your program, click the control, and you should see your first transition take place!

Transitioning States in XAML

It is possible to transition states without adding any procedural code, by using the GoToStateAction behavior. This can be very useful when you are building custom templates that you want to apply across numerous projects, and don't want the baggage of a full-blown UserControl. Use the Assets library to locate this behavior (see Figure 5–60).

Figure 5–60. The GoToStateAction allows you to transition states using markup.

Drag the behavior directly onto the UserControl (you may drop it either on the artboard or on the tree of markup shown by the Objects and Timeline panel). Once you are done, you will see the set of objects shown in Figure 5–61.

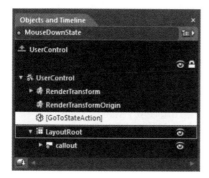

Figure 5–61. The GoToStateAction behavior, ready for configuration

Select this element, and use the Properties panel (make sure you are not still in the Events area) to configure the behavior. The Trigger section allows you to pick which event will be monitored, which for this example we will assume is the MouseEnter event. The Common Properties section allows you to pick the custom state to transition to (MouseOverState in this example). Figure 5–62 shows the final configuration of this GoToStateAction behavior object.

Figure 5–62. The GoToStateAction behavior configured for transition

Now run your project once again, and verify that your second state transitions when the mouse cursor is over the control.

VSM: Further Resources

Your examination of styles and templates ala Blend is complete. To be sure, there are other aspects of these topics that you will want to explore, but you should feel (much) more comfortable with the core operations at this point. If you are interested in learning more about the Visual State Manager, be sure you look up the topic "Define different visual states and transition times for a user control" within the Blend User Guide (see Figure 5–63).

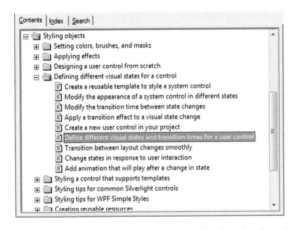

Figure 5–63. The Blend documentation has further details of the VSM and UserControl creation.

■ **Source Code** The **BlendUserControl** project can be found under the Chapter 5 subdirectory.

Summary

This chapter covered a number of topics, all of which focused on the process of customizing the look and behavior of a WPF or Silverlight control. You began by examining the role of styles. As you learned, styles allow you to ensure that a family of related controls (specified via the TargetType attribute) has the same set of property settings. You also learned about a number of tools supplied by the Blend IDE that can simplify the creation (and application) of your styles.

Next, you learned about the role of control templates. Recall that a *template* provides a way for you to completely restyle how a control renders its visual display. At this time, you learned how to use Blend to extract a copy of a control's default template. Even more interesting, this part of the chapter also showed you how the IDE provides a very simple way to generate a template from an existing graphic.

When you create templates, you are also very likely to add back "visual cues" to give the end user some level of interactivity. As shown in this chapter, WPF projects can add such interactivity using the original trigger framework, whereas Silverlight projects use an alternative mechanism termed the Visual State Manager (VSM). As of .NET 4.0, WPF has a VSM implementation as well.

We wrapped things up by examining the role of custom UserControl classes, which provide a way to build new controls by aggregating existing controls. Here, you learned how you can extract a new UserControl from an existing set of UI elements, and then define custom states (and transitions) using the VSM.

CHAPTER 6

■ ■ ■

Blend Data Binding Techniques

The Blend IDE has a number of tools that allow you to connect data values (from a variety of sources) to user interface components. Formally speaking, this process is termed *data binding* and is supported in both the WPF and Silverlight[1] APIs (although each API has slightly differing levels of data binding support). In this chapter, you will examine a number of Expression Blend data binding techniques, and some related coding techniques as well.

You'll begin by examining the concept of *control-to-control* data binding operations. As the name suggests, this approach to data binding allows you to connect the value of a *source* control property to the value of a *destination* control property in your application. During this discussion, you will also learn the distinction between one-way and two-way data binding operations and learn how to convert data values as they pass between the source and destination by authoring custom *conversion classes*.

Next up, you will learn how to bind values from non-UI objects (such as business objects in your program, or XML documents) to properties of GUI objects. Here, you will learn about the Blend Data panel and see a number of ways in which you can visually connect the values of class properties to UI elements.

This chapter will also examine the role of *data templates*. Similar to a control template (see Chapter 5), a data template allows you to define a custom set of rendering instructions to be used during a data binding operation, complete with nested layout mangers, graphical objects, and animations.

To wrap things up, you'll examine how to create new custom stores of data using Blend, and learn the role of Blend sample data, which you can insert into a WPF or Silverlight application. Not only can sample data help you further investigate various Blend data binding techniques using a well-defined set of starter data (and code), but it can also serve as useful placeholder data during the prototyping process.[2]

■ **Note** Although Blend offers a rich data binding framework, a number of scenarios require authoring a fair amount of procedural code, which is beyond the mission of this text. However, I'll point you to some useful resources at the conclusion of this chapter if you wish to explore the topic of code-centric data binding in greater detail.

---

[1] And as you will see in Chapter 7, the Windows Phone 7 programming model also supports data binding.

[2] See Chapter 8.

The Role of Data Binding

GUI controls are often the target of various data binding operations. Simply put, *data binding* is the act of connecting a control's properties to other data values. By doing so, you can simplify your coding efforts, as the UI will automatically display the current state of the properties that they are connected to. Consider the following examples:

- You could bind the value of a Boolean class property to a CheckBox.

- You could fill a DataGrid object with data contained in a custom collection.

- You could populate a ListBox with values from an XML document.

When employing data binding, you must be aware of the distinction between the *source* and the *destination* (also termed the *target*) of the binding operation. As you might expect, the source of a data binding operation refers to where the data is coming from (an object property, an XML node, etc.), while the destination (or target) refers to a property of a UI element (a CheckBox, TextBox, and so on) that will receive and use the source data. To clarify this important distinction, the previous bulleted list could be refined as so:

- A Boolean source value could be bound to the IsChecked destination property of a CheckBox control.

- A destination DataGrid object could be filled with data from a custom collection source.

- A destination ListBox object could be filled with data from a source XML document based on an XPath statement.

Truth be told, using the data binding infrastructure is always optional. If a developer were to create his or her own data binding logic, the connection between two object properties would typically involve handling various events and authoring procedural code to connect the source and destination. For example, if you had a ScrollBar on a Window that needed to display its value on a Label, you might handle the ScrollBar's ValueChanged event and update the Label's Content property accordingly.

In many cases, WPF and Silverlight data binding allows you to establish these connections entirely through XAML. While this is true to a large extent, there are certainly times when you will need to author some additional procedural code as well (as you will see).

Control-to-Control Data Binding

To begin examining how Blend can be used to establish data binding operations, our first example will illustrate how you can bind the value of one control property to the value of a second control property (i.e., control-to-control data binding). This technique can be very useful when you want to ensure that a control refreshes its value based on a user selection.

Building the Example UI

Fire up Expression Blend and create a new WPF application project[3] named **ControlToControlBinding**. For this example, let's assume that your Window maintains two

---

[3] The techniques shown in this example would be more or less identical for a Silverlight application project, so select a Silverlight application project if it tickles your fancy.

StackPanel objects (both of which have the Orientation property set to Horizontal), each of which contains a Slider control and a Label control. These StackPanel objects are grouped in a larger StackPanel control, giving you a "stack of stack panels." Use the Assets panel and artboard to create the UI shown in Figure 6–1 (note the Content property value of each Label; you will configure the Slider objects in just a moment).

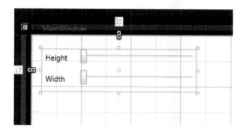

Figure 6–1. *The initial user interface*

■ **Note** Friendly reminder! Recall from Chapter 4 that you can right-click a set of controls selected on the artboard and group them into a new layout manager by using the Group Into menu option. As well, don't forget that you can perform basic Copy/Paste operations on the artboard (or the Objects and Timeline panel).

Behind the scenes, the Blend IDE generates XAML that looks something like the following (your exact markup may differ based on additional settings you made on the objects):

```
<StackPanel HorizontalAlignment="Left" Margin="28,40,0,0"
            Orientation="Vertical"
            VerticalAlignment="Top" Width="248">
  <StackPanel Height="33" Orientation="Horizontal"
              d:LayoutOverrides="Width">
    <Label Content="Height" Width="61"/>
    <Slider Width="187"/>
  </StackPanel>
  <StackPanel Height="33" Orientation="Horizontal"
              d:LayoutOverrides="Width">
    <Label Content="Width" Width="61"/>
    <Slider Width="187"/>
  </StackPanel>
</StackPanel>
```

Select each Slider control on the artboard (via a Ctrl+click operation), and then use the Properties panel to set the Maximum property to the value 200 and the Minimum property to the value 10 (you can find these properties in the Common Properties section of the Properties panel; and don't forget the Search feature). You should now find that each Slider control has been defined using markup such as so:

```
<Slider Width="187" Maximum="200" Minimum="10"/>
```

These Slider controls will be used to change the size of a different UI element on your artboard via a data binding operation. To complete the initial user interface, draw a graphic of your choosing on your artboard, such that it is part of the LayoutRoot Grid object. I chose to use the triangle geometry found within the Shapes category of the Assets library, as shown in Figure 6–2.

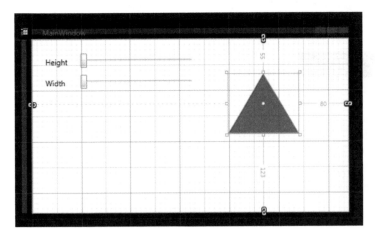

Figure 6–2. *The final user interface*

Creating New Data Bindings

When you want to use Blend to bind values from one control property to another control property, your first step is to select the control that will be the target (a.k.a. the destination) of the data binding operation (the triangle in this example). Select this UI element on your artboard now, and then locate the Height property in the Layout section of the Properties panel. Once you have done so, click the Advanced options button (the small square icon) to the right of the Height property text area (see Figure 6–3).

Figure 6–3. *Activating the advanced options of the Height property*

From the menu that opens, shown in Figure 6–4, select the Data Binding menu option.[4]

---

[4] You can also configure data binding operations using the Element Property Binding menu option, as shown later in this chapter.

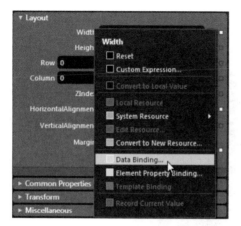

Figure 6–4. *Activating the Data Binding menu option*

You will be presented with the Create Data Binding dialog box, shown in Figure 6–5. As you can see, this dialog box has the following three tabs on the top, which allow you to configure three different types of data sources. In a nutshell, your options break down as follows:

- *Data Field*: This tab can be used to select a .NET object or XML document data[5] as the source of data.

- *Element Property*: This tab allows you to select a UI object property as the source of data.

- *Data Context*: This tab allows you to select from a *data context* already defined in your application as the source of data. As clarified later in this chapter, a data context allows a parent container (such as a layout manager) to define a data source that all child elements can use free of charge.

You will examine each of these data binding concepts as you progress through the chapter, but for the time being, select the middle, Element Property tab. As just mentioned, this tab is where you can "connect" a source object's property value to the destination you selected on the artboard. Using the tree view on the *left*, locate and select the first Slider object, as shown in Figure 6–5. Then, using the tree view on the *right*, select the Value property.

---

[5] As examined in more detail later in this chapter, the Silverlight API has little support for XML data binding operations. Therefore, the +XML button on the Data Field tab is disabled for Silverlight projects.

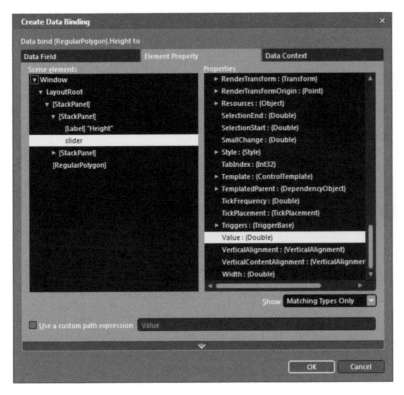

Figure 6–5. Connecting the Height property of the triangle to the Value property of the Slider

---

■ **Note** For this example, I did not bother to give fitting names to my UI elements, in which case Blend provides default names such as `slider`, `slider1`, and so forth.

Click the OK button, and repeat the process just explained to bind the `Width` property of your shape to the `Value` property of the second `Slider` control. Then, if you run your application, you should find that you can change the size of the shape by moving the sliders! Not bad for a few mouse clicks. You might want to change the `Minimum` and `Maximum` values of each `Slider` object and observe the new behavior.

Back in Expression Blend, if you select the shape geometry and examine the Properties panel, you will see that the `Height` and `Width` properties are each surrounded by a yellow bounding box, as shown in Figure 6–6. This is Blend's visual cue that these properties are being set by a data binding operation.

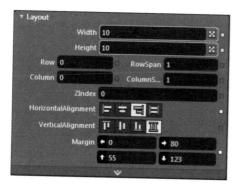

Figure 6–6. The bound properties appear in yellow bounding boxes.

Viewing the Generated Markup

If you open the XAML editor, you can see what the Create Data Binding wizard has done on your behalf, as shown next. Notice how your destination object (the geometrical shape) makes use of an XAML markup extension named {Binding}. The markup extension has two key components. First, we find the name of the source property (the Value property of the Slider objects). Second, we have the ElementName attribute, which specifies the name of the source object (the two Slider objects).

```
<ed:RegularPolygon Fill="#FFADOBAF" HorizontalAlignment="Right"
    InnerRadius="1" Margin="0,55,80,123" PointCount="3"
    Stretch="Fill" Stroke="Black"
    Width="{Binding Value, ElementName=slider1}"
    Height="{Binding Value, ElementName=slider}"/>
```

Essentially, this markup states "the Width property will be assigned to the Value property of the slider1 object, while the Height property will be assigned to the Value property of the slider object."

Converting Data Types

The current example works just fine, as the underlying data type of the Slider's Value property is compatible with the underlying data type of the Height and Width properties (all properties operate on a numeric value, specifically a double data type).

However, what if you want to connect properties that are in some way incompatible, and want to transform the values? For example, what if you want to change the color of your geometric shape based on the position of a third Slider control? When you think about this for a moment, the problem becomes clear: the Value property of the Slider is a numeric (double) value, but the Fill property of the geometry requires a brush object! When you want to convert a value to a new data type, you can do so by authoring a custom class to handle the conversion, and then register this class in the markup.

Add a new Slider control and a new Label control to your artboard (where you place these new items is up to you). Set the Content property of the Label to the value Shade and configure the Slider object so that it has a maximum value of 255 and a minimum value of 0. As well, make sure the SmallChange property of the Slider has been set to the value of 1. Once you are done, the new controls should look something like so (note I've once again arranged my controls in a new horizontal StackPanel):

```
<StackPanel Height="33" Orientation="Horizontal"
            d:LayoutOverrides="Width">
  <Label Content="Shade" Width="61"/>
  <Slider x:Name="slider2" Width="187"
          Maximum="255" SmallChange="1"/>
</StackPanel>
```

Creating a Custom Data Conversion Class

Before we configure the new binding, we need to author a custom class that will be consulted during the data binding operation. Insert a new C# class into your project using the Project ➤ Add New Item menu option of the Blend IDE. In the resulting New Item dialog box, add a new class named DoubleToSolidBrushConverter.cs (see Figure 6–7).

■ **Note** This part of the example assumes you are comfortable with C# programming. If this is not the case, you may wish to examine the provided solution code for this project as you read this section.

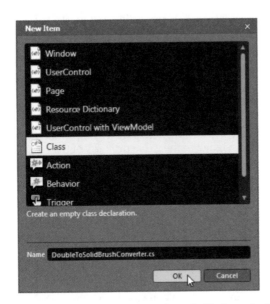

Figure 6–7. Inserting a new C# code file into the Blend project

A "converter class" must implement a specific .NET interface named IValueConverter. This interface defines two methods, Convert() and ConvertBack(). The Convert() method is called during one-way data binding operations, while ConvertBack() is called for two-way data binding operations (more information on data binding modes is presented in just a bit). While both methods must be accounted for in your class, you can return null from either method if a given data conversion is unnecessary. For this example, we are only concerned with a one-way data binding operation, so update your class as so:

```
public class DoubleToSolidBrushConverter : IValueConverter
{
  public object Convert(object value, Type targetType, object parameter,
                        System.Globalization.CultureInfo culture)
  {
    double currValue = (double)value;
    byte valueAsByte = (byte)currValue;

    Color color = new Color();
    color.A = 255;
    color.G = valueAsByte;
    return new SolidColorBrush(color);
  }

  public object ConvertBack(object value, Type targetType,
                            object parameter,
                            System.Globalization.CultureInfo culture)
  { return null; }
}
```

Recall, the goal of the Convert() method is to transform the incoming double value sent by the Slider into a custom brush object. As you can see, we are able to nab the incoming original source value (a double) via the object parameter. We then cast this value into a byte data type (which is expected by the new Color object), and use this new value to configure a SolidColorBrush object set to a given shade of green (based on setting the G [green] property of the SolidColorBrush object).

■ **Note** Before proceeding with this example project, rebuild the source code using Project ➤ Build Project. If you do not build your application, you will not be able to locate your custom class in the step to follow.

Selecting a Conversion Class in Blend

Now that we have this class in place, we can refer to it when establishing the data binding operation in XAML. Open MainWindow.xaml in the Blend designer and select the geometry object (the triangle) on the artboard once again, but this time, click the Advanced options button (the small square icon) for the Fill property (located in the Brushes section of the Properties panel). Once you have done so, activate the Data Binding menu option as you did earlier in this example when configuring the Height and Width properties, and select the Element Property tab as before.

Next, select the new Slider control from the tree of elements on the left of the Create Data Binding dialog box, and attempt to look for the Value property within the tree on the right. You might be surprised that it appears to be missing! This is because, by default, the Element Property tab of the Create Data Binding dialog box will show you only *compatible data types*. Use the Show drop-down list box on the bottom of the dialog box to pick the All Properties setting. At this point, pick the Value property (see Figure 6–8).

Figure 6–8. You need to select All Properties to view a seemingly incompatible property.

We can use this same dialog box to specify our custom conversion class. To do so, expand the advanced properties area at the bottom of the dialog box, and click the "Add new value converter" button (Figure 6–9 shows only the relevant [bottom] portion of the larger dialog box).

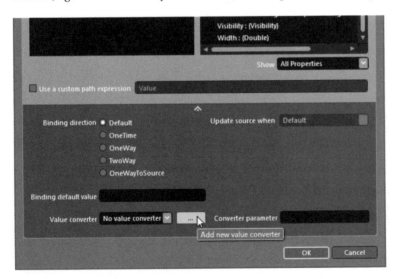

Figure 6–9. You can specify converter classes using the advanced properties area.

Once you click this button, you should find your custom `DoubleToSolidBrushConverter` class listed, as shown in Figure 6–10. (If you can't find your class in this dialog box, you most likely forgot to build your project; see the previous Note.)

Figure 6–10. *Selecting your custom conversion class*

Now, run your program! You should see that the color of your geometry changes when you move the thumb of your new slider (see Figure 6–11).

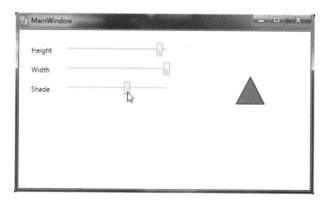

Figure 6–11. *Converting a double to a solid color brush*

Viewing the Generated Markup

If you examine the generated markup, you will see that your custom conversion class has been declared as a `Window`-level object resource:

```
<Window.Resources>
  <local:DoubleToSolidBrushConverter
      x:Key="DoubleToSolidBrushConverter"/>
</Window.Resources>
```

The `local:` prefix shown here was generated by Blend when you selected your conversion class. As you may know, when you want to describe a custom class in XAML, you must define an XML namespace that maps to the .NET namespace that defines the custom class. If you view the opening `<Window>` tag of this example, you'll see that `local:` maps to the root .NET namespace of this project:

```
<Window xmlns="http://schemas.microsoft.com/winfx/2006/xaml/presentation"
   ...
   xmlns:local="clr-namespace:ControlToControlBinding"
   ...
>
```

In any case, this resource is referenced by the `Converter` attribute of the `{Binding}` markup extension of the shape geometry (be aware that I broke the full markup extension across multiple lines for readability, which you should not do in your project):

```
<ed:RegularPolygon Fill="{Binding Value,
   Converter={StaticResource DoubleToSolidBrushConverter},
   ElementName=slider2}"
   ...
/>
```

So far, so good! Next, let's examine the role of data binding *modes*.

Understanding Data Binding Modalities

Data binding operations support a `Mode` attribute, which allows you to define how the source and destination are kept in sync during the life of the application. By way of example, you may wish to ensure that the destination is updated when the source changes, but not vice versa. Or, perhaps you do want to make sure that if the destination changes, the source is updated automatically. Specifically, the `Mode` attribute can be set to any of the values shown here:

- `OneWay`: When the source changes, the destination is updated.

- `TwoWay`: When the source changes, the destination is updated, *and* if the destination changes, the source is updated.

- `OneWayToSource`:[6] This is sort of a "reverse" `OneWay` setting. If the destination is changed, the source is updated, but not vice versa.

- `OneTime`: The destination is updated with the source value when the application starts, and then all binding logic is forgotten.

---

[6] The `OneWayToSource` mode value is not supported in Silverlight.

Let's examine some of the more common data binding modes.

Configuring Data Binding Options with Blend

To illustrate some common Mode options, add a few final controls to your current artboard; specifically, add a final Label control (with the Content property set to Change Number), a final Slider control (all the default settings are fine), and a final TextBox named myTextBox (again, the default settings are fine).

Now let's bind the Value property of the new Slider to the new TextBox's Text property; however, this time we will use an alternative approach to using the Data Binding menu option/Create Data Binding dialog box to do so. First, select the TextBox on your artboard, and locate the Text property in the Properties panel. Once you have done so, click the Advanced options button and then select the Element Property Binding option (see Figure 6–12).

***Figure 6–12.** The Element Property Binding option is an alternative way to define a data binding.*

Once you select this menu option, you'll notice that your mouse cursor has changed its display, looking somewhat like a bull's-eye symbol, as shown in Figure 6–13. This icon signifies that you can now click an artboard control that represents the *source* of the data binding operation. Go ahead and click the new Slider control.

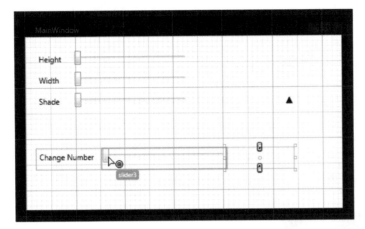

Figure 6–13. Selecting the Slider as the target for the Element Property Binding operation

Once you have done so, you can select the Value property using the drop-down list box in the resulting dialog box. As well, open the advanced settings area (via the downward arrow icon on the bottom of the dialog box), and notice you have a set of binding modes to pick from; select the OneWay option for the time being (see Figure 6–14).

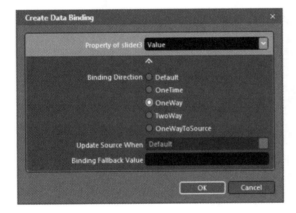

Figure 6–14. Setting a one-way binding mode

Configuring a Two-Way Data Bind

If you run your application, you will be able to verify that the text area updates when the Slider's thumb is repositioned. However, try typing into the text area a value that is within the range of the final Slider control (say, the value 100). You should *not see* the Slider's thumb change position, as a one-way data binding operation only updates the destination based on the source, not the other way around. If, however, we reconfigure the binding as a two-way data binding operation, you can indeed change the thumb's position when you enter new data into the text area.

When you want to tweak the settings for any of your data bindings, locate a currently configured property (the Text property in this example), click the Advanced options button, and select the Data Binding menu option as usual. From here, you can elect to set TwoWay binding mode, as well as define when the source property should be updated. Notice in Figure 6–15 that I opted to update the Slider when the TextBox loses focus.

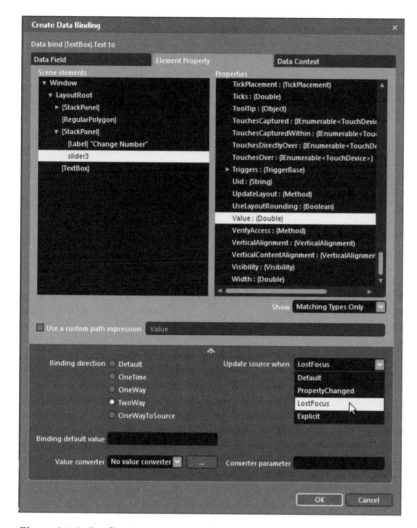

Figure 6–15. *Configuring a two-way binding mode*

Now, you should be able to verify that if you type a value into the text area, the slider changes position when the TextBox loses focus (such as when you tab off the control). If you check out the modified XAML, you'll find that the TextBox control's Text property has been configured as follows (note the Mode attribute in particular):

```
<TextBox ...
    Text="{Binding Value, ElementName=slider3, Mode=TwoWay,
           UpdateSourceTrigger=LostFocus}"/>
```

■ **Note** When you run this program, you'll notice that the text area displays the underlying floating-point number of the `Value` property. If you wanted to display only whole numbers, you would need to build (and register) a second data conversion class. See if you can create and register a new class to solve the problem (the solution for this project provides the required code and markup).

I won't go into the details of the `OneTime` and `OneWayToSource` options (as they are less commonly used), so check out the .NET Framework documentation for further details if you are interested. In any case, that wraps up our first data binding example. At this point, I hope you feel comfortable establishing bindings between related control properties. Next up, let's see how to connect properties from non-UI objects to control elements.

■ **Source Code** The **ControlToControlBinding** project can be found under the Chapter 6 subdirectory.

Binding to Properties of Non-UI Objects

The previous example illustrated a few ways to connect UI property values to other UI property values via control-to-control data binding. While this is certainly useful, there are many situations where you might wish to bind property values from *non-UI objects* to a graphical user interface.

For example, you might have a collection of business objects that needs to be shown in a `DataGrid` control. Maybe you are building an application that needs to display data within an XML document in a set of `ListBox` controls. To begin understanding how Blend can be used to connect to non-UI properties, our next example will illustrate how to build a collection of custom object property values for various UI elements.

Creating a Custom Collection of (Custom) Objects

Create a brand new WPF (or Silverlight) application project named **CollectionDataContext**. Insert a new class named `PurchaseOrder` using the Project ➤ Add New Item menu option. Update this class to support a handful of properties (of your choice) and a custom constructor to set these values. Here is one possible example:

```
public class PurchaseOrder
{
  public PurchaseOrder(){}
  public PurchaseOrder(int amt, double cost, string desc)
  {
    Amount = amt;
```

```
    TotalCost = cost;
    Description = desc;
  }

  public int Amount { get; set; }
  public double TotalCost{ get; set; }
  public string Description{ get; set; }
}
```

While you could use Blend to connect the values of these three properties to a UI object based on a single instance of the PurchaseOrder class, you will most likely want to bind a *collection* of these objects to UI elements.

Thus, define a second class named PurchaseOrders (note the plural name of this new class). You can add this class to the same C# code file if you wish, or add another new class to your project using Project ➤ Add New Item.

Update this class to extend the ObservableCollection[7] class, which can be very useful when working with data binding operations, given that this class will automatically "refresh" bindings when the contents change (e.g., items are added, removed, or changed). Finally, ensure that when your collection comes to life, a few objects will be added to the collection upon startup (I have paid homage to my personal four-legged friends who are upon me at this time):

```
public class PurchaseOrders :
  System.Collections.ObjectModel.ObservableCollection<PurchaseOrder>
{
  public PurchaseOrders()
  {
    // Add a few items upon startup.
    this.Add(new PurchaseOrder(5, 50.00, "Mikko's Cat Nip Treat"));
    this.Add(new PurchaseOrder(5, 50.00, "Saku's Best Dog Bone"));
    this.Add(new PurchaseOrder(1, 2.50, "Extra Bland Tofu"));
  }
}
```

Now that we have a custom collection of business objects, we can construct a user interface that will display the data of each member of the collection (remember, what we are really doing is mapping the properties of the individual PurchaseOrder objects in the collection to UI element properties). For example, we could bind each PurchaseOrder object property to a set of drop-down list boxes. We could map the entire collection onto a DataGrid. Whichever way you wish to go, the Blend IDE simplifies matters by enabling you to use the *Data panel.*

Defining an Object Data Source with the Data Panel

When you want to use Blend to bind to a custom non-UI object (such as our PurchaseOrders collection), your first step is to use the Data panel to establish a new *object data source.* Locate and open the Data panel (mounted on the right side of the IDE by default), click the "Create data source" button, and, from the drop-down list, pick Create Object Data Source, as shown in Figure 6–16.

---

[7] ObservableCollection is in the System.Collections.ObjectModel namespace.

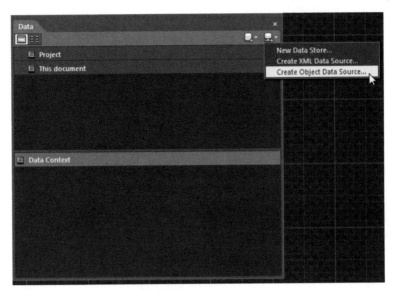

Figure 6–16. *The Data panel allows you to establish data sources for the current project.*

At this point, you are presented with a new dialog box, where you can select from a large variety of .NET object types, including any custom classes that are part of your current application.

■ **Note** If you do not see your custom class, you have forgotten to build your project!

In Figure 6–17, notice I have collapsed all nodes of the standard libraries for readability; the key here is that the correct assembly (named the same as your project) will show you your custom classes. This being said, pick the PurchaseOrders collection, and notice that the suggested name of your new data source (on the upper portion of the current dialog box) is PurchaseOrdersDataSource (which is fine, but feel free to rename it if you wish).

Figure 6–17. *Selecting our PurchaseOrders collection*

Once you click the OK button, examine the contents of your Data panel, shown in Figure 6–18, and you will see that your new object data source is displayed, showing you the properties of the subobject in the collection.

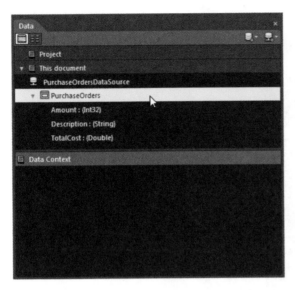

Figure 6–18. *The Data panel shows you each data source used within your current application.*

If you now examine the markup of your initial `Window` (or, if you are using a Silverlight project, your initial `UserControl`), you'll notice that the IDE has defined a new object resource (see Chapter 2) that maps to your custom collection object:

```
<Window.Resources>
  <local:PurchaseOrders x:Key="PurchaseOrdersDataSource"
                        d:IsDataSource="True"/>
</Window.Resources>
```

This resource will be used throughout the data binding operation.

Binding the Entire Collection to a ListBox

At this point, we can define a UI that will display the property values yielded from the object data source. Simply put, once you have established a data source via the Data panel, each aspect of the displayed tree can be dragged to the artboard to generate a new UI control that is automatically bound to the data store.

If you examine the top-left area of the Data panel, you will notice two buttons. The leftmost button (selected by default) activates List mode of the currently selected data source. When your data source is configured in List mode, you can drag a given property or object from the Data panel and it will be displayed in a new `ListBox` control. The button to the right configures the data source to work in Details mode, which will be examined later in the chapter.

Assuming you are in the default List mode, if you were to select the `PurchaseOrders` node in the Data panel and drop it onto your artboard, you would find that a single `ListBox` control is added, which shows all properties for each object in the collection. If you were to try this yourself, you'd see a UI similar to that shown in Figure 6–19.

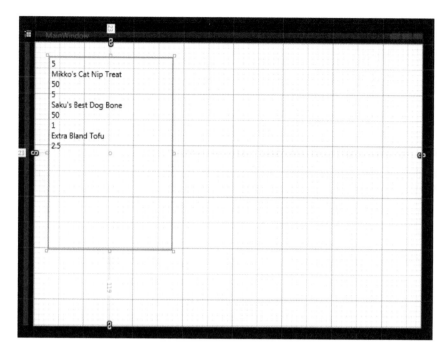

Figure 6–19. *A single ListBox containing all object data*

At first glance, it might not seem very useful to bind an entire collection of objects to a single ListBox, given that each list entry shows each object property value one after the other. While it is true that the currently displayed UI is not very helpful, WPF and Silverlight both support the ability to build *data templates* that can stylize how a data binding should be displayed in the destination control.

For example, we could create a data template such that we don't simply see stacks of string data, but also see additional bits of descriptive text, graphics, animations, or what have you. Essentially, anything you would do when building a control template (see Chapter 5) can be done within a data binding operation. More details about data templates are coming in a moment. Until then, let's solidify the role of a *data context*.

Examining the Role of the Data Context

If you open the XAML editor, you will notice that the `<Grid>` layout manager (`LayoutRoot`) has a new `DataContext` attribute, which is assigned a binding expression that binds it to the name of the `Window`-level object resource, `PurchaseOrdersDataSource`. When a layout manager sets the `DataContext` attribute, any child element is able to use this source of the data (which is our `PurchaseOrders` object) during a data binding operation:

```
<Grid x:Name="LayoutRoot" DataContext="{Binding Source=
    {StaticResource PurchaseOrdersDataSource}}">
    ...
</Grid>
```

You will also notice that the `ListBox` in the `<Grid>` sets two properties of interest, `ItemsSource` and `ItemTemplate`. The `ItemsSource` property may appear to be odd, in that it has only an empty {Binding} markup extension. This simply marks the source of ListBox data as the result of a data binding operation, which is truly defined by the related data template (described next):

```
<ListBox ItemTemplate="{DynamicResource PurchaseOrderTemplate}"
        ItemsSource="{Binding}"
  ...
/>
```

A First Look at Data Template Markup

The resource identified by the ItemTemplate property is a new object resource that was put in place when you dragged and dropped the PurchaseOrders node from the Data panel onto the artboard. Again, you will learn more about data templates (and how to customize them) later in this chapter, so don't worry too much about details just yet.

```
<DataTemplate x:Key="PurchaseOrderTemplate">
  <StackPanel>
    <TextBlock Text="{Binding Amount}"/>
    <TextBlock Text="{Binding Description}"/>
    <TextBlock Text="{Binding TotalCost}"/>
  </StackPanel>
</DataTemplate>
```

Viewing the Bound Data Context

Last but not least, if you view the Data panel once again, you'll notice that the lower portion of the window shows a new data context node (see Figure 6–20). Essentially, the upper portion of the Data panel simply lists the full set of data sources that could be used, whereas the lower portion shows which data sources are currently in use (a.k.a the data contexts).

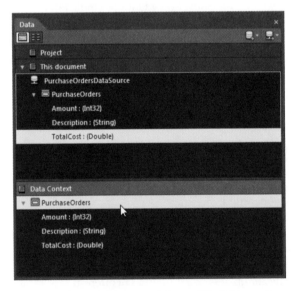

Figure 6–20. The Data panel shows "live" data contexts.

Quick Project Cleanup

Now that you have a better feel for what the IDE generates if you drop an entire collection onto the artboard, press Ctrl+Z so that your `Window` definition is back to a default look and feel. Once you are done, verify that your markup no longer has the `ListBox` control, but does maintain the object data source:

```
<Window
  xmlns="http://schemas.microsoft.com/winfx/2006/xaml/presentation"
  xmlns:x="http://schemas.microsoft.com/winfx/2006/xaml"
  x:Class="CollectionDataContext.MainWindow"
  x:Name="Window"
  Title=" MainWindow"
  Width="640" Height="480">

  <Window.Resources>
    <local:PurchaseOrders x:Key="PurchaseOrdersDataSource"
                          d:IsDataSource="True"/>
  </Window.Resources>

  <Grid x:Name="LayoutRoot"/>
</Window>
```

Binding Individual Properties to ListBox Controls

If you were to drag an individual property from the Data panel to the artboard, there would be a new `ListBox` (assuming you are in the default List mode of the Data Panel) that displays the selected property value of the data source. For example, let's say that you want to define three `ListBox` controls that will hold the property values for each `PurchaseOrder` object in your collection. To achieve this via Blend, select the `Amount` property in the Data panel and drag it onto the artboard for your current `Window`. You'll see that when you drag over a single property, the IDE automatically generates a new `ListBox`. Figure 6–21 shows my artboard after I dragged the `Amount`, `Description`, and `TotalCost` properties onto it (and resized the current `Window` and `Grid` objects a tad).

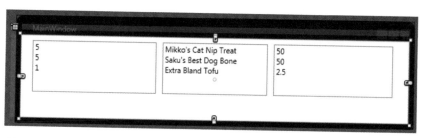

Figure 6–21. *Three ListBox controls bound to custom object properties*

Binding the Collection to a DataGrid

At this point, you have seen that if you drag a property (or the entire collection) from the Data panel to the artboard, the IDE will display data in related `ListBox` controls by default. Other UI controls can also be the drop target of the Data panel, of course, provided that you add the control first.

To illustrate, locate the DataGrid control within your Assets library, and draw one on your Window, somewhere below the current ListBox controls. Next, select the PurchaseOrders node in your Data panel (not the individual properties beneath this node) and drag it onto the new DataGrid object. Once you do, you'll see that the content of your collection is automatically displayed, as shown in Figure 6–22.

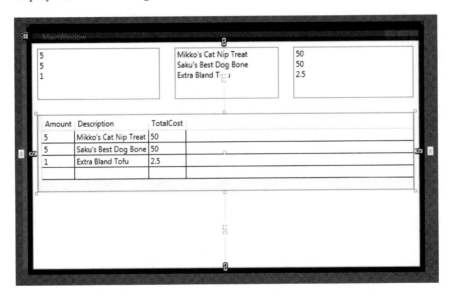

Figure 6–22. *Binding the entire collection to a UI DataGrid*

If you examine the generated markup, you'll see that the DataGrid is still leveraging the data context defined by LayoutRoot, this time mapping object properties to individual <DataGridTextColumn> elements:

```
<Grid x:Name="LayoutRoot" DataContext="{Binding
      Source={StaticResource PurchaseOrdersDataSource}}">
...
  <DataGrid Margin="8,112,8,120" AutoGenerateColumns="False"
            ItemsSource="{Binding}">
    <DataGrid.Columns>
      <DataGridTextColumn Binding="{Binding Amount}" Header="Amount"/>
      <DataGridTextColumn Binding="{Binding Description}"
                          Header="Description"/>
      <DataGridTextColumn Binding="{Binding TotalCost}"
                          Header="TotalCost"/>
    </DataGrid.Columns>
  </DataGrid>
</Grid>
```

Manipulating the Collection at Runtime

Recall that our custom PurchaseOrders collection extended a parent class named
ObservableCollection. This collection has the unique ability to refresh UI data bindings if the
contents of the collection change (items are added, removed, or updated). To wrap up the first
example, add a new Button control to your Window's artboard and handle the Click event via the
properties window.

Now recall that when you first defined your object data source, the IDE added to your main
Window an object resource named PurchaseOrdersDataSource that maps to an instance of your
PurchaseOrders collection. When the application is run, the collection object is created using
the default constructor.[8] So, if you want to gain access to this same class instance, you simply
have to locate the item by key name in your resource container. Consider the following Click
event hander that will add a new PurchaseOrder object to the collection:

```
private void btnAddNewObject_Click(object sender,
  System.Windows.RoutedEventArgs e)
{
  // First, get our object resource.
  PurchaseOrders myOrders =
    (PurchaseOrders)this.Resources["PurchaseOrdersDataSource"];

  // Now, generate some random values for the numerical properties.
  Random r = new Random();
  int amount = r.Next(50);
  double cost = r.NextDouble();

  // Finally, add the new random test item.
  myOrders.Add(new PurchaseOrder(amount, cost, "TEST ITEM!"));
}
```

Here, for simplicity, I am generating some random data to account for the cost and amount
of a test item, but I am sure you can extend this project with some new text entry controls to
gather unique values if you wish. In any case, if you run your application and click your Button
control a few times, you will see that the ListBox and DataGrid objects automatically update!
See Figure 6–23.

---

[8] In markup, it is only possible to call the default constructor of any object.

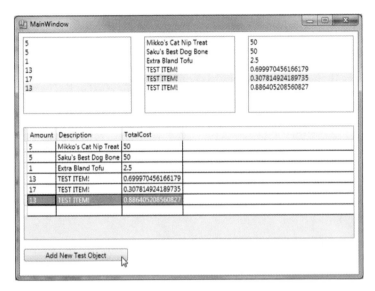

Figure 6–23. Adding, and rebinding, new orders

That wraps up the current example. Next up, let's examine the role of *data templates*.

■ **Source Code** The **CollectionDataContext** project can be found under the Chapter 6 subdirectory.

Working with Data Templates

Our next example will reuse our current PurchaseOrder and PurchaseOrders classes to illustrate how Blend can facilitate the creation of custom data templates. Create a new WPF application project named **FunWithDataTemplates**, and then use Project ➤ Add Existing Item to copy over the C# file (or files) that contains your business object and custom collection.

After ensuring that you have built your project, create a new object data source connection to your PurchaseOrders object, as you did in the previous example, and drag the PurchaseOrders node from the Data panel onto the Window's artboard. At this point, you should see the same display as shown previously in Figure 6–19. Recall that the IDE generated a default data template (as a Window resource in MainWindow.xaml) that is used by the ListBox to display each property value in a simple, unstyled TextBlock:

```
<DataTemplate x:Key="PurchaseOrderTemplate">
  <StackPanel>
    <TextBlock Text="{Binding Amount}"/>
    <TextBlock Text="{Binding Description}"/>
    <TextBlock Text="{Binding TotalCost}"/>
  </StackPanel>
</DataTemplate>
```

Editing a Data Template

When you want to modify this default data template, you first need to open the Resources panel and locate the template by name, as shown in Figure 6–24. Once you have done so, open it for editing by clicking the Edit resource button.

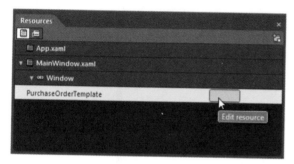

Figure 6–24. *Locating a data template in the Resources panel*

Locate the Objects and Timeline panel and select the first `TextBlock` (see Figure 6–25).

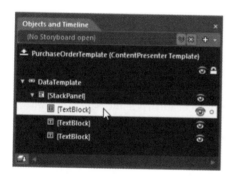

Figure 6–25. *Selecting the first TextBlock in the data template for editing*

Styling Items in a Data Template

At this point, you are free to use the Properties panel to change any settings you wish in order to style how the `Amount` property will be displayed in the `TextBlock`. By way of a few suggestions, change the `Foreground` property to a new color value, and maybe tinker with the font settings using the Text section of the Properties panel. Here is how I configured my first `TextBlock`:

```
<TextBlock Text="{Binding Amount}" Foreground="#FFE91616"
           FontWeight="Bold" FontSize="18.667"/>
```

Now, if you run your program, you will see that each `Amount` property looks somewhat more interesting (see Figure 6–26).

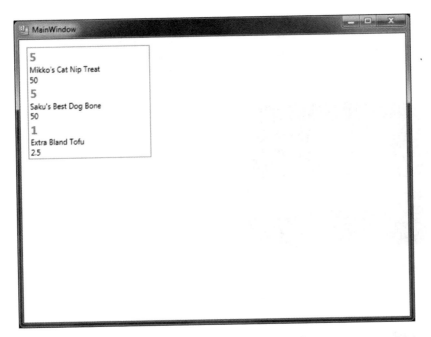

Figure 6–26. Our first attempt at styling our data template

Defining Composite UI Elements for a Data Template

Adding a bit of color is fine, but the underlying object properties are still rather nondescript (what does this large, red 5 mean exactly?). Return to the Objects and Timeline panel for your data template, and select the first TextBlock once again. Right-click this node, and group this item into a new nested StackPanel by selecting Group Into ➤ StackPanel.

Once you have done so, set the Orientation property of this new StackPanel to Horizontal. Finally, add a new Label control above the existing TextBlock (remember, you can drag and drop tree nodes to new locations). Once you are done, the Objects and Timeline panel tree should look like Figure 6–27.

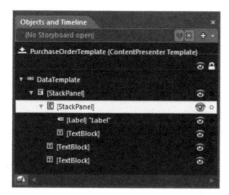

Figure 6–27. The first item in the template is now a nested StackPanel.

Before moving on, set the `Content` property of your `Label` control to `Amount`. If you examine the editor for the data template, you will notice that everything is very small in size, so use the artboard controls on the lower left (or the mouse wheel) to zoom way into the designer. You will see that your new nested layout manager and its control are not positioned correctly. To tidy things up, set the `Width` property of your new `Label` to `70`.

Use this same general process to add a bit of flair to the remaining two `TextBlock` controls in the data template. Again, you will most likely need to group each in a nested layout manager (again, using the Group Into menu option of the Objects and Timeline panel), and then add a few new items of your choosing.

Figure 6–28 shows my final Objects and Timeline panel (and a portion of the zoomed-in artboard) for each part of my template. Notice that I have reordered the nested `StackPanel` objects so the amount and cost are listed before the product description. Also notice I have added a small graphic to "point to" the product description.

Figure 6–28. The final data template layout

The underlying XAML looks like so (yours will most certainly differ to some level, but you see the general idea):

```xml
<DataTemplate x:Key="PurchaseOrderTemplate">
  <StackPanel>
    <StackPanel Orientation="Horizontal" >
      <Label Width="70" Content="Amount" BorderBrush="#FF309914"
             FontWeight="Bold" FontStyle="Italic"/>
      <TextBlock Text="{Binding Amount}" Foreground="#FFE91616"
                 FontWeight="Bold" FontSize="18.667"
                 d:LayoutOverrides="Width"/>
    </StackPanel>
    <StackPanel Orientation="Horizontal" >
      <Label Width="70" Content="Cost" FontWeight="Bold"
             FontStyle="Italic"/>
      <TextBlock Text="{Binding TotalCost}" Foreground="#FF1031E7"
                 FontWeight="Bold" FontSize="18.667"
                 d:LayoutOverrides="Width"/>
    </StackPanel>
    <StackPanel Orientation="Horizontal">
      <ed:BlockArrow Fill="#FF5A5AC2" Height="11" Orientation="Right"
                     Stroke="#FF1030E4" Width="15"
                     StrokeThickness="2"/>
      <TextBlock Text="{Binding Description}"
                 d:LayoutOverrides="Width"
                 Foreground="#FFAD11DE"/>
    </StackPanel>
  </StackPanel>
</DataTemplate>
```

An important point to note is that when you are editing any data template, you can return to the Window (or UserControl) designer by clicking the "Return scope to Window/UserControl" button in the Objects and Timeline panel, as shown in Figure 6–29.

Figure 6–29. Returning to the window designer from the data template designer

Return to the artboard, and you will see the results of your tinkering (see Figure 6–30). If you run the application, you will see that, sure enough, you can select a given item in your stylized list box data display.

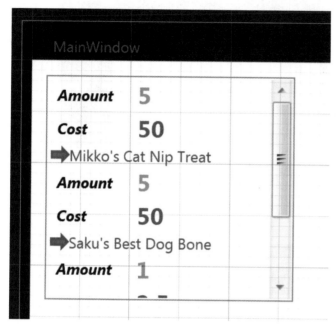

Figure 6–30. *Our final data template display*

Creating Control Templates Containing Data Templates

To wrap up our customized data template, I'd like to point out that you are free to create *control templates* (see Chapter 5) that contain embedded *data templates*. Why might you want to do this? Well, suppose you want to ensure that when the user selects one of the items in the ListBox, the selected StackPanel of data changes in some manner (such as a bounce animation or what have you). Furthermore, suppose you want to have a number of these ListBox controls on the same window.

■ **Note** In this section, you will be using the States panel, which was examined in Chapter 5. Refer to the section "Working with the VSM via the States Panel" for a quick refresher if required.

If you are attempting to add interactivity to a data template, one easy way to do so is to right-click the control that is currently using your data template (the ListBox control in our example) and, under the Edit Additional Templates menu option, opt to edit a copy of the "generated item container" (see Figure 6–31).

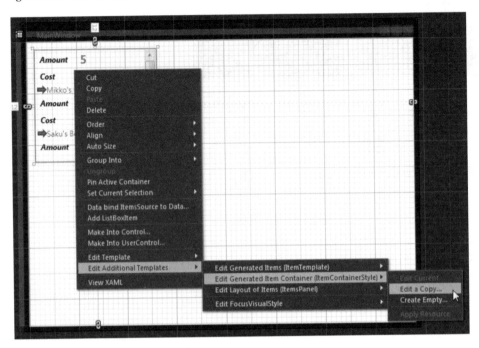

Figure 6–31. Editing a copy of our ListBox's item container template

Essentially, this IDE option generates a new `ListBox` style that allows you to define how the `<ContentPresenter>` will display its data under various conditions (when an item is selected, unselected, receives mouse events, and many other possible notifications). Activate this menu option now, and in the Create Style Resource dialog box, name your style `myListStyle` and save it as a `Window`-level resource (see Figure 6–32).

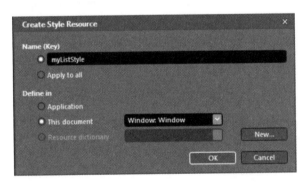

Figure 6–32. Naming and storing the new style resource

Adding Interactivity to the Template

Examine your Objects and Timeline panel and notice that you can see the internal `<ContentPresenter>`. Select this node in the tree. Recall that our goal is to add some interactivity to the control template, and therefore we need to work with triggers or the Visual State Manager (VSM) as explained in Chapter 5. Here, we will opt for the use of the VSM.

Open the States panel and you will notice that a number of default visual states are already listed. Pick the `Selected` state from the list, as shown in Figure 6–33, to activate the state editor.

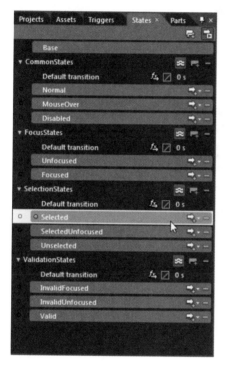

Figure 6–33. Viewing the intrinsic visual states of the ListBox template

Now that you have selected the `Selected` state (pardon the redundancy!), you can make any changes you wish to the `<ContentPresenter>`. I chose to reduce the X and Y scaling to 0.85 using the Scale tab (setting the X and Y values to 0.85) of the Transform section, as shown in Figure 6–34.

Figure 6–34. Shrinking the size of the selected list item

Next, I added a bounce effect. To do so, begin by adding a new transition into the `Selected` state in the States panel, as shown in Figure 6–35.

Figure 6–35. Adding a new state transition

Next, use the related animation easing editor to add a bounce effect of your liking, as shown in Figure 6–36.

Figure 6–36. Adding a bounce effect when transitioning to the Selected state

Last but not least, make sure you set a proper time duration for the animation to occur, as the default value of zero basically means you will not see the animation effect at all! As you can see in Figure 6–37, I set a value of one second.

Figure 6–37. Setting a time duration for the effect

Now, run your application and select items in your list. You should see a nice bouncing effect for the whole set of composite items defined by your data template. How useful is a bouncing composite list item? Well, I'll let you be the judge of that.

In any case, this example has illustrated a number of interesting ways to customize how a data binding operation looks and feels. As I am sure you've guessed, data templates can be styled in a large number of ways. I hope this example has helped you become comfortable with the nuts and bolts of using the Blend IDE to customize the look of your data binding operations.

■ **Source Code** The **FunWithDataTemplates** project can be found under the Chapter 6 subdirectory.

Defining a WPF XML Data Source

If you are a .NET developer, you are well aware that the platform supports various ways to programmatically manipulate XML data, such as the original System.Xml namespace as well as the LINQ to XML API. If your WPF or Silverlight applications need to modify XML data at runtime (add new elements, delete elements, update elements, etc.), then you will most certainly need to drop down to procedural code. However, the Blend IDE also provides a way to bind UI elements to data that is contained in an XML document, by using the XML Data Source option of the Data panel.

■ **Note** Unfortunately, the ability to bind XML data to UI elements via an XML data source is available only for WPF applications. Of course, it is certainly possible to manipulate XML data in a Silverlight program, but to do so, you will need to rely on procedural code. Look up the topic "XML Data" within the Silverlight documentation for information and code examples regarding XML data and Silverlight applications.

Given that direct XML document data binding is only available under WPF, create a new WPF application project named **WpfXmlDataBinding**. If you have an XML document you would like to manipulate, you are free to use that specific *.xml file; however, for this example, I will assume you are using the following I636.15Onventory.xml file (which is included in the code download for the current example of this chapter):

```
<?xml version="1.0" encoding="utf-8"?>
<Inventory>
  <Product ProductID ="0">
    <Cost>5.00</Cost>
    <Description>
    Eight Times the sugar and twice the caffeine
    </Description>
    <Name>Super Spazz Soda Pop</Name>
    <HotItem>true</HotItem>
  </Product>
  <Product ProductID ="1">
    <Cost>10.00</Cost>
    <Description>A soothing night time cookie</Description>
    <Name>Sleepy Time Cookies</Name>
    <HotItem>true</HotItem>
  </Product>
  <Product ProductID ="2">
    <Cost>15.00</Cost>
    <Description>It's Tofu, what can you say?</Description>
    <Name>Joe's Tofu</Name>
    <HotItem>false</HotItem>
  </Product>
</Inventory>
```

Insert this file (or your custom XML file) into your current project using Project ➤ Add Existing Item. Once you have done so, you should see this file within the Projects panel.

■ **Note** It is not mandatory to include an XML data file in your project in order to bind to it with the Data panel, but this does make it easy to open the file within Blend for editing.

Adding an XML Data Source

First open `MainWindow.xaml` in the artboard designer, and then locate the Data panel and opt to add a new XML data source, as shown in Figure 6–38.

Figure 6–38. Adding a new XML data source

In the resulting Create XML Data Source dialog box, shown in Figure 6–39, browse to whichever XML document you wish to use (again, here I am assuming the `Inventory.xml` file). Name your new XML data source `InventoryXmlDataStore` and store the object resource in the current document.

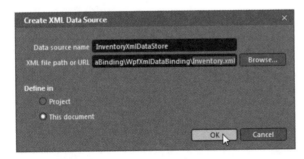

Figure 6–39. Mapping to your XML document

Click the OK button. At this point, your Data panel should look something like what you see in Figure 6–40.

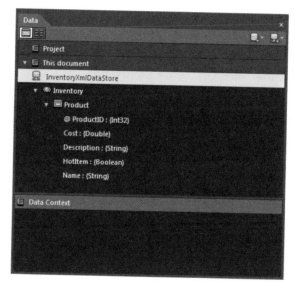

Figure 6–40. *The XML data source*

If you examine the XAML data located in `MainWindow.xaml`, you will notice that a new resource of type `XmlDataProvider` has been defined:

```
<Window.Resources>
  <XmlDataProvider x:Key="InventoryDataSource"
                   Source="\Inventory.xml"
                   d:IsDataSource="True"/>
</Window.Resources>
```

Binding XML Data to UI Elements via XPath

Now that we have established our XML data source, we can drag and drop the nodes from the Data panel onto the artboard, just like we did when we created an object data source. Thus, if you drag the entire `Product` node to the artboard, the IDE will generate a `ListBox` that displays all data for each XML element. Notice that the `ItemsSource` property has been bound to the `<Products>` node using an XPath expression:

```
<ListBox HorizontalAlignment="Left"
  ItemTemplate="{DynamicResource ProductTemplate}"
  ItemsSource="{Binding XPath=/Inventory/Product}"
  Margin="89,65,0,77" Width="200"/>
```

As well, the generated template (specified by the `ItemTemplate` property) uses some additional XPath expressions to connect the various attributes and subnodes of the `<Product>` node:

```
<DataTemplate x:Key="ProductTemplate">
  <StackPanel>
```

```
  <TextBlock Text="{Binding XPath=@ProductID}"/>
  <TextBlock Text="{Binding XPath=Cost}"/>
  <TextBlock Text="{Binding XPath=Description}"/>
  <CheckBox IsChecked="{Binding XPath=HotItem}"/>
  <TextBlock Text="{Binding XPath=Name}"/>
  </StackPanel>
</DataTemplate>
```

Again, similar to when you are working with an object data source, you can also drag individual attributes (such as `ProductID`) or subnodes (`Cost`, `Description`, etc.) directly to the artboard to generate `ListBox` controls that display only that subset of data. Thus, if you drag the `HotItem` node to the artboard, the IDE will generate a new `ListBox` control using a new related data template:

```
<!-- The ListBox -->
<ListBox HorizontalAlignment="Right"
         ItemTemplate="{DynamicResource ProductTemplate1}"
         ItemsSource="{Binding XPath=/Inventory/Product}"
         Margin="0,78,54,64" Width="200"/>

<!-- The data template-->
<DataTemplate x:Key="ProductTemplate1">
  <StackPanel>
    <CheckBox IsChecked="{Binding XPath=HotItem}"/>
  </StackPanel>
</DataTemplate>
```

To be sure, you will want to modify these data templates using the techniques examined earlier in the chapter. In any case, as you can see, the general process of working with an XML data source is very similar to working with an object data source, so you should be in good shape.

■ **Note** The Blend User Guide includes an interesting tutorial that illustrates how to use the XML data source to bind to an RSS feed. Look up the topic "Try it: Create an RSS news reader" if you are interested.

Before we move on to the final major topic of this chapter (creating new data stores and sample data), the next example illustrates a second way you can use the Data panel. As you will see, it is possible to quickly build a "list details" display by enabling the Details mode feature of the Data panel.

■ **Source Code** The **WpfXmlDataBinding** project can be found under the Chapter 6 subdirectory.

Creating a List Details Data Binding

Our data binding examples thus far showed how data items in the Data panel will map to new `ListBox` controls. However, right next to the List Mode button is a Details Mode button (see Figure 6–41) that will place the data source into Details mode.

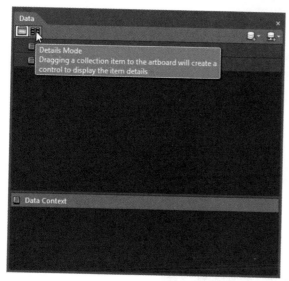

Figure 6–41. The Data panel can toggle between List mode and Details mode.

When you select Details mode, you will find that when you drag individual properties from the Data panel to the artboard, the data value is captured within a `TextBlock` control (rather than a `ListBox`). As well, if you drag a parent node to the artboard, the IDE will generate markup that allows you to cycle through the "details" of a selected item (a full example of doing so is provided in just a moment).

To illustrate this aspect of the Data panel, create a new WPF (or Silverlight) application project named **ListDetailsDataBinding**. Next, add to your project the C# file that contains your `PurchaseOrder` and `PurchaseOrders` classes, build your project, and then use the Data panel to define a new object data source that maps to your custom `PurchaseOrders` class.

Creating the User Interface

Ensure that you are still in the default List mode of the Data panel, and drag the `Description` node to the artboard to generate a `ListBox` that shows you the text description of each item (I've also added a `Label` control to describe the contents of this control). Click the Details Mode button of the Data panel and select all three properties (`Amount`, `Description`, and `TotalCost`) using a standard Shift+click operation (see Figure 6–42).

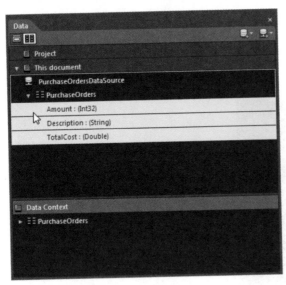

Figure 6–42. Selecting multiple items from the Data panel in Details mode

Once these items are selected, drag them to the artboard. At this point, your artboard should look something like that shown in Figure 6–43.

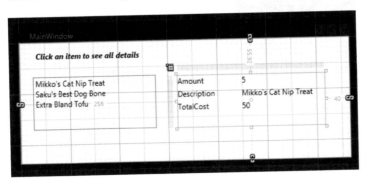

Figure 6–43. Our list-details UI

Because you have dragged and dropped multiple items from the Data panel, the IDE generated a `Grid` object that contains a set of related `TextBlock` controls. If you examine the Objects and Timeline panel, you will see the tree of UI elements shown in Figure 6–44.

Figure 6–44. *Dragging multiple items from the Data panel to the artboard results in a Grid of controls.*

Now, run your project! You will see that when you click any item in the `ListBox`, the full details of the selected item are shown in the details area (the `Grid` of `TextBlock` controls). Not too shabby, eh? Of course, you are free to change the layout of the items in the sub-`Grid`, modify the related data templates, and what have you. I'll allow you to modify the generated UI markup as you see fit, but let's take a look at the data binding markup.

Examining the Generated Markup

When you dragged the initial `Description` node from the Data panel, the IDE generated basic markup that established a data context for the root `Grid` object that maps to your custom collection. As well, the `ListBox` control uses a simple data template to display the values from the `Description` properties. Here is the relevant markup *before* you added additional items in Details mode:

```
<Window
... >
  <Window.Resources>
    <CollectionDataContext:PurchaseOrders
      x:Key="PurchaseOrdersDataSource" d:IsDataSource="True"/>
    <DataTemplate x:Key="PurchaseOrderTemplate">
      <StackPanel>
        <TextBlock Text="{Binding Description}"/>
      </StackPanel>
    </DataTemplate>
  </Window.Resources>

  <Grid x:Name="LayoutRoot" DataContext="{Binding Source=
    {StaticResource PurchaseOrdersDataSource}}">
    <ListBox HorizontalAlignment="Left"
            ItemTemplate="{DynamicResource PurchaseOrderTemplate}"
            ItemsSource="{Binding}" ... />
```

```
    </Grid>
</Window>
```

Once you added the remaining detail items, the sub-`Grid` defined its own data context that binds to the `SelectedItem` property of the `ListBox`. Each of the contained `TextBlock` controls uses the expected `{Binding}` markup extension to connect to a given object property from the collection (note that Blend automatically named each item, as we did not explicitly set the `Name` property). Here is some partial markup:

```
<Grid DataContext="{Binding SelectedItem, ElementName=listBox}"
        Margin="257,53.92,36,0"
        d:DataContext="{Binding [0]}" Height="97" VerticalAlignment="Top">
    <TextBlock HorizontalAlignment="Left" VerticalAlignment="Top"
            Width="100" Text="Amount"/>
    <TextBlock Text="{Binding Amount}" HorizontalAlignment="Left"
            VerticalAlignment="Top"
            Width="150" Margin="104,0,0,0"/>
...
</Grid>
```

■ **Note** The second `DataContext` property (marked with a d tag prefix) is used by the Blend designer surface, and is not required for the data binding operation to perform its work.

Figure 6–45 shows my final application in action.

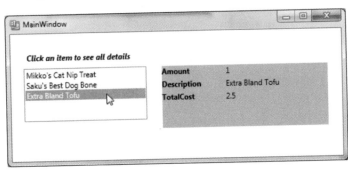

Figure 6–45. A list-details data binding operation

■ **Source Code** The **ListDetailsDataBinding** project is included under the Chapter 6 subdirectory.

Exploring the Role of Sample Data

Many of the examples thus far in this chapter have used a customized collection of `PurchaseOrder` objects, which we manually created using the C# code editor. As it turns out, it is not uncommon for a developer to need to work with some temporary data during the construction of the user interface. For example, perhaps the *real* data will come from a relational database...which is currently being constructed by your friendly DBA. Or, perhaps the exact business objects to be used by the program are currently little more than a collection of UML class diagrams.

When you are building a WPF or Silverlight application with Blend, you can elect to insert what is known as *sample data*. As the name suggests, this provides a way for you to visualize the UI even when the live data is unavailable. As well, Blend sample data can be useful during the process of learning more about data binding techniques in general.

■ **Note** Sample data is also useful when you are using SketchFlow to prototype your applications. You'll learn about SketchFlow prototyping in Chapter 8.

Inserting Sample Data into a Project

Create a new WPF or Silverlight application project named **FunWithSampleData**.[9] Open the Data panel and elect to insert sample data into your project (see Figure 6–46). Leave all the settings in the resulting dialog box at their defaults.

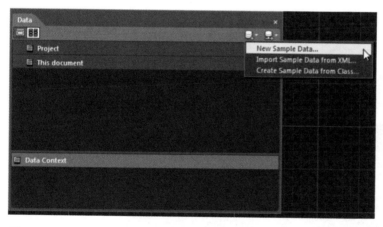

Figure 6–46. Inserting sample data

At this point, your Data panel has been populated with a number of testing items, including a custom collection (which extends `ObservableCollection`) and a few default properties (named `Property1` and `Property2`). Double-click the current `Collection` node and rename this to `PersonCollection`. Likewise, rename your first two properties to `FirstName` and `LastName` (which is currently a Boolean value, but we will change this in a moment). Figure 6–47 shows the Data panel after these adjustments.

---

[9] Unlike most other projects in this book, I did not supply a solution for this project, as it is little more than a "create and examine" example.

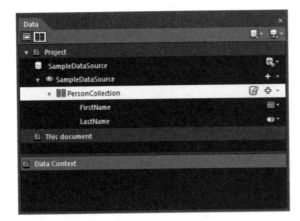

Figure 6–47. Renaming the initial items

Adding Additional Properties

You can add additional properties to your data store using the New Property button. If you click the drop-down arrow, you will see you the four choices shown in Figure 6–48.

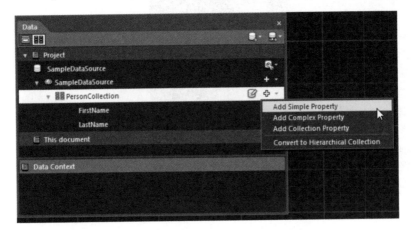

Figure 6–48. Adding additional properties

The first three choices break down as so (the fourth is discussed a bit later):

- *Add Simple Property*: Use this option to add a String, Number, Boolean, or Image property. By default, a String property is added, but this can be changed after creation.

- *Add Complex Property*: Use this option to create a property that can contain child properties (in other words, a new class with custom properties).

- *Add Collection Property*: Use this option to create a new class extending ObservableCollection.

Add a new "simple property" named `Picture`, which will automatically default to a String data property.

Modifying the Data Types and Values

Once you have added properties, you can further configure their data types. The first approach is to change properties values by clicking the embedded property drop-down editor. Figure 6–49 shows how we can change the `Picture` property to an Image. Do know that the Image property can be configured to select a specific image file (such as pictures of various people), but don't bother; the IDE will use some sample images by default.

Figure 6–49. Modifying individual property settings

In addition, you can configure all property data types if you click the "Edit sample values" button, as shown in Figure 6–50.

Figure 6–50. Editing all property values

Use the resulting Edit Sample Values dialog box to change the `LastName` property from a Boolean value to a String data type, as shown in Figure 6–51. Notice that each property is being set to a set of default string data and image files (after all, this is in fact *sample* data). Also note that you can change how many test records you wish to have generated.

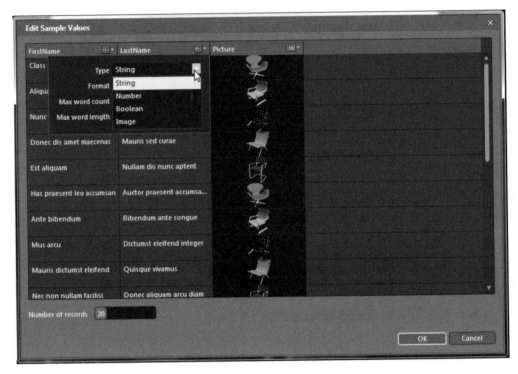

Figure 6–51. The Edit Sample Values dialog box

Binding Sample Data to the UI

At this point in the chapter, I am sure you know the next step. You can drag and drop elements from the Data panel onto the artboard. Make sure you double-check whether the Data panel is in List mode or Details mode, as inserting sample data defaults to Details mode. In Figure 6–52, you can see the end result of dragging the `PersonCollection` node on to a `DataGrid` control (while the Data panel was in List mode).

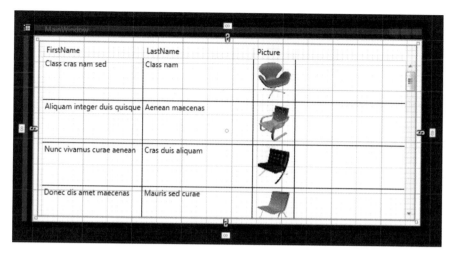

Figure 6–52. Visualizing the sample data on a DataGrid

Also note that you have the option to convert your sample data from a flat list of objects to a hierarchal format (see Figure 6–53).

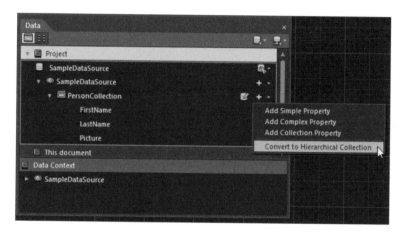

Figure 6–53. Converting sample data to a hierarchal format

Figure 6–54 illustrates the same data (which is now in a hierarchal format) bound to a new TreeView control.

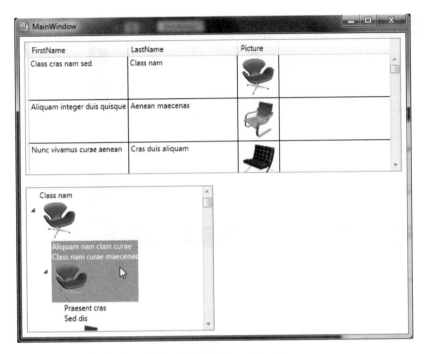

Figure 6–54. Displaying hierarchal data in a TreeView

Learning More About Sample Data

If the topic of sample data is of interest to you, and I suspect it will be during the prototyping phase of new WPF or Silverlight projects,[10] be aware that the Blend User Guide has a whole section on the topic, which builds upon the topics examined here. Look up "Creating sample data" for more information (see Figure 6–55).

---

[10] See Chapter 8 for details of using SketchFlow during application prototyping.

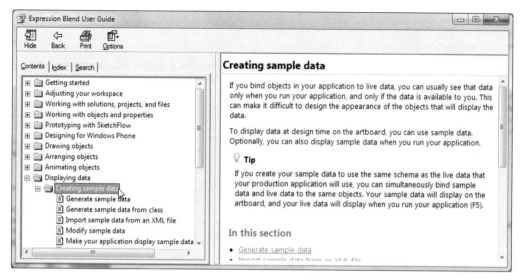

Figure 6–55. More details regarding Blend sample data can be found here.

Data Binding: A Brief Word on Final Topics

Over the course of this chapter, you have learned a number of data binding techniques, including how to bind control properties to other control properties; bind to custom collections; construct data templates; configure list-detail displays; and work with sample data. To be sure, there are other data binding–centric topics that I have not covered. Here is a rundown of a few items you may wish to explore yourself.

Binding to Relational Database Data

Perhaps the most common location for an application's data is a relational database. As you may know, the .NET platform provides a very comprehensive data access API named ADO.NET. Using this programming model, you can manipulate relational database tables in a variety of ways (the connected layer, the disconnected layer, the Entity Framework, and so forth).

Typically, data access logic is bundled into a dedicated .NET library, and referenced by the external applications (a WPF Window, a custom WCF service, or what have you). When you are referencing a data access library from a Blend project, you can create a new object data source that will invoke specific methods on the data objects to fetch data. The result set is then bound to a UI element via the Data panel.

I will not walk you through the process of building a Blend UI that uses data access libraries, as this would require building a database and authoring a good deal of procedural C# code. If you would like to learn more about using ADO.NET to build a data library (and how to leverage it in your Blend projects), look up the topic "Try it: Display data from a sample SQL database" in the Blend User Guide (see Figure 6–56). Here you will find a detailed tutorial that will walk you through the process.

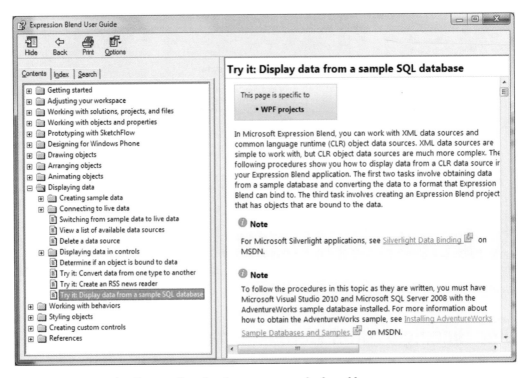

Figure 6–56. More details regarding database access can be found here.

The Role of Blend Databound Project Templates (MVVM)

I also want to briefly point out that Blend WPF and Silverlight projects (as well as Windows Phone 7 projects, provided you have installed the necessary templates [see Chapter 7]) can be created to make use of a very popular design pattern termed Model-View-ViewModel (MVVM). This design pattern helps you build applications in which the UI layer and business logic layer are as loosely coupled as possible. If you select a Databound project template, your starter code will follow the MVVM design pattern. Figure 6–57 shows the Silverlight Databound project type within the Blend New Project dialog box.

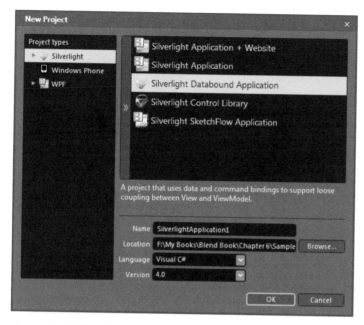

Figure 6–57. The Blend Databound projects follow the MVVM design pattern.

While learning MVVM is certainly a good idea for any WPF or Silverlight programmer, this topic is way outside the mission of this text. As you may know, working with MVVM can entail using a number of more advanced programming techniques. If you are interested in learning more about MVVM, my first bit of advice is to create a new Blend Databound project and examine the generated starter code.

I also recommend that you read the very useful MSDN magazine article titled "WPF Apps with the Model-View-ViewModel Design Pattern"[11] (the same techniques would work with a Silverlight project). This article will give you a solid understanding of why MVVM is so popular, and explain the overall architecture. Do be aware, however, that this particular article is targeted toward experienced .NET programmers.

Summary

This chapter examined a number of ways in which Blend can help you connect data source values to user interface elements. It began by investigating the role of control-to-control data binding. You learned how to use the Create Data Binding dialog box, learned how to build (and register) custom data conversion classes, and learned about the role of one-way and two-way data binding operations.

Next, you learned how you can use the Blend Data panel to create object data sources. Here, you created a custom collection of objects, which were bound to various UI elements. You then learned how to customize the way a data binding operation will be displayed using custom data templates. As shown, you can build a custom data template using many of the same techniques you use when building a custom control template.

---

[11] See http://msdn.microsoft.com/en-us/magazine/dd419663.aspx.

I wrapped things up with a quick preview of Blend sample data. This feature of the IDE allows you to define and use "mock" data as a simple placeholder for the "real" data that may not be available when constructing your UI. Last but not least, I pointed out from a high level a few final topics that are important (MVVM, for example) but outside the scope of this text.

■ ■ ■

CHAPTER 7

Designing for Windows Phone 7

At the time of this writing, Windows Phone 7 is Microsoft's latest handheld device, which stands as a direct competitor to Apple's iPhone platform (as well as other popular handhelds). From a .NET programmer's point of view, building applications for Windows Phone 7 is a very enticing proposition, as the native toolkit is in fact based on Silverlight![1] Given this fact, you can build a Windows Phone 7 application using C#, VB, XAML, Visual Studio 2010, Expression Blend, and the same general programming model as you would use when building a WPF or web-centric Silverlight application.

The first topic of this chapter illustrates how to install the necessary Windows Phone 7 SDK, which will update Visual Studio 2010 and Expression Blend 4 with the necessary libraries, templates, and IDE extensions. Once your machine has been configured with the correct development bits, you will be given a guided tour of the new project types and the new aspects of the Blend IDE that enable application development for the Windows Phone 7 platform.

Given that a vast majority of topics covered in Chapters 1 through 6 of this book apply directly to Windows Phone 7 development, the remainder of this chapter will have you create and modify each of the primary Windows Phone project types (simple, panorama, and pivot), which will illustrate various aspects of Windows Phone 7 development.

■ **Note** While Windows Phone 7 uses essentially the same programming model as Silverlight proper, you will need to learn about a number of phone-centric programming techniques to complete the puzzle (such as the navigation framework, how to interface with the handheld device, and so on). Given that the mission of this book is to teach you how to use the Blend IDE to design UIs (rather than to teach you how to implement complete software solutions), I will keep the coding techniques to a minimum. However, I will point you to a number of useful online resources at the conclusion of this chapter so that you can explore the topic further on your own.

Installing the Windows Phone 7 SDK

Microsoft's Windows Phone 7 device was released to the world after the release of Expression Blend 4 (as well as Visual Studio 2010). Therefore, if you want to create Windows Phone 7 projects, you must download and install the free Software Development Kit (SDK; formally

---

[1] Formally termed Silverlight for Windows Phone.

called the *Windows Phone Developer Tools*). Although there are many locations on the Web from which you can download and install the SDK, perhaps the simplest approach is to access the download area of the Expression Blend home page. Open a web browser and navigate to the following URL:

```
http://www.microsoft.com/expression/windowsphone
```

In Figure 7–1, you can see the design of this web page at the time of writing, which could be changed in the future. In any case, locate and click the "Download the Developer Tools" link.

Figure 7–1. *The Windows Phone 7 SDK can be freely downloaded from the Expression Blend web site.*

Next, you will be asked to download a small executable program that will begin the installation process (see Figure 7–2). Click the Run button to proceed.

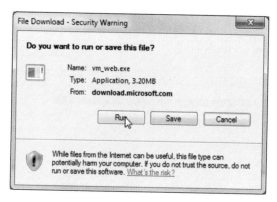

Figure 7–2. Running the initial installer

■ **Note** If you get an error informing you that the installer cannot run in Compatibility mode, download the installer once again, but this time save the application to your desktop. Next, right-click the executable and select the "Run as Administrator" menu option.

Once this installer is downloaded, click the Run button (once again) from the new dialog box that springs up, and this will start the formal installation process. After you accept the license agreement, click the Install Now button (see Figure 7–3) to install the full set of Windows Phone 7 development tools.

Figure 7–3. Installing the Windows Phone 7 SDK

The entire setup process can take awhile; go grab a snack and pop back in half an hour or so (perhaps longer depending on your Internet connection speed). You might be asked to reboot your machine, so make sure you do so if so prompted (I'll be waiting...).

■ **Note** I recommend that you perform a standard Windows Update on your machine after installing the Windows Phone 7 SDK. I needed to download a number of service packs after installation.

Examining the New Bits

Once the installation process is complete, your development machine will have a number of new tools and templates that you can use. However, exactly what is installed will be based on your current machine configuration. The Windows Phone 7 installer is smart enough to install only the bits you currently do not have installed. If you had a completely new machine (with no trace of Visual Studio, Blend, or the .NET/Silverlight platforms), you would end up with the following items:

- Visual Studio 2010 Express

- Microsoft .NET Framework version 4.0

- The latest version of Silverlight

- The Windows Phone 7 emulator

- A free "Windows Phone 7" version of Expression Blend[2]

- Microsoft XNA Game Studio 4.0

Note that if you currently have Visual Studio 2010 on your development machine, the installer will not bother to add a copy of Visual Studio 2010 Express, but will update your installation with new Windows Phone 7 project templates. On a related note, if you already have Expression Blend, you will not get the free "Windows Phone 7 Only" version of Blend, but your existing Blend installation will be updated with the Windows Phone 7 project templates.

You will also find that the Windows Phone 7 emulator is installed under the Windows Start button as well; however, you won't typically need to activate this directly. When you are building a Windows Phone 7 project with Expression Blend or Visual Studio 2010, the emulator launches automatically to host your application.

The Role of Microsoft XNA Game Studio 4.0

If you click the Windows Start button, you will find a new folder for Microsoft XNA Game Studio 4.0. Essentially, XNA Game Studio 4.0 is a programming environment that allows you to use Visual Studio (not Expression Blend!) to create games for Windows Phone, the Xbox 360 console, and Windows-based computers. XNA Game Studio includes the XNA Framework, which is a set of managed libraries (a.k.a. .NET assemblies) designed for game development

---

[2] Microsoft has been kind enough to build a special (and free) version of Expression Blend that exclusively targets Windows Phone 7 projects (called, appropriately, Expression Blend for Windows Phone). Again, understand that this free version will not allow you to build WPF- or Silverlight-proper applications.

based on Microsoft .NET Framework, as well as a number of Visual Studio 2010 project templates.

Now, be very aware that you can certainly build video games for Windows Phone 7 (as well as Silverlight/WPF applications in general) without using XNA Game Studio. It is completely possible to create games using nothing more than the .NET 4.0/Silverlight APIs and the tools and techniques you have learned over the course of this book. However, XNA Game Studio provides you with additional, more powerful libraries to build much more sophisticated video game software.

Although this book will not directly address XNA Game Studio, the following web site will be very useful if you are interested in exploring this platform further. Here you will find numerous tutorials regarding game development, including articles on artificial intelligence (AI) algorithms, incorporating physics into your games (collision detection, chase camera angles, etc.), and numerous other topics.

```
http://create.msdn.com/en-us/education/roadmap
```

On a final note about XNA Game Studio, once you have installed the Windows Phone 7 SDK, you will find a new set of Visual Studio 2010 project templates at your disposal. As you can see in Figure 7–4, you can target a variety a platforms (Xbox 360, Windows Phone 7, or the Windows OS itself).

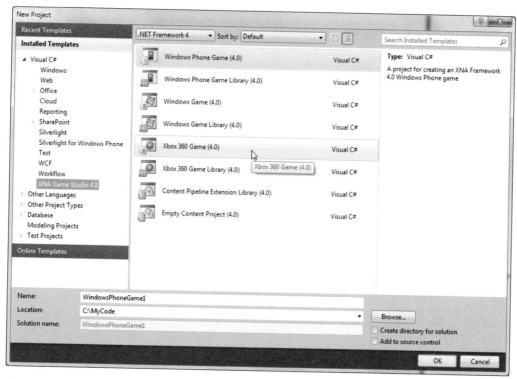

Figure 7–4. *XNA Game Studio includes a number of new Visual Studio project templates.*

Installing the Windows Phone 7 Documentation

If you intend to dive deeply into the Windows Phone 7 programming model, I recommend that you update your local .NET Framework 4.0 documentation help system to fetch the Windows Phone 7 documentation. Assuming you have previously installed Visual Studio 2010,[3] use the Windows Start button to navigate to All Programs ➤ Microsoft Visual Studio 2010 ➤ Visual Studio Tools, and from there, open the Manage Help Settings tool. At this point, you can elect to install local help documentation[4] (see Figure 7–5).

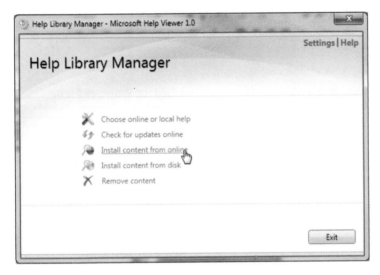

Figure 7–5. *Preparing to install the Windows Phone 7 SDK documentation*

Last but not least, you can now opt to install any part of the .NET help system (including Windows Phone 7 or Silverlight help; see Figure 7–6).

---

[3] If you do not want to install the documentation locally, you can view the same help system online at http://msdn.microsoft.com.

[4] If you have not installed the .NET Framework 4.0 documentation locally, you can use the Manage Help Settings tool to do so.

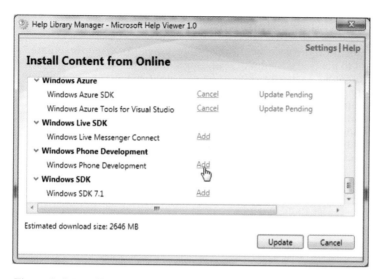

Figure 7–6. Installing the Windows Phone 7 SDK documentation

■ **Note** It is a good idea to run the Manage Help Settings tool every few weeks or so, as it will detect any updates to the documentation and allow you to download the freshest information.

After the SDK documentation has been installed, you can launch your local .NET documentation and search for the topic "Silverlight for Windows Phone," as shown in Figure 7–7.

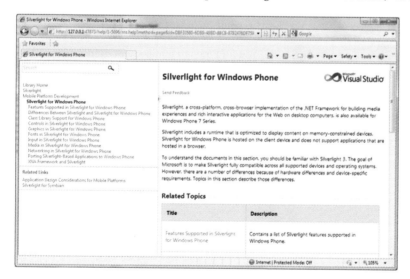

Figure 7–7. The Silverlight for Windows Phone portal

A Survey of Key Windows Phone 7 Namespaces

Although this chapter will not focus on the programming-specific aspects of Windows Phone 7 development, I do at least want to provide a roadmap regarding some of the new APIs you will encounter. Recall that when you build a Windows Phone 7 application, you are in fact building a Silverlight program. Therefore, if you have programmed Silverlight (or WPF) applications in the past, you will feel right at home.

This being said, the Windows Phone 7 SDK does include a handful of new .NET assemblies (such as `Microsoft.Phone.dll` and `Microsoft.Phone.Interop.dll`) that define a number of new .NET namespaces. Table 7–1 provides a brief overview of some (but not all) of these phone-centric namespaces. Be sure to consult the .NET Framework 4.0 documentation for full details.[5]

Table 7–1. *A Survey of Core Windows Phone 7 Namespaces*

Windows Phone Namespace	Meaning in Life
Microsoft.Devices	Defines a small number of types that allow you to program directly against the Windows Phone 7 device itself. For example, there are types that allow you to make the device vibrate, gather information regarding which version of the platform is on the device, and so forth.
Microsoft.Devices.Radio	Provides programmatic access to the FM Radio aspect of the handheld device.
MicrosoftDevices.Sensors	Provides access to APIs to access the accelerometer.
Microsoft.Phone.Controls	Defines a number of phone-centric controls, including the types to build panorama and pivot displays. You'll learn about these navigation models later in the chapter.
Microsoft.Phone.Notification	Allows your Windows Phone 7 applications to receive data sent via the Microsoft Push Notification Service.
Microsoft.Phone.Tasks	Defines a number of types that allow you to interact with key services of the handheld device, including the integrated camera, e-mail program, and telephone service.

---

[5] At the conclusion of this chapter, I'll point you to some online resources where you can download Windows Phone 7 sample projects that use these new assemblies and namespaces.

Viewing the New Blend Projects

Launch Blend and choose File ➤ New Project; you should find in the New Project dialog box a new Windows Phone node, shown in Figure 7–8, that defines a variety of project types.

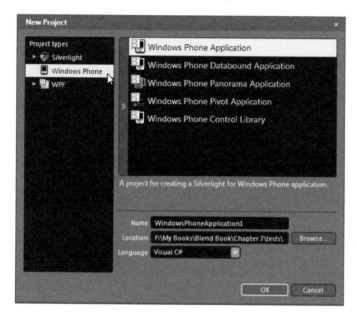

Figure 7–8. The Blend Windows Phone project templates

Table 7–2 documents these new project templates of Expression Blend. As you can see, they are similar (but not identical) to their WPF and Silverlight counterparts.

Table 7–2. Windows Phone Project Templates of Expression Blend

Windows Phone Project Template	Meaning in Life
Windows Phone Application	This is a simple project template for creating a Silverlight for Windows Phone application.
Windows Phone Databound Application	This template is also for creating a Silverlight for Windows Phone application, but it uses View and ViewModel objects to provide loose coupling between your presentation and data logic (see Chapter 6).
Windows Phone Panorama Application	This template uses the Panorama control to create a panorama-style application (more information is provided later in the chapter).

Windows Phone Project Template	Meaning in Life
![Windows Phone Pivot Application]	This template uses the `Pivot` control to create a tabbed-style application (more information is provided later in the chapter).
![Windows Phone Control Library]	This template is for creating custom controls that can be reused across other Windows Phone applications.

You'll learn more about these different types of project templates as you progress through the chapter, but in a nutshell, a panorama-style application allows you to build a long, horizontal canvas of UI elements, which can be smoothly panned within the view port of the phone, whereas a pivot-style application allows the end user to "flip" between a set of related UI pages, similar to the act of flipping pages in a book (typically with much more animation, however).

The Updated Blend User Guide

On a related note, be aware that once you install the Windows Phone 7 SDK, your local Expression Blend User Guide is updated with a new set of related tutorials and walkthroughs, as shown in Figure 7–9.

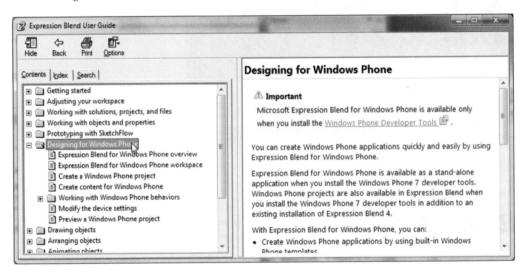

Figure 7–9. The updated Blend User Guide

Consider What You Already Know...

You may be surprised that this new part of the Blend User Guide is quite sparse. This is actually good news! As mentioned earlier, a vast majority of what you have already learned in this book applies directly to Windows Phone 7 development. For example, when building a Windows Phone 7 application, you will still be able to use Expression Blend to

- Create and interact with vector graphics (see Chapter 2)

- Package up and use object resources (see Chapter 2)

- Work with animations and easing effects (see Chapter 3)

- Build UIs with controls, layout managers, and behaviors (see Chapter 4)

- Create styles, templates, and UserControls (see Chapter 5)

- Use the Data panel to bind to data, and create custom data templates (see Chapter 6)

Remember, one of the biggest benefits of building software for Windows Phone 7 is that the underlying API is based on the exiting Silverlight platform (which in turn is based on WPF technologies). In fact, the Silverlight for Windows Phone documentation contains a specific topic regarding how to port an existing Silverlight application to the Windows Phone 7 platform. Search for the topic "Porting Silverlight-Based Applications to Windows Phone" if you are interested.[6]

Viewing the New Visual Studio 2010 Projects

Even though this chapter will not require you to use Visual Studio 2010, allow me to quickly point out that if you access the Visual Studio 2010 File ➤ New Project menu option, you will see a new Silverlight for Windows Phone 7 node under your programming language of choice (see Figure 7–10).

---

[6] On a related note, look up the topic "Differences Between Silverlight and Silverlight for Windows Phone." As you will see, there are a number of important differences to be mindful of, as these two toolkits are not 100 percent identical.

Figure 7–10. *The Visual Studio 2010 Windows Phone 7 project templates*

As you can see, these are the same Windows Phone 7 project template types as found in Expression Blend. Just like a WPF or Silverlight-proper application, you are free to start a new Windows Phone 7 project using either Expression Blend or Visual Studio 2010, and then open the code base into either tool as you see fit.[7]

Exploring the Windows Phone Application Project Type

Now that you have configured your development machine with the necessary programming tools, let's take things out for a test drive and create a new Windows Phone Application project type using Expression Blend. Select this project type in the New Project dialog box, and name your project **FirstPhoneApp**.

The Windows Phone Artboard

The first thing you will notice is that the artboard automatically displays a "phone page" that contains the application UI you are constructing, an example of which is shown in Figure 7–11.[8]

---

[7] In this chapter, I'll focus only on the Expression Blend project templates; however, be sure you take a moment to create a new sample project via Visual Studio 2010.

[8] In the Silverlight for Windows Phone 7 SDK, each phone display page is of type `PhoneApplicationPage`, which is a member of the `Microsoft.Controls.Phone` namespace.

Figure 7–11. *The Windows Phone artboard*

If you examine the Objects and Timeline panel, you will notice that (like a WPF or Silverlight project), your main layout manager is a `Grid` object named `LayoutRoot`. This `Grid` is carved into two rows, the first of which contains a `StackPanel` (named `TitlePanel`) to hold the basic display text on the top, and the second of which contains a sub-`Grid` object (named `ContentPanel`), where you can design your UI. The initial markup for this layout system looks like so:

```
<!--LayoutRoot is the root grid where all page content is placed-->
<Grid x:Name="LayoutRoot" Background="Transparent">
  <Grid.RowDefinitions>
    <RowDefinition Height="Auto"/>
    <RowDefinition Height="*"/>
  </Grid.RowDefinitions>

  <!--TitlePanel contains the name of the application and page title-->
```

```
<StackPanel x:Name="TitlePanel" Grid.Row="0" Margin="12,17,0,28">
  <TextBlock x:Name="ApplicationTitle" Text="MY APPLICATION"
             Style="{StaticResource PhoneTextNormalStyle}"/>
  <TextBlock x:Name="PageTitle" Text="page name" Margin="9,-7,0,0"
             Style="{StaticResource PhoneTextTitle1Style}"/>
</StackPanel>

<!--ContentPanel - place additional content here-->
<Grid x:Name="ContentPanel" Grid.Row="1" Margin="12,0,12,0"/>
</Grid>
```

The Windows Phone System Styles

If you examine the definition of the TextBlock objects closely, you can see they automatically use a few Windows Phone 7 styles (PhoneTextNormalStyle and PhoneTextTitle1Style). As you learned in Chapter 5, WPF ships with a set of Simple Styles that can be used as a starting point for customization. In a similar manner, a Windows Phone application can (and typically should, according to UI best practices) use a set of built-in System Styles. You can view these default styles in the Assets library/Assets panel, as shown in Figure 7–12.

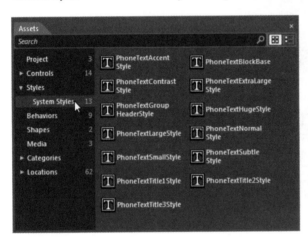

Figure 7–12. *The Windows Phone System Styles*

When you are designing your UI, you can connect these styles to controls using the Properties panel, as already explained in Chapter 5. Or, more simply, select a style from the System Styles category of the Assets library and drop it on your artboard (go ahead and try to drag a few style objects onto the ContentPanel Grid object and see the end result, but delete the items once you are finished).

Creating a List-Details View with the Data Panel

At this point you can use just about any number of techniques shown in this book to create your user interface. Here, we will build an example application that uses a variety of techniques, including working with the Data panel, creating a custom template, and building a simple animation.[9]

First, we want to import the `PurchaseOrder` and `PurchaseOrders` classes created in Chapter 6, by using Project ➤ Add Existing Item.[10] Once you have done so, build your project (via Project ➤ Build Project) and then use the Data panel to create a new object data source that connects to your custom `PurchaseOrders` collection. Recall from Chapter 6 that you can create a new object data source as follows:

1. Click the "Create data source" drop-down button on the Data panel.

2. Select the Create Object Data Source option.

3. Select the class (`PurchaseOrders` in our example) from the resulting dialog box.

Once you have established your object data source, drag the `Description` node in the Data panel to the second `Grid` object (named `ContentPanel` by default). Next, click the Details Mode button located in the upper-left corner of the Data panel, and then select each node under `PurchaseOrders` from the Data panel and drag your selection to the artboard to create a list-details relationship.

Once you are done, the artboard should look similar to Figure 7–13. Feel free to resize, reposition, or configure any of your items (via the Properties panel) as you so choose. Here, I've changed the `Background` property of the `ContentPanel Grid`, and tinkered with the position of my various UI elements.

---

[9] Because these topics have been examined in detail in previous chapters, here I will only give high-level instructions. Please consult the appropriate section of this text for more details.

[10] Recall we used these classes as a source for various data binding operations.

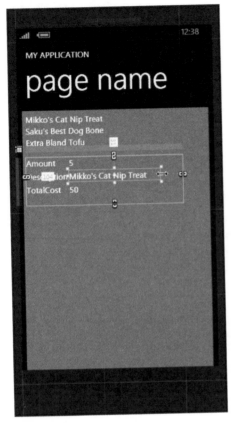

Figure 7–13. *Leveraging the data binding engine*

Creating an Interactive Graphic

Windows Phone 7 projects also support the capability to create interactive graphics; however, your choice of default shapes is somewhat limited. You still can use the Pen and Pencil tools (see Chapter 2) to create freeform data. As well, you can still select from the Rectangle, Line, and Ellipse tools to render basic geometries.[11]

Here, add a new Canvas layout manager to your ContentPanel Grid object. Remember, you can either drag and drop items from the Assets panel (but not via the Assets library) to the Objects and Timeline panel, or select the item and draw it on the artboard via the mouse.[12]

Draw an Ellipse in your new Canvas, and add a new MouseDragElementBehavior object to the Ellipse. To do so, locate this behavior within your Assets panel (under the Behaviors category), select it, and drag it on top of the Ellipse currently on your artboard.

---

[11] See Chapter 2 for details on working with the graphics tools of Expression Blend.

[12] See Chapter 4 for details on working with layout managers and controls in the Blend IDE.

Next, select this new `MouseDragElementBehavior` object in your Objects and Timeline panel, and then check the `ConstrainToParentBounds` property located in the Properties panel (see Figure 7–14).

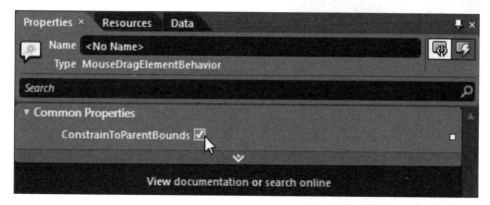

Figure 7–14. *Configuring the MouseDragElementBehavior*

At this point, you can run your application (via F5 or Ctrl+F5). As you can see, the Windows Phone 7 emulator will launch automatically and host your application! You should be able to interact with your graphic via the mouse, and view the details for each list item.

Creating a Custom Control Template

The final concept we will leverage in this application project is the "control template from graphic" trick you learned about in Chapter 5. Be sure to refer to the section "Creating a Stylized Template from a Graphic" in Chapter 5 for full details. Here is a quick refresher to prime the pump.

First, use the Pen tool to create a geometric shape on the lower portion of the `ContentPanel` `Grid` object, and then right-click the item and choose Make Into Control (see Figure 7–15).

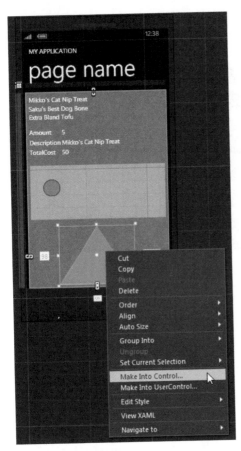

Figure 7–15. *Defining a new template from an existing graphic*

In the resulting Make Into Control dialog box, shown in Figure 7–16, select the Button control type, name it (I named mine `TriangleButton`), and elect to store this new object resource at the application level.

Figure 7–16. *The TriangleButton template*

At this point, your template is displayed within the IDE using the template designer. Recall you are free to change UI properties, add interactivity using the Visual State Manager and States panel (again, see Chapter 5 for details), and so forth. Take a few moments to tinker with this template, and once you are satisfied, rebuild your project via Project ➤ Build Project.

■ **Note** In the downloadable solution for this example, I added a visual state to my template. Specifically, when clicked, the template shrinks by a tiny amount via a graphical transformation. As well, I added a BounceOut easing function to make the template a bit more visually interesting.

Handling the Click Event

The last step for the current project is to handle the Click event for your newly generated Button control (which was at one point a simple triangle graphic). Use the Events button of the Properties panel to handle this event, and then author the following event handler logic:

```
private void Button_Click(object sender,
  System.Windows.RoutedEventArgs e)
{
  MessageBox.Show("Yippy! My phone app rocks!");
}
```

Configuring the Emulator via the Device Panel

Before we run our application, open the `MainPage.xaml` file into the Blend artboard. Take a moment to open the Windows Phone 7 Device panel, via the Window menu of the Blend IDE (see Figure 7–17).

Figure 7–17. *Opening the Device panel*

This (new) area of the Blend IDE, shown in Figure 7–18, allows you to configure a number of settings regarding how your Windows Phone 7 application should be handled when the project is executed. By default, the IDE uses the Windows Phone 7 emulator that was installed with the SDK, but you can also connect to a physical compatible device if you happen to own one. As well, you can use the Device panel to change the display orientation and color theme.

Figure 7–18. *The Device panel allows you to control how your project launches.*

So, with just a few lines of markup (and one line of C# custom code), we have created a simple illustrative phone project that uses data binding, vector graphics, mouse activity, and a custom control template. Figure 7–19 shows the application you've just created running in the emulator (you can see that I changed the text of the `TextBlock` controls in the `TitlePanel` layout manager).

■ **Note** If you position your mouse cursor over the upper-right portion of the emulator, a set of emulator controls appears. You can use these controls to change the orientation of the emulator, zoom the display, and close the emulator itself.

Figure 7–19. Your first Windows Phone 7 application

■ **Source Code** The **FirstPhoneApp** project can be found under the Chapter 7 subdirectory.

Exploring the Panorama Application Project Type

The previous example used the simplest of all Windows Phone 7 templates, the Windows Phone Application project type. By default, this type of application consists of a single UI display page, which you can compose to your liking. Of course, this single page could consist of a layout manager that displays dynamic content (via a set of custom UserControl objects), but generally speaking, all of the UI content is constrained within the device screen.

As an alternative, the Windows Phone 7 platform also provides the *Windows Phone Panorama Application* project type. Panoramic applications offer a unique way to view the UI content of your application, by using a long, horizontal display that extends beyond the confines of the device screen.

When the user uses their finger (for a real phone; you'll use the mouse to achieve a similar effect), the view port will smoothly scroll to the next part of the larger graphic using layered animations, which smoothly pan at different speeds, similar to parallax effects. Figure 7–20 captures the idea behind a panorama display. Notice that the entire display area is quite larger than the view port of the Windows Phone 7 device screen.

Figure 7–20. *A panorama display allows the user to scroll between related views.*

To understand the building blocks of a Windows Phone 7 panorama display, let's modify the starter code generated by the Blend IDE. Using the File ➤ New Project menu option, create a new Windows Phone Panorama application project named **PanoramaDemoApp**.

Examining the Initial Tree of Objects

Take a look at the Objects and Timeline panel and notice that your LayoutRoot Grid object defines a single child object of type Panorama. This object is responsible for smoothly transiting between its set of PanoramaItem objects, of which there are currently two, each of which contains a single ListBox (see Figure 7–21).

Figure 7–21. *The initial tree of objects*

Now, run your application (press F5 or Ctrl+F5). Once the emulator loads, you can use your mouse to "swipe" to the left or right to smoothly scroll the device view port and see the data in each PanoramaItem object. Close the emulator once you have experimented for a moment or two.

Viewing the PanoramaItem Markup

Back in Blend, open the XAML editor for your MainPage.xaml artboard, and notice that each PanoramaItem object has been configured to pull data from a related data template; for example:

```xml
<!--Panorama item one-->
<controls:PanoramaItem Header="first item">
  <!--Double line list with text wrapping-->
  <ListBox ItemsSource="{Binding Items}" Margin="0,0,-12,0">
    <ListBox.ItemTemplate>
      <DataTemplate>
        <StackPanel Margin="0,0,0,17" Width="432">
          <TextBlock Text="{Binding LineOne}" TextWrapping="Wrap"
            Style="{StaticResource PhoneTextExtraLargeStyle}" />
          <TextBlock Text="{Binding LineTwo}" TextWrapping="Wrap"
            Margin="12,-6,12,0"
            Style="{StaticResource PhoneTextSubtleStyle}" />
        </StackPanel>
      </DataTemplate>
    </ListBox.ItemTemplate>
  </ListBox>
</controls:PanoramaItem>
```

■ **Note** These data templates are pulling hard-coded data from the application's ViewModel class. Check out the MainViewModel.cs file located in the ViewModels folder of your project if you are interested.

Each `PanoramaItem` object is contained within a single `Panorama` control that is responsible for the scrolling animation and the task of displaying the correct UI content in the device screen. In addition to maintaining the `PanoramaItem` objects, the `Panorama` control also establishes which image file to use as the background. By default, new Windows Phone Panorama application projects use a sample file added to your project named `PanoramaBackground.png`. As you can see, an `ImageBrush` object (see Chapter 2) is used to paint the surface background:

```
<!--Panorama control-->
<controls:Panorama Title="my application">
  <controls:Panorama.Background>
    <ImageBrush ImageSource="PanoramaBackground.png"/>
  </controls:Panorama.Background>

  <!--PanoramaItem controls listed here -->
  ...
</controls:Panorama>
```

Changing the Panorama Background

Now, let's change the default background image with a custom image file. Select the `Panorama` object in the Objects and Timeline panel, and locate the `Background` property. Figure 7–22 shows the current property value.

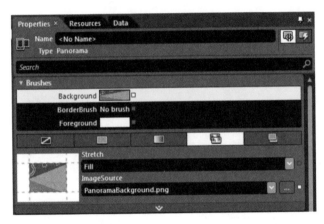

Figure 7–22. *The initial image data for the Panorama object*

Before we can change this background, we need a custom graphic. If you are following along, open a digital image file of your choosing into the Windows Paint application, which you can start by choosing Start ➤ All Programs ➤ Accessories ➤ Paint in Windows. Once you have done so, resize the image to 1024 × 768 pixels in size (which is the size of the original image) by clicking the Resize and Skew button (or simply press the Ctrl+W keyboard shortcut; see Figure 7–23).

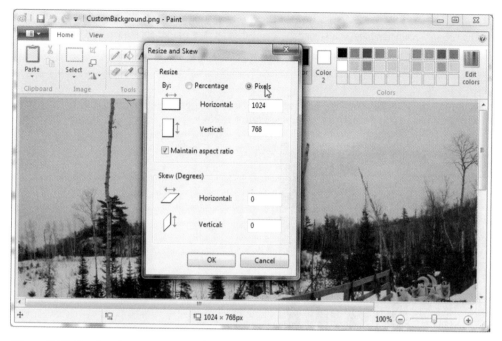

Figure 7–23. Configuring a custom graphic using the Windows Paint program

Save this modified image as a PNG file to a convenient location on your computer's hard drive, via a standard Save operation. Return to Expression Blend, and change the `Background` property of the `Panorama` control to specify your custom graphic, by clicking the ellipsis button next to the `ImageSource` property text area, as shown in Figure 7–24.

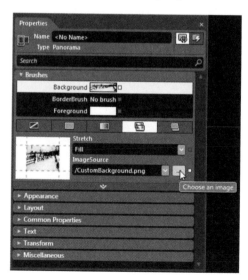

Figure 7–24. Choosing an image for the Panorama object

■ **Note** The IDE will recommend that you embed the image data into the current application as a binary resource. For this example, your choice does not matter.

Now, run your program once again, and you will see *your* graphic scrolling in the background, thanks to the Panorama object (see Figure 7–25).

Figure 7–25. A custom background image!

Adding a New PanoramaItem Object

The final modification we will make to this project is to add a third `PanoramaItem` to the collection maintained by the `Panorama` parent node. The simplest way to do so is to right-click the `Panorama` object in the Objects and Timeline panel and select the Add PanoramaItem menu option, as shown in Figure 7–26.

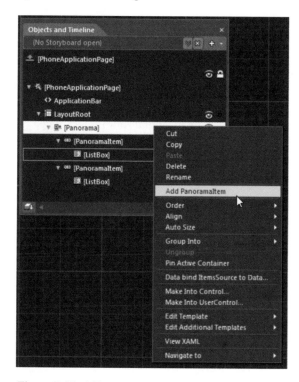

Figure 7–26. *Adding a new PanoramaItem object*

As soon as you activate this menu option, the artboard displays the new `PanoramaItem` object, to which you can add any number of controls, graphics, or what have you. The default XAML is shown here:

```
<controls:PanoramaItem Header="item4">
  <Grid/>
</controls:PanoramaItem>
```

For this sample application, you might want to change just the `Header` property of the `PanoramaItem` object (via the Properties panel) and perhaps add a new control or graphic to the `Grid` layout manager (really, anything will do here; you just need something to test). I opted for a single `Button` control and handled the `Click` event to show a message box via `MessageBox.Show()`. Now, run your program once again, and you should be able to scroll smoothly between each of your `PanoramaItem` objects, while your custom graphic passes in the background.

■ **Source Code** The **PanoramaDemoApp** project can be found under the Chapter 7 subdirectory.

Exploring the Pivot Application Project Type

Another standard navigation system provided by the Windows Phone 7 SDK is termed a *pivot application*. Essentially, this flavor of application is a fancy tab-control system, where the user can switch between different (related) views of information either by clicking the styled tab at the top of the device screen, or via input gestures such as a horizontal pan (tap and drag to the left or right) or a horizontal flick of the finger (tap and quickly swipe your finger to the left or right).

Under this programming model, the root layout manager (a Grid) maintains a Pivot object, which is responsible for maintaining the pages of data, each represented by a PivotItem object. When you create a new Windows Phone Pivot application using the Blend New Project dialog box (I named my project **PivotDemoApp**), the initial tree of objects looks like the example shown in Figure 7–27.

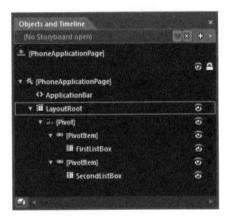

Figure 7–27. *The initial tree of objects for a new pivot application*

The Grid object of each PivotItem maintains a ListBox control that displays hard-coded test data, similar to what you examined in the previous panorama project. Thus, the unmodified artboard for your MainPage.xaml file looks like what you see in Figure 7–28.

Figure 7–28. The initial pivot application artboard

Adding a New PivotItem

Like the `PanoramaItem` object, each `PivotItem` can be configure using the Properties panel. For example, the `Header` property can be used to change the display of each tab. If you wish to modify the starter code, you might begin by selecting each `PivotItem` in your Objects and Timeline panel and changing the `Header` property accordingly. As well, feel free to delete the `ListBox` controls in each sub `Grid` to build any sort of UI you wish (using any of the techniques shown in this text).

If you want to add a new `PivotItem`, simply right-click the `Pivot` node in the Objects and Timeline panel and select Add PivotItem (see Figure 7–29).

Figure 7–29. *Adding a new PivotItem*

Designing the Pivot GUI Layout

At this point, you are free to design your UI in any way you choose. For my new `Pivot` object, I've created a simple "smiley face" graphic using the Ellipse and Pen tools. I then grouped all of these items into a new `Grid` layout manager by selecting (via a Shift+right-click) each part of the graphic on the artboard and activating the Group Info menu option, as shown in Figure 7–30.

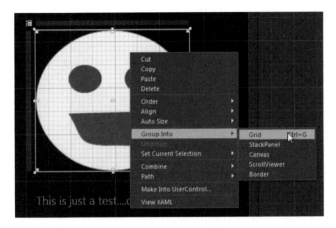

Figure 7–30. *Designing the layout of the new page of data*

Once you have grouped your items, name the new `Grid` object `mrHappyGrid` by using the Properties panel; we will interact with this layout manager using the `ControlStoryboardAction` behavior in just a moment. As you can also see in Figure 7–30, I added a simple `TextBlock` control to the parent `Grid` that displays some basic informational text (specifically, "This is just a test....only a test").

Transforming the Grid

Let's use the Blend Animation editor to create a new storyboard object to transform our layout manager and the contained graphics. Chapter 3 provides detailed information regarding the Blend animation editor, but here is a brief overview of the steps I took for the current example (of course, feel free to animate your `Grid` in any way you choose):

1. Click the New Storyboard button in the Objects and Timeline panel and name the storyboard `FlipHappyDude`.

2. Select the `mrHappyGrid` layout manager in the Objects and Timeline panel.

3. Using the animation timeline, add two keyframes, at the zero-second marker and two-second marker (using the "gray egg" button).

4. Locate the Transform section of the Properties panel and change the X and Y values of the Rotation Projection transformation to the value 360 (see Figure 7–31).

5. Select the last keyframe in the animation editor and use the Properties panel to apply an easing effect. (I've opted for an Elastic Out effect, as shown in Figure 7–32, but you can apply whatever you like.)

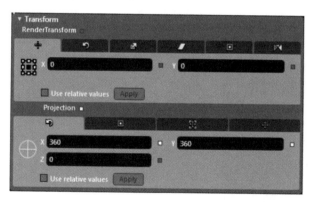

Figure 7–31. *The storyboard will transform the Grid object using a transformation.*

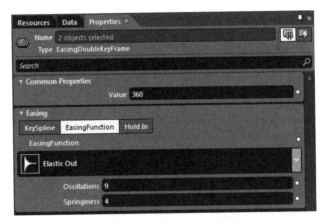

Figure 7–32. The final keyframe of the storyboard will use an animation easing effect.

Click the Play button of the Objects and Timeline animation editor to test the transformation of your `Grid` and the contained graphical data. Once you are happy with the results, move to the next section.

Controlling the Storyboard in XAML

While we could author code to start our storyboard, let's leverage one of Expression Blend's built-in behavior objects. Locate the `ControlStoryboardAction` behavior[13] within your Assets panel (see Figure 7–33) and drag this item onto the `mrHappyGrid` object found in your Objects and Timeline panel.

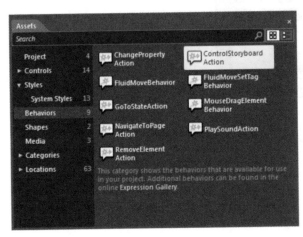

Figure 7–33. Adding a new ControlStoryboardAction behavior to the mrHappyGrid

---

[13] This behavior was first examined in detail in Chapter 3.

Select the new `ControlStoryboardAction` node in the Objects and Timeline panel, and use the Properties panel to click the "Artboard element picker" tool of the `SourceName` property (see Figure 7–34).

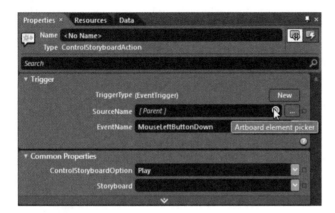

Figure 7–34. *Use the artboard element picker to select the element that will interact with the storyboard.*

Next, click one part of your graphic (I'm clicking the left eyeball). Pick an initiating event via the `EventName` property and fitting values for the `ControlStoryboardOption` and `Storyboard` properties. In Figure 7–35, you can see that I have configured my behavior to start the `FlipHappyDude` storyboard when the left mouse button clicks in the proper `Ellipse` object.

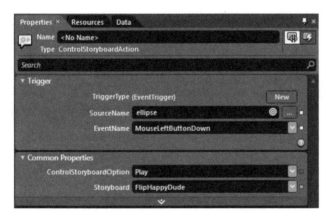

Figure 7–35. *The fully configured ControlStoryboardAction behavior*

And there you have it! If you run your program, you can click the header of your new tab (or slide the pages via the mouse), click the left eyeball of your happy dude, and see the result of your animation.

■ **Source Code** The **PivotDemoApp** project can be found under the Chapter 7 subdirectory.

Learning More About Windows Phone Development

Although the examples shown in this chapter were quite simple, collectively they illustrated a number of useful Blend (and Silverlight) programming techniques. While this is true, I am sure you would like to see some more real-world samples, which of course entails real-world code and, sadly, is outside the scope of this text. However, to wrap up this chapter, allow me to point out a few useful online resources you might wish to consult to learn more about building Silverlight applications for Windows Phone 7.

MSDN Windows Phone Sample Projects

MSDN online (http://msdn.microsoft.com) is your first stop to learn more about Windows Phone 7 development. Once you navigate to this main page, you will find a graphical link to the online development portal; simply click the phone icon (see Figure 7–36).

Figure 7–36. MSDN online is your entry point to Windows Phone 7 development.

Scroll down to the bottom of the resulting the web page and click the link to the Windows Phone Development MSDN web portal (see Figure 7–37).

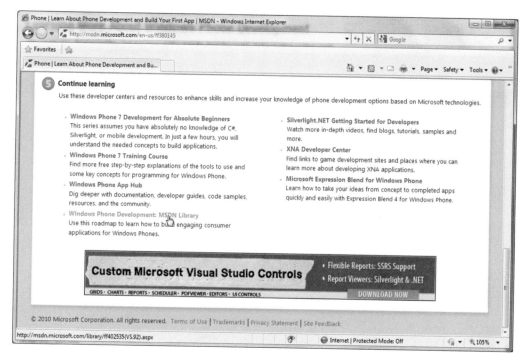

Figure 7–37. Linking to the Windows Phone Development MSDN online documentation

As shown in Figure 7–38, by clicking the Code Samples link, you will find a number of sample projects to download, which you can then load into either Expression Blend or Visual Studio 2010.

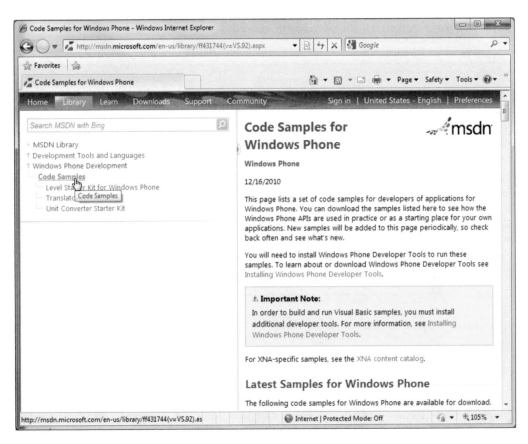

Figure 7–38. Sample projects!

In the code download folder for this text, I've included one illustrative sample project from this site, the Weather Forecast Sample project. If you open and run this project, you'll see that the Windows Phone emulator fires up and allows you to check out the weather conditions in a variety of cities, via an XML web service (I modified the starter code, to show the current weather in my fair city of Minneapolis, Minnesota; Figure 7–39).

Figure 7–39. *Quite warm for this time of year, thank you very much!*

■ **Source Code** The modified Weather Forecast Sample project (**WeatherForecast**) can be found under the Chapter 7 subdirectory.

The App Hub Web Site

Another useful web site for Windows Phone 7 (and XNA Game Studio for that matter) development is the App Hub site, located at http://create.msdn.com. Here, you will find a very rich community of independent developers who are interested in creating, uploading, and (hopefully) profiting from Windows Phone 7 and Xbox 360 applications. You can create a custom profile, and for a modest price ($99 USD each year), you can post applications to Windows Phone Marketplace or Xbox LIVE Marketplace. In addition, this site provides even more sample projects, online video tutorials, and various promotional events. Figure 7–40 shows the home page for the App Hub web site.

Figure 7–40. *The App Hub site is another useful Windows Phone 7 site.*

Well, that should leave you in a good position for further exploration if you are interested. With this, you are ready to move onto the final chapter of this book and learn about the role of *SketchFlow*. As you are about to see, the Expression Blend IDE has a whole other set of tools that enables rapid prototyping of WPF and Silverlight applications.

Summary

This chapter was rather short and sweet, given that the process of using Blend to construct user interfaces for a Windows Phone 7 device is just about identical to the process of building UIs for a WPF or Silverlight application. Nevertheless, this chapter did point out a few important aspects of developing for this handheld device.

After you were shown how to install the necessary Windows Phone 7 SDK, you examined the various project templates provided by Expression Blend. The first example had you construct a simple Windows Phone application project, where you were able to use the same data binding, animation, and control template techniques illustrated in previous chapters.

You then learned about two standard Windows Phone 7 application navigational schemes, specifically a panorama application and a pivot application. You created each of these project types, and modified the default markup and code (just a bit) to get a taste of building these particular UIs. The chapter wrapped up by pointing out a few useful online resources, where you are free to dive into numerous aspects of programming a full-featured Windows Phone 7 application.

■ ■ ■

CHAPTER 8

Prototyping with SketchFlow

The Ultimate edition of Expression Studio ships with a component of the Blend IDE that is called *SketchFlow*. This aspect of Blend allows you to generate interactive prototypes for WPF- and Silverlight-based projects. This chapter begins with a brief introduction to the role of prototypes in the context of a software development life cycle. You then will learn the key aspects of designing with SketchFlow by dissecting an Expression Blend sample application.

The reminder of this chapter will walk you through the process of creating a working prototype for a typical online shopping application using Silverlight.[1] You will learn how to work with various SketchFlow-specific tools (such as the Map panel), see how you can generate project requirements from a SketchFlow prototype, and discover how you can use the prototype as the starting point for the envisioned production software.

■ **Note** Remember, SketchFlow is available only in Expression Studio Ultimate Edition. Thankfully, the free 60-day trial edition of Expression Studio Ultimate also includes the SketchFlow prototyping environment.

The Role of Application Prototyping

Every once in a while, a software developer may have the chance to build a small-scale application, such as a simple in-house configuration tool, or maybe a personal pet project such as a video game, digital media organizer, or contact manager. Such projects are often created by a single individual and typically do not require any sort of formal vision statement, data dictionary, requirements document, or other artifacts. Rather, a programmer might dive right in using the "code and fix" model of software development (e.g., just start hacking away and fix errors as they come up).

Thankfully, most programmers (and management teams) understand just how important a formal software development project life cycle truly is when attempting to create a large-scale coding effort. For example, many companies use the Rational Unified Process (RUP) model, which formalizes key iterative phases that a software project typically goes through during the development effort. RUP (and many other software development methodologies) encourages the early use of *application prototyping* to mock up how the finished product might look and feel.

---

[1] As you might suspect, the process of working with SketchFlow to prototype a WPF application is more or less identical to that of prototyping a Silverlight application.

Building application prototypes is a great way to get feedback from the client and user base regarding how the user interface should be laid out and how well they like basic functionality of the software. Over the years, developers have whipped together prototypes using various tools, including the GUI designers of Visual Studio. While this is all well and good, application prototyping has a few "hidden dangers," some of which you may have experienced first-hand. For example:

- The client might easily consider the prototype to be the "real" software, as the UI often very closely resembles a functional user interface on the surface.

- Prototypes are often discarded once client feedback has been obtained. This requires developers to essentially re-create the same UI in a new production-level project.

- Many prototyping tools have neither a way to incorporate client feedback directly into the project itself nor a way to generate formal documentation from these initial design notes.

- If a client wanted to make their own modifications to the prototype, they not only would need the prototyping tool installed on their machine, but would also need to be comfortable using the tool itself.[2]

Ideally, there would be a tool that could be used to build a UI that *clearly* shows the user that this is an initial crack at a working solution, rather than a feature-complete product. As well, this tool would enable clients to directly embed their personal comments into the project, and enable developers to use this data when generating documentation. Even better, the tool would enable the client to view and interact with the prototype, even if they do not own a copy of the prototyping tool used to create it. Fortunately, the Expression Blend IDE provides these very features (as well as many other features) via SketchFlow.

The Role of SketchFlow

As the name suggests, SketchFlow is a set of tools that allows a development team, and the software stakeholders, to rough out a software prototype for WPF- and Silverlight-based applications.

When you create a WPF or Silverlight SketchFlow project, you will be happy to see that you can construct the UI using the same tools and techniques you've learned over the course of this book. For example, you can add controls to the artboard via the Assets library, configure their look and feel via the Properties panel, incorporate graphics and animations into the prototype, and whatnot.

What makes SketchFlow unique is that it also provides some additional tools that allow you to map out and iterate the flow of an application UI and the transition from one "application state" to another. For example, using the SketchFlow Map panel, you can quickly create a set of UI layouts that will be displayed as an end user activates menu items, or advances through a wizard-like layout via Next and Previous buttons. As well, you can easily change the sequence of these transitions as you elicit feedback from the client.

In addition to mapping out your application's UI flow, Microsoft has intentionally designed the default style of each control for a SketchFlow project to look simple and generic, to clearly denote that this is a *prototype* rather than the final software product. Using the intrinsic Sketch Styles, Sketch Shapes, and Mockup Controls (all of which can be found in the Assets library), you can design a UI that will help focus the user on the overall flow and layout of your

---

[2] And if this tool happens to be Visual Studio, I am sure you can image how intimidating this IDE would be to a nontechnical individual.

prototype, rather than on minutia-level details such as font sizes, background and foreground colors, and so forth. Figure 8–1 shows a WPF `Window` constructed using several of these SketchFlow styles and Mockup Controls.

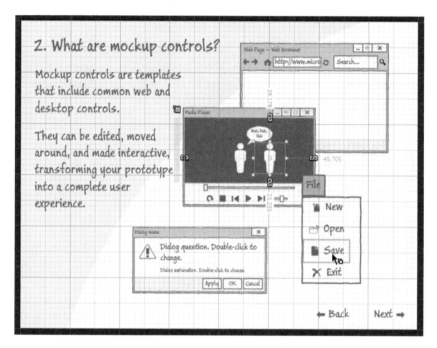

Figure 8–1. *SketchFlow styles are intentionally simple, to help keep your client focused on the big picture.*

Another excellent aspect of SketchFlow is that it is built in such a way that client feedback can be gathered and recorded while you are in the process of building and demonstrating the prototype. While you can certainly use Expression Blend annotations to do so (see Chapter 1), the SketchFlow Player provides a more powerful and interactive way to record user feedback. Clients can test multiple scenarios and provide comments for the development team by annotating their experience as they navigate the prototype. You'll see this tool in action a bit later in this chapter.

■ **Note** The SketchFlow Player is freely distributable and does not require a full installation of Expression Blend on the client machine. Furthermore, the SketchFlow Player is able to host WPF desktop prototypes as well as Silverlight web-centric prototypes.

As you work through this chapter, you will also see that a SketchFlow prototype can be used as a starting point for the "real" application you intend to develop. Thus, instead of throwing away your prototype, you can replace the SketchFlow styles as you see fit, scrape out all user feedback into a dedicated Microsoft Word document, and start to elaborate the details of your software project. Always remember that SketchFlow prototypes are not just simple drawings, but are fully functioning WPF or Silverlight applications. If you make the necessary modifications, you can convert your prototype into a production project and continue to build out the final application.

■ **Note** Although not covered in this chapter, be aware that the SketchFlow Player can be configured to automatically upload client and developer annotations to a named SharePoint server. This can be very useful when you wish to store important data in a centralized location. Search for the topic "Publish to SharePoint" in the Blend User Guide for more information.

Examining a SketchFlow Prototype Sample

Now that you have a better idea of what you can do with SketchFlow, let's look at this tool in action. However, we will not be building a custom prototype just yet. Rather, I'd like to offer a guided tour of some key SketchFlow tools via one of the built-in sample projects. In this way, you can see SketchFlow working in the context of a larger, real-world example. To begin, launch Expression Blend and choose Help ➤ Welcome Screen. Click the Samples tab, and select the **PCGamingSketch** sample project[3] (see Figure 8–2).

---

[3] I encourage you to explore each of the SketchFlow example projects (which have the word "Mockup" or "Sketch" in their name) while reading this chapter. They showcase the usefulness of this technology quite well.

Figure 8–2. Blend ships with several SketchFlow sample projects.

Exploring the SketchFlow Map Panel

Once the sample project has loaded, you will notice a new aspect of the Blend IDE, the
SketchFlow *Map panel*, which can be found docked below the artboard. Figure 8–3 shows the
content of the Map panel for the **PCGamingSketch** application.

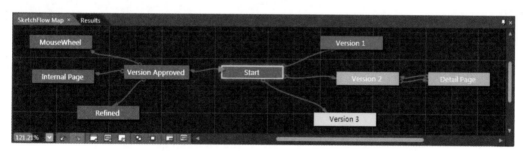

Figure 8–3. The SketchFlow Map panel

The SketchFlow Map panel is a graphic editor in which you can define the structure, flow,
navigation, and composition of an application. Unlike the artboard (which allows you to focus
on the UI content for a given `Window` or `UserControl`), the SketchFlow Map panel allows you to
focus on the overall structure of the application.

Each node in the SketchFlow Map panel represents a specific "screen" in your prototype,
which typically correlates to a specific `Window` or `UserControl`. In the **PCGamingSketch** project,

note that the set of leftmost nodes are named `MouseWheel`, `Internal Page`, `Refined`, and `Version Approved`.

Collectively, these nodes represent a set of screens that shows the final approved UI of the initial GUI mockups for the application.[4] If you double-click any of these nodes (or any node in the SketchFlow map for that matter), you will open the related screen within the artboard for viewing. Figure 8–4 shows the screen representing the `Version Approved` node.

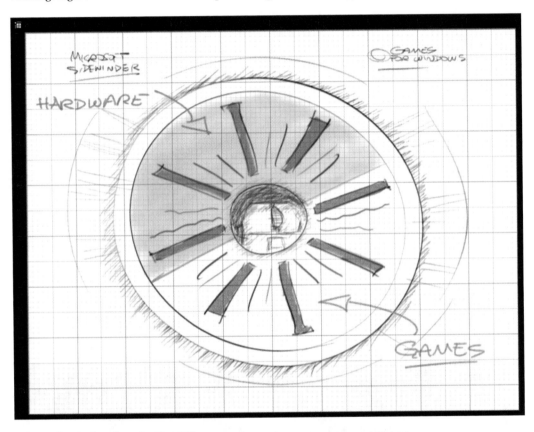

Figure 8–4. *Each node in the SketchFlow map represents a screen in your prototype.*

If you were to open the `Refined` node (see Figure 8–5), you would find a formal UI layout constructed using the expected Silverlight layout managers (such as the `Grid` and `Canvas`) and numerous UI controls (`TextBlock`, custom components, etc.) and Blend behaviors.

---

[4] Most of these screens, however, were not created via the SketchFlow control set. Rather, the screens use several `Image` controls used to hold `*.png` and `*.jpg` files that were created in a dedicated graphics tool such as Expression Design or Adobe Illustrator.

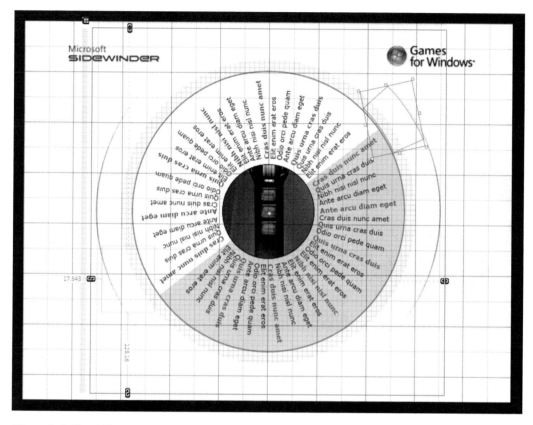

Figure 8–5. SketchFlow prototypes can contain screens created with "real" components.

Notice that the nodes under discussion in the SketchFlow Map panel shown in Figure 8–3 are connected using directional arrows. For example, the `Version Approved` node has three outbound arrows that connect to the three leftmost nodes. These relationships represent the basic flow of the UI, and can be tested using the SketchFlow Player's navigation editor (you will see how to do so later in the chapter).

As well, you can use various navigation behaviors to quickly model this flow via user interactions (button clicks, menu selections, etc.). Best of all, these navigational relationships can be changed on-the-fly using the Blend IDE. You will learn how to use the navigation editors as you progress through this chapter.

The Role of the Start Node

Note that the `Start` node in Figure 8–3 has a specific green arrow icon on the upper left of the node (shown in detail in Figure 8–6). When you create a new SketchFlow application, you will automatically be provided with an initial screen node marked in this manner, which represents the initial screen to show upon prototype startup.

Figure 8–6. *The Start node is marked with a green arrow icon.*

If you wish to change the startup node, you simply need to right-click any node and select the "Set as Start" menu option. Once you have done so, the green arrow icon moves to the selected node. By way of example, assign the `Version Approved` node to be the startup item (see Figure 8–7), but be sure to reset the `Start` node as the startup node before moving on.

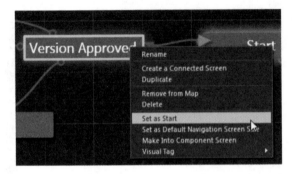

Figure 8–7. *Changing the Start node*

Color Coding

You can assign a unique color to each node, which can be useful when you wish to identify visually a set of related nodes. A node's color has no impact on the runtime behavior of your prototype; however, by default, the color blue represents a Navigation screen and the color green represents what is termed a Component screen. As explained later in this chapter, Component screens allow you to define a chunk of repeatable UI content (such as a navigation menu) that will be displayed on multiple Navigation screens.

You can change the color of any node by hovering your mouse cursor over it to expose the node editing tray, as shown in Figure 8–8, and then using the integrated color editor on the far right.

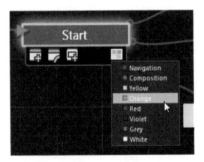

Figure 8–8. *Each node can be assigned an arbitrary color.*

Creating and Connecting Nodes

The node editor can also be used to create new connected nodes (and the related screen), connect the current node to an existing screen, and create a new Component screen (again, more details regarding Component screens are provided later in the chapter). If you hover your mouse cursor over any node, you will see that each of these options is mapped to a specific button (see Figure 8–9).

Figure 8–9. *The node editor can be used to create and connect nodes.*

■ **Note** It is possible for two nodes to navigate to each other in a bidirectional manner, as is the case for the Version 2 and Detail Page nodes on the SketchFlow Map panel shown earlier in Figure 8–3.

As you are adding and connecting nodes via the Map panel, you will certainly need to change the UI flow during the prototyping process. To do so, simply click either end of the arrow on the connection line and relocate it accordingly. When doing so, be mindful of the fact that the "circle end" of a connection represents a screen that is navigated *from*, while the "arrow end" of a connection represents a screen navigated *to*.

■ **Note** On a related note, you can right-click any connection line and choose Delete to delete it completely.

Assigning Transition Styles

Once you have a set of connected nodes, you have the option of assigning transition effects, which can provide a bit of eye candy to the prototyping effort. Before we execute this prototype, right-click the connection between the Start and Version 1 nodes and select a transition style of your liking (see Figure 8–10). Repeat the process for the other three outbound connections of the Start node.

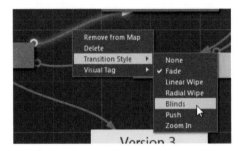

Figure 8–10. *You can assign various transition effects to any screen navigation.*

Testing the Prototype with the SketchFlow Player

Let's test the prototype using the SketchFlow Player by pressing Ctrl+F5 (or F5). Since **PCGamingSketch** is a Silverlight prototype, the Player will load into your browser, at which point the node marked as Start will appear as the active screen.

Navigating Screens

The left side of the Player UI consists of two key areas. On the top, you find the navigation pane, which can be used to display screens based on the connections and transitions you created back on the SketchFlow Map panel. Recall that from the Start screen, the user can navigate to four outbound screens (Version 1, Version 2, Version 3, and Approved Version). If you wish, you can also click the Map button to view a read-only display of this same map, as shown in Figure 8–11.

Figure 8–11. *The SketchFlow Player in action*

Take a few moments to explore by clicking each screen link in the Navigate panel or, alternatively, by clicking a node in the SketchFlow map.

■ **Note** You can click the Home button located above the Navigate panel to return to the prototype's Start screen.

Once you are on a given screen, you may notice that the Navigate panel displays some transition behaviors or animation sequences that can be started when clicked. These effects were added to the screen using various SketchFlow behavior objects and custom animations, using the Blend IDE. Figure 8–12 shows the transitions found on the Version 2 screen.

Figure 8–12. Screens that use behaviors and animations can be triggered using the Navigate panel.

■ **Note** Any animation or behavior can also be executed by clicking the portion of a screen that uses it (as defined in the prototype). For example, if you click the `Version 2` node, you can use the vertical Games or Hardware area of the `Version 2` screen to see the same animation sequence.

Adding Feedback to the Prototype

Remember, the main purpose of the SketchFlow Player is to provide a way for clients to provide useful feedback on the prototype. To facilitate this, clients can use the My Feedback panel mounted on the lower left of the Player, shown in Figure 8–13. Here, a client can enter textual input, as well as select from a set of drawing tools (ink, highlighting, and eraser) to draw and annotate portions of a screen. Furthermore, when the client selects the ink or highlight tool, they have various options to configure the size and color of the visual annotation. Notice in Figure 8–13 my large orange arrow, and how it is possible to dock and undock the SketchFlow Player tool panel.

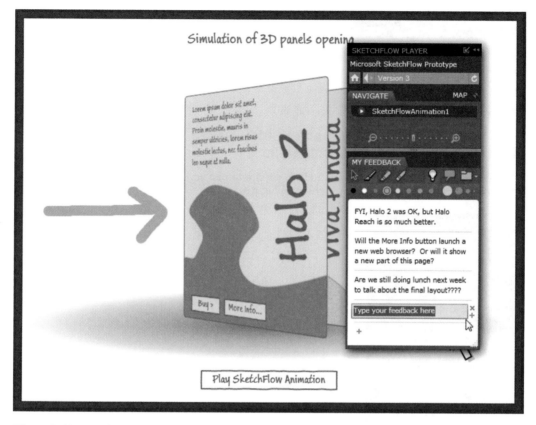

Figure 8–13. *Providing textual and graphical feedback*

Exporting Prototype Feedback

Client feedback is recorded automatically, and you can leave both text and ink feedback on each screen throughout the prototype. When you have finished adding feedback, you can save the feedback via the Folder button on the My Feedback panel. For this example, use the text and graphics tools to author some basic feedback on a few screens, similar to what you saw in Figure 8–13. Once you have done so, elect to export your feedback (see Figure 8–14) as a file named **MyFeedback**,[5] saved to your Windows desktop (or wherever you choose).

---

[5] Prototype feedback files are saved with a `*.feedback` file extension. Not surprisingly, this file contains an XML description of the data.

Figure 8–14. *Exporting feedback to an external file*

Importing Client Feedback into Blend

To view feedback back within the Blend IDE, you first must activate the SketchFlow Feedback option, located under the Window menu (see Figure 8–15).

Figure 8–15. *Client feedback can be viewed in Blend, once you enable the option.*

Once you have done so, the SketchFlow Feedback panel becomes active within the IDE. To add the XML data to this viewer (and thus on the artboard for a given page), click the plus button, click Add (see Figure 8–16), and locate the exported file.

Figure 8–16. *You can add *.feedback files via the SketchFlow Feedback panel.*

At this point, you will see rendered feedback appear on the artboard. The SketchFlow Map panel will display a light-bulb icon for each screen that contains client input. Figure 8–17 illustrates this, and also shows that the user text annotations can be seen using the SketchFlow Feedback panel (docked on the left side of this particular screenshot).

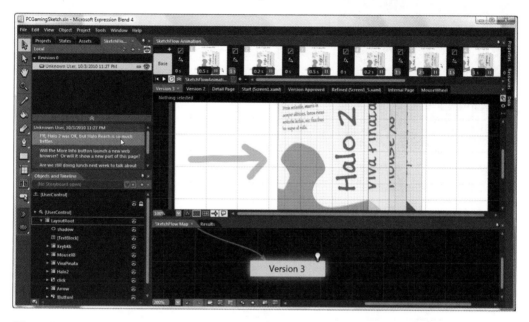

Figure 8–17. *Viewing client feedback within a Blend project*

Generating Microsoft Word Documentation

Before we turn our attention to creating a prototype from the ground up, I'd like to point out that the Blend SketchFlow IDE also provides a way to generate a Microsoft Word document that captures each screen and stakeholder annotation in the prototype. As you might guess, this document can serve as a beginning template for the product documentation. Generating this documentation is no more complex than choosing File ➤ Export to Microsoft Word (see Figure 8–18).

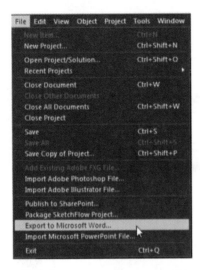

Figure 8–18. Exporting a SketchFlow prototype to Microsoft Word

SketchFlow ships with its own Microsoft Word template; however, as you can see in Figure 8–19, you are free to specify a custom template, as well as configure a few additional options (most importantly, including stakeholder feedback).

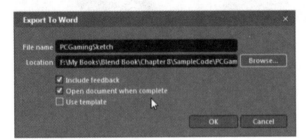

Figure 8–19. Configuring export options

Once you have exported the data, flesh out the full description as you see fit.

■ **Source Code** The modified **PCGamingSketch** project can be found under the Chapter 8 subdirectory.

Creating a Silverlight Prototype

Let's create a custom SketchFlow prototype application that models some typical screens one might see in an online sales application. Begin by creating a new Silverlight SketchFlow application project named **OnlineStoreApp** from the New Project dialog box (see Figure 8–20).

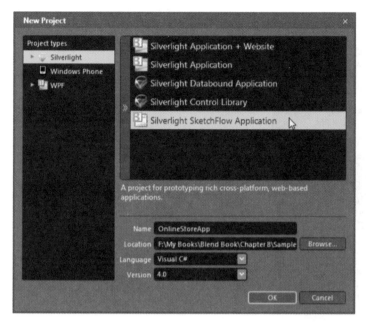

Figure 8–20. *Creating a new Silverlight SketchFlow application project*

Upon creation, you will see that you are provided with a single screen (named `Screen 1`) configured as the prototype startup screen. Using the SketchFlow Map panel, rename this initial screen to **MainScreen** by right-clicking the map node and selecting the Rename option (see Figure 8–21).

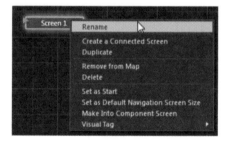

Figure 8–21. *Renaming screen nodes*

Examining the Project Files

A SketchFlow project is organized a bit differently than a typical WPF or Silverlight application. Activate your Projects panel and notice that your Solution contains two related projects, as shown in Figure 8–22. The first project (named **OnlineStoreApp**) contains the overall application logic represented by the `App.xaml` and `App.xaml.cs` source files. In addition, this project references several Expression Blend SketchFlow assemblies (all prefixed with `Microsoft.Expression`).

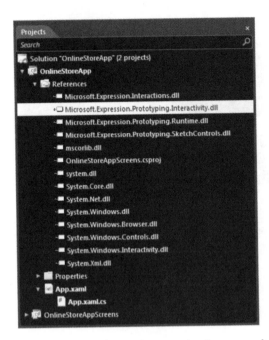

Figure 8–22. *The first project contains the core application logic.*

The second project (named **OnlineStoreAppScreens**) references the same prototyping assemblies, and will be the location for each screen you add to your application via the Map panel. Currently, you can see your `MainScreen` present and accounted for. In addition, this project will define a few additional items of interest:

- `SketchStyles.xaml`: This XAML file contains styles for the SketchFlow UI elements.

- `Sketch.Flow`: This XML document contains data that is read by the Map panel to display nodes and their connections. You typically do not need to directly edit this file as it will be updated automatically when working with the SketchFlow IDE.

- *Fonts folder*: This folder stores a few SketchFlow font types used by the supplied styles.

Figure 8–23 shows the breakdown of this second project.

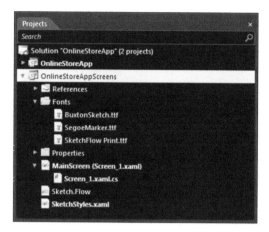

Figure 8–23. *The second project stores screens, styles, fonts, and mapping data.*

The SketchFlow styles will be applied automatically when you use the prototyping controls in your Assets library. However, if you are curious, you can view each of these styles by examining the Resources panel. As described in Chapter 2, you can double-click any of these resources to edit and modify their appearance; however, for this example I'll assume you will not be doing so.

Creating a Component Screen

When building a WPF or Silverlight application, a common practice is to create a navigation system that is common to a set of related `Window`/`UserControl` objects. This navigation system could be a traditional menu system, or you could create a custom navigation scheme consisting of animated graphics, a tree-like navigation system, or what have you.

SketchFlow *Component screens* allow you to define such a navigation scheme, which can then be connected to any screen that requires the navigation UI. Internally, a Component screen is a custom `UserControl` object (for both WPF- and Silverlight-based projects) that is added to the layout manager of the item making use of it. This is certainly a useful approach, because if you wish to change the look and feel of your navigation system, you only need to change the Component screen UI, and the remaining nodes will be refreshed upon the next build.

■ **Note** Component screens are not limited to navigation systems. You can use Component screens to model any sort of repeatable UI content (footers on the bottom of a window, a set of common input controls, or what have you).

To begin, hover your mouse cursor over the `MainScreen` node to open the node configuration tool, and click the "Create and insert a Component screen" button (see Figure 8–24).

Figure 8–24. *Creating a new Component screen*

Once you have done so, rename the new node to **NavSystem** and drag it away from the `MainScreen` node for readability purposes. Notice that Component screen nodes are green in color by default, and use a green connection arrow that points *from* the Component screen node *to* the screen that uses it (see Figure 8–25).

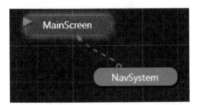

Figure 8–25. *The Component screen is connected to your main screen.*

If you were to view the artboard for the `MainScreen` node, you would see that the navigation system is present on the designer. If you view the underlying XAML, shown next, you can see that the `UserControl` that represents this navigation system has been added to the root layout manager (your exact markup may differ from what you see here, based on how you positioned your items):

```
<Grid x:Name="LayoutRoot" Background="White">
  <local:NavSystem HorizontalAlignment="Left" VerticalAlignment="Top"
      d:IsPrototypingComposition="True" Margin="83,8,0,0"/>
</Grid>
```

Now, ensure that the artboard for your `NavSystem` screen is active in the IDE. Using the Assets library, locate the Sketch Styles section under the Styles category. Here, you will find each of the prototyping controls typically used in a SketchFlow project. While you are free to use any control in your prototype, recall that one benefit of these SketchFlow styled controls is that they clearly inform the client that this is a *working prototype*, not a production-ready UI. Figure 8–26 shows these styled components (all of which have a `-Sketch` suffix).

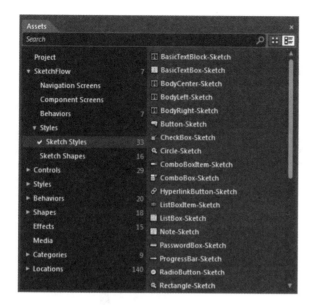

Figure 8–26. *The Sketch Styles controls*

Also notice that the Styles category of the Assets library provides a set of styled shapes (`Ellipse`, `Rectangle`, etc.) that also support this prototype look and feel. Because these styles have been set to be the default,[6] they will automatically be used when you select an item on the Tools panel. This all being the case, use the Tools panel (or Assets library) to build a navigation system (in the `NavSystem` screen, remember) consisting of three colored geometries of your liking. In Figure 8–27, you can see I've opted to arrange some star-shaped geometries and some informational `TextBox` controls.

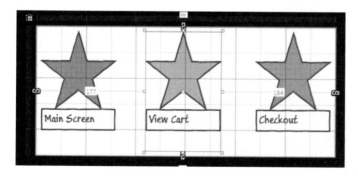

Figure 8–27. *A simple navigation system*

The goal is to allow the user to navigate to any of three specific screens by clicking the corresponding star shape. While you could handle various mouse events and code for such situations, the Blend IDE can automate this process using various SketchFlow behaviors. Before

---

[6] See Chapter 5 for details on setting a default style.

we build these additional screens, complete your `MainScreen` by adding a simple blurb of descriptive text via the `TextBlock` control (see Figure 8–28).

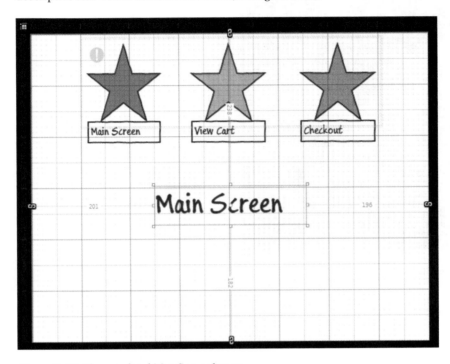

Figure 8–28. *The completed MainScreen layout*

Creating Additional Screens

Using the Map panel, create two new screens by right-clicking any blank area and selecting the Create a Screen menu option (see Figure 8–29). Rename these screens to **ViewCart** and **Checkout** when you are finished.

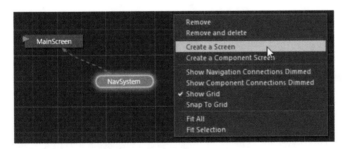

Figure 8–29. *Two currently unconnected screens*

For the `ViewCart` screen, add some descriptive text, a placeholder graphic (I just used a large gray square) for the shopping cart, and a `Button` control. Figure 8–30 shows a possible layout.

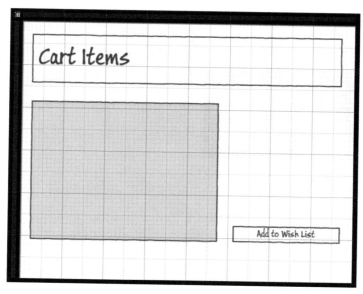

Figure 8–30. *The layout of the ViewCart screen*

The `Checkout` screen, shown in Figure 8–31, is equally simple.

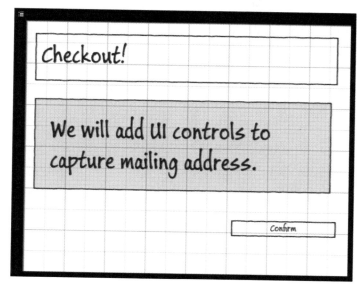

Figure 8–31. *The layout of the Checkout screen*

Replicating the Navigation GUI

Now that the ViewCart and Checkout screens are stubbed out, we can add the navigation GUI to each layout manager. To do so, we can use the Map panel once again. When you wish to connect a Component screen to a new node, use your mouse to drag the *entire* Component screen node on top of the screen that will make use of it. Once you are done, you should find that your prototype map looks similar to Figure 8–32.

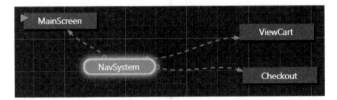

Figure 8–32. *The updated prototype map*

■ **Note** Of course, now that each screen contains the navigation system, you will certainly want to tweak the size and layout of your existing components on the Checkout and ViewCart screens.

Using the NavigateToScreenAction Behavior

We now need to account for the fact that the correct screen must launch when the user clicks a given star graphic. The simplest way to do so is to leverage some unique context menus of the artboard. Open the artboard for your NavSystem component and right-click the star that will take the user to the main screen. From there, use the "Navigate to" menu to select the MainScreen option (see Figure 8–33). Repeat this process to map the remaining star graphics to their respective screens.

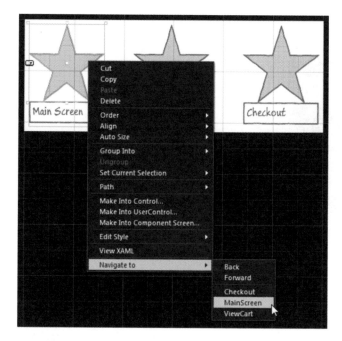

Figure 8–33. *Connecting elements to a navigation action*

So, what exactly did the IDE do based on these actions? If you look at the XAML for your NavSystem component, you will see that the navigation logic is handled by a SketchFlow behavior object named NavigateToScreenAction. For example, here is the markup for the first star graphic:

```
<ed:RegularPolygon ed:GeometryEffect.GeometryEffect="Sketch"
    InnerRadius="0.47211" PointCount="5" Stretch="Fill"
    Stroke="{StaticResource BaseBorder-Sketch}"
    StrokeThickness="2"
    UseLayoutRounding="False" Height="120" Fill="#FFCE8585">
  <i:Interaction.Triggers>
    <i:EventTrigger EventName="MouseLeftButtonDown">
      <pi:NavigateToScreenAction
          TargetScreen="OnlineStoreAppScreens.Screen_1"/>
    </i:EventTrigger>
  </i:Interaction.Triggers>
</ed:RegularPolygon>
```

You could also connect elements to navigation actions by manually adding a SketchFlow behavior from the Assets library (located under the Behaviors section of the SketchFlow category), and then configuring it with the Blend Properties window.

On a related note, like any element on the artboard, you can locate these behaviors from the Objects and Timeline panel and then change the settings. For example, consider Figure 8–34, which shows you how the NavigateToScreenAction behavior was configured by default. Here you can see that the MouseLeftButtonDown trigger is the instigating event; however, you are free to change these default settings as you see fit.

Figure 8–34. You can use the Properties panel to configure any SketchFlow behavior.

■ **Note** Details of each of the SketchFlow behaviors can be found within the Blend User Guide. Simply look up the topic "Working with SketchFlow Behaviors." Not too surprisingly, SketchFlow behaviors work similarly (if not identically) to the behavior objects you have used throughout this text.

In any case, at this point you will find that your Map panel not only shows that each screen is using the Component screen, but also shows the navigation connection lines (see Figure 8–35).

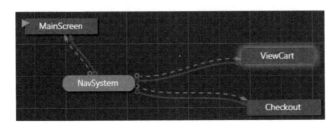

Figure 8–35. The final navigation map

Now, launch your prototype by pressing the F5 key! You should find that you can navigate between each screen by using the SketchFlow Player Navigate panel and by clicking a given star graphic (see Figure 8–36).

Figure 8–36. *Our prototype in action*

Incorporating Prototype Interactivity

The SketchFlow IDE provides a lightweight version of the Blend animation editor (described in Chapter 3) that you can use to incorporate interactivity into a given prototype. You can certainly use the full-blown animation editor for a prototype created with SketchFlow, but the SketchFlow Animation panel is tightly integrated into the prototyping environment and is therefore somewhat easier to use.

For our example, let's add some interactivity to the Checkout screen. Begin by opening the Checkout artboard and adding a Block Arrow Up - Sketch shape to the existing layout (see Figure 8–37), which will represent (in exaggerated terms) the mouse cursor of the user.

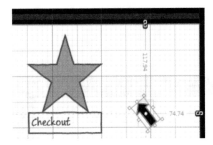

Figure 8–37. Adding a mock mouse cursor

Next, locate the SketchFlow Animation panel, which is mounted (by default) at the top of the designer (see Figure 8–38).

Figure 8–38. The SketchFlow Animation panel

Click the + button (also shown in Figure 8–38) to create a new SketchFlow animation storyboard. Once you have done so, you are free to rename this animation storyboard to a more fitting description (such as "AnimateArrow") via the drop-down list at the bottom of the SketchFlow Animation panel.

In any case, similar to the full-blown Blend animation editor (see Chapter 3), the lightweight SketchFlow Animation panel is based on changing the properties of UI elements in a keyframe-by-keyframe manner. To add new keyframes to the animation sequence, select a given keyframe in the SketchFlow Animation panel and click the + button (or use the – button to delete the selected keyframe) located in the upper right of a selected keyframe (see Figure 8–39).

Figure 8–39. Adding new keyframes

Add three keyframes to your current storyboard. The general idea here is that you can select any keyframe in the SketchFlow Animation panel and make changes to the storyboard as you see fit. As you make changes to the artboard of a selected keyframe, the data will be recorded, again, much like the full-blown Blend animation editor.

In Figure 8–40, you can see I have added three keyframes to this animation. The first keyframe simply captures the default screen state with the mock mouse cursor in the default position. Now, if you select the second keyframe, you can relocate the mock mouse cursor over the `Button` control. Next, select the third and final keyframe, which changes the `Button`'s background color to signify the idea of clicking the button.

Figure 8–40. *Changing the "mouse icon" across three frames*

In you wish to get even fancier with your animation prototype, you can also configure a given keyframe with animation easing effects (bounce, spring, etc.) and transitions (fade, wave, and so forth). If you wish to add an easing effect to a given keyframe, click the button pointed to in Figure 8–41.

Figure 8–41. *Each keyframe can be configured using easing functions.*

On a related note, if you wish to add a transition for a given keyframe, click the *fx* button pointed to in Figure 8–42.

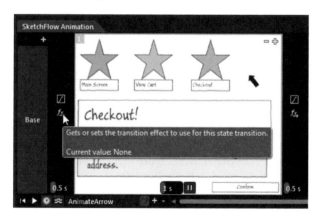

Figure 8–42. *Each keyframe can also be configured using transitions.*

Using the PlaySketchFlowAnimationAction Behavior

After you have tinkered with various animation effects, run the prototype once again. If you navigate to the Checkout screen, you will be able to play your animation via the Navigate panel (see Figure 8–43).

Figure 8–43. *Playing your prototype animation*

If you would like to start this animation (or any animation) via user input, you can use the PlaySketchFlowAnimationAction behavior, located within the SketchFlow ➤ Behaviors section of your Assets library. Select this element, and drag it to the Objects and Timeline panel, specifically on top of the [UserControl] tree node for the Checkout screen (see Figure 8–44).

Figure 8–44. *Adding a PlaySketchFlowAnimationAction element*

Next, select this element and use your Properties panel to configure a trigger for the Loaded event that starts the animation in question (see Figure 8–45). If you run your prototype and navigate to the Checkout screen, you should now see your animation start automatically.

Figure 8–45. Configuring the PlaySketchFlowAnimationAction element

So there you have it! You have completed your simple prototype using various aspects of the SketchFlow IDE. To be sure, our example prototype is much simpler than you would find in a real-world software project, but you now should feel comfortable with the overall process of generating prototypes with SketchFlow, capturing user comments, exporting these comments to a dedicated Microsoft Word document, and managing the SketchFlow Map panel.

■ **Note** Try to add some user comments to your prototype, as you did when examining the **PCGamingSketch** sample project earlier in this chapter. As well, try to generate a Word document based on your prototype (again, as you did earlier in the chapter).

To complete this chapter, I'd like to close by examining the following topics:

- How to package a prototype to use the standalone SketchFlow Player
- How to use your prototype as the starting point for a production application

---

■ **Source Code** The **OnelineStoreApp** project can be found under the Chapter 8 subdirectory.

Packaging a Prototype

As you were working through this chapter, you saw that when you run your SketchFlow prototype using the Blend IDE, the SketchFlow Player launches automatically. However, what are you to do when you want to ship the prototype to an interested stakeholder who does *not* have a copy of Expression Blend? Thankfully, it is possible to create a standalone player that can be sent to a client, by choosing File ➤ Package SketchFlow Project (see Figure 8–46).

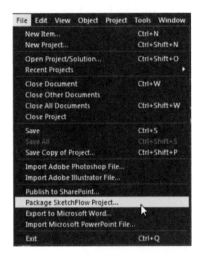

Figure 8–46. *Packaging your prototype to use the standalone SketchFlow Player*

Once you activate this menu option, simply specify a location and name for the generated player. Since we have created a Silverlight SketchFlow prototype, our generated file set consists of an HTML file and an XAP binary (as well as an ASP.NET web page). The client can simply double-click the HTML file to view the prototype in their browser (see Figure 8–47).

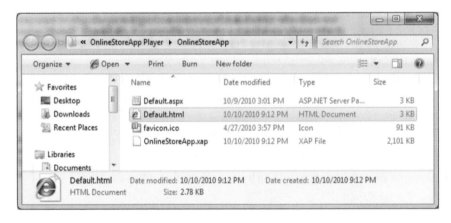

Figure 8–47. *The generated file set*

■ **Note** If you were to package a WPF SketchFlow prototype, you would end up with an executable file (*.exe).

Moving a Prototype into Production

Once you have gathered and documented client feedback, modified your prototype accordingly, and received any necessary sign-off, you can convert your SketchFlow prototype to a "real" Silverlight or WPF project. The first step is to save a copy of the current prototype via the File ➤ Save Copy of Project menu option.

Now, assuming you are operating on a copy of the current prototype, be aware that there is no automatic "Convert prototype to Production" button in the Blend IDE. When you wish to strip out the prototyping-centric aspects of the code base, you must do so manually. While the Blend User Guide provides step-by-step details of how to convert Silverlight and WPF prototypes to a production body of code, I'll describe the process here.

■ **Note** The process of converting a WPF prototype is a tad different from the process of converting a Silverlight prototype. Look up the topic "Convert into a production project" within the Blend User Guide for details.

Modifying the *csproj Files

The first step you must take to transform a prototype to a production application is to modify the `*.csproj` file of the project in your solution that contains your `App.xaml` and `App.xaml.cs` files. For the current example, this would be the `OnlineStoreApp.csproj` file. Open this file in a simple text editor, and completely delete the following XML elements:[7]

```
<ExpressionBlendPrototypingEnabled>
    False
</ExpressionBlendPrototypingEnabled>
<ExpressionBlendPrototypeHarness>
    True
</ExpressionBlendPrototypeHarness>
```

Once you have done so, save and close the file. Next, open the `*.csproj` file for the secondary project of your solution that contains the prototype screens (in this example, that would be `OnlineStoreAppScreens.csproj`). Locate and delete these same two lines of XML, and once again save the file when you are finished.

Updating the Root Project Assembly References

Open your modified solution back into the Blend IDE, and use the Projects tab to delete the `Microsoft.Expression.Prototyping.Runtime.dll` assembly (see Figure 8–48).

---

[7] I would have to guess that forthcoming versions of Expression Blend and Visual Studio will change the underlying schema of the C# project file. Here I am assuming you are using Blend 4/Visual Studio 2010, so consult the Blend User Guide if this is not the case.

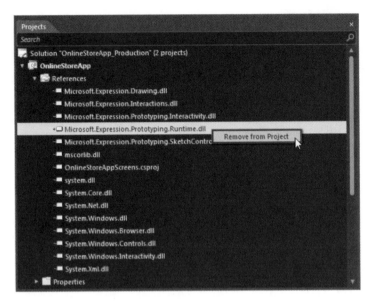

Figure 8–48. Deleting the SketchFlow runtime library

Next, using the Project ➤ Add Reference menu option of the Blend IDE, add a reference to the Silverlight 4.0 `System.Windows.Controls.Navigation.dll` assembly, located by default under the `C:\Program Files\Microsoft SDKs\Silverlight\v4.0\Libraries\Client` folder.

■ **Note** If you are using a 64-bit version of Windows, use **Program Files(x86)** in your path rather than `Program Files`.

As you might be guessing, delete the `Microsoft.Expression.Prototyping.Runtime.dll` assembly and add the `System.Windows.Controls.Navigation.dll` assembly for the secondary project (again, `OnlineStoreAppScreens.csproj` in this example) as well.

Modifying the App.xaml.cs File

Open your `App.xaml.cs` file for editing. You'll notice an assembly-level attribute at the top of your code file right before the declaration of the `App` class type. Comment out this line completely:

```
[assembly: Microsoft.Expression.Prototyping.Services.SketchFlowLibraries
  ("OnlineStoreApp.Screens")]
```

As well, locate the current implementation of the `Startup` event handler. Delete (or comment out) the current line of code, and replace it with the following, substituting the name of the XAML file (`Screen_1.xaml`) with whichever XAML resource you wish to display upon startup. As well, change the name of the project (`/OnlineStoreApp.Screens`) with the name of the project containing the individual screens.

```
private void Application_Startup(object sender, StartupEventArgs e)
{
  // Comment out the current line!
  // this.RootVisual = new
  // Microsoft.Expression.Prototyping.Workspace.PlayerWindow();

  // Add this code statement, but update the XAML file name!
  this.RootVisual = new Frame()
  {
  Source = new
    Uri("/OnlineStoreApp.Screens;component/Screen_1.xaml",
      UriKind.Relative)
  };
}
```

■ **Note** The name to specify after the / of the Uri string is the same name that was passed into the SketchFlowLibraries attribute you commented out.

At this point, your project will no longer use the SketchFlow Player. Thus, if you run the Silverlight application, it will load into a browser just like a typical XAP file would do. The only other bit of cleanup you might wish to do is to swap out the SketchFlow styles with your own; however, I'll leave that detail to you! Figure 8–49 shows the final result of our transformation.

Figure 8–49. Our XAP file

■ **Source Code** The **OnlineStoreApp_Production** project can be found under the Chapter 8 subdirectory.

Summary

The final chapter of this book explored the role of SketchFlow in the software development life cycle. As mentioned at the opening of this chapter, the process of creating application prototypes is a very common task during the process of gathering user requirements. Expression Blend allows you to build interactive prototypes for WPF and Silverlight applications that can be modified and extended on-the-fly, ideally when you are working with the software stakeholders directly.

As you have seen, a SketchFlow solution consists of two projects, one of which contains all of the screens (e.g., Window and UserControl objects) that can be strung together using the Map panel. Recall that a Component screen allows you to build a custom UserControl that can be incorporated into any number of additional screens. In our examples, we used Component screens to model a simple navigation system; however, you can use Component screens for any sort of repeatable UI. This chapter also examined the "micro" animation editor of a SketchFlow solution, as well as a number of useful behaviors that can simplify the prototyping process.

You also learned how to use the SketchFlow Player to capture user feedback. Last but certainly not least, this chapter also illustrated how a SketchFlow solution can be used as a starting point for formal requirements documentation as well as starter code for the production application.

Index

■■■

■ Special Characters and Numbers

+Event button, 104
+Property button, 104
2D graphical transformations, 64–69
  applying
    in code, 68–69
    at design time, 66–68
  building initial UI, 64–66
2D images, mapping to 3D planes, 70–71
3D graphical transformations, 69–81
  in Silverlight, 79–81
  in WPF, 69–79
    controlling camera in code, 77
    mapping 2D images to 3D planes, 70–71
    using light editors, 75–77
    using properties panel, 73–74
    Viewport3D object in, 71–75
    ZAM 3D tool, 78–79
3D planes, mapping 2D images to, 70–71

■ A

ActivateStateAction behavior object, 157
Add Collection Property option, 264
Add Complex Property option, 264
Add New Item menu option, 228
Add new value converter button, 230
Add PanoramaItem option, 299
Add PivotItem option, 301
Add Simple Property option, 264

advanced configuration options, viewing of, 19
Advanced options button
  Brushes editor, 81
  Properties panel, 224, 233
AI (artificial intelligence) algorithms, 277
Alignment Settings, 143
All Properties setting, Create Data Binding dialog box, 229
Ambient node, 75
AmbientContainer, 75
Amount property, 243, 247, 259
AnimateCircle storyboard, 90, 97, 117
animating layout, for Pivot Application Project, 303–304
AnimationEasingEffects project, 110
animations, 87–118
  and behavior objects in XAML, 115–118
    ControlStoryboardAction behavior object, 116–118
    SimpleBlendAnimations example, 115–116
  in code, 96–98
  effects in, 109–114
    applying, 111–113
    executing at runtime, 114
    initial layout, 110
    initial storyboards, 111
    KeySpline editor, 113
  with Objects and Timeline panel, 16
  services for, 87–88
  testing, 94
  viewing markup for, 94

workspace layout for, 88–96
adding keyframes, 91–92
capturing object property changes, 92–93
creating storyboards, 89–90
managing storyboards, 90–91
storyboard properties, 94–95
testing animations, 94
viewing markup for, 94
zooming timeline editor, 96
WPF specific techniques, 98–109
motion paths, 98–102
using triggers, 102–109
annotations, viewing of, 12–13
App class type, 344
App Hub web site, resources for Windows Phone 7 development, 309–310
Appearance category, 18
Appearance editor, modifying shapes using, 40–41
Application location, 82
Approved Version screen, 320
App.xaml.cs files, modifying, 344–346
artboard, 93, 284–285
artboard controls, 11
Artboard element picker tool, 305
artboard tools, changing Viewport3D object using, 74–75
artboard visual designer, 10–14
annotations on, viewing, 12–13
rendering effects, 12
UI positioning with snap grid, 12
XAML from, 14
zooming in, 11–12
ASP.NET framework, 34
ASP.NET web page, 342
assembly references, updating, 343–344
Assets library, 25–28
Shapes section, 39–40
Tools panel, 22, 121
Assets panel, 28, 54
AutoReverse check box, Properties panel, 95
AutoReverse property, 125

B

Background color, 144
Background property, 85, 186, 287, 296–297
Background value, 186
backgrounds, for Panorama Application Project, 296–298
BasedOn attribute, 168
BasicControlStyle, 165–167
bear Canvas, 62
bear_paper.design file, 56
bear_paper.xaml data, 60
bear_paper.xaml file, 57, 61–62
Begin() method, 97
<BeginStoryboard> element, 102
behavior objects, 156–162
MouseDragElementBehavior object, 159–162
in XAML, 115–118
ControlStoryboardAction behavior object, 116–118
SimpleBlendAnimations example, 115–116
behaviors, 87
Behaviors category, 26
BigGreenButton style, 168
binDebug directory, 156
Binding markup extension, 227, 232, 242
Blend Animation editor, 303
Blend New Project dialog box, 270, 300
Blend Panorama Application Project. See Panorama Application Project
Blend Pivot Application Project. See Pivot Application Project
Blend Projects Templates, for Windows Phone 7, 280–283
Blend Properties panel, 182
Blend User Guide, for Windows Phone 7 SDK, 282–283
Blend Welcome Screen, 5, 8
Blend Windows Phone Application Project. See Windows Phone Application Project
Blend Windows Phone project templates, 281
BlendControlContent project, 124
Block Arrow Up - Sketch shape, 337
block elements, 148

Blocks (Collection) property, 151

Border class, 134

Border container, 160

Border control, 161

Border object, 160

BorderBrush property, 160

BorderThickness property, 160

Bounce Out effect, 112

BounceOut function, 291

bound data contexts, viewing, 242

brush animation, 87

brush-centric properties, 42

brush options

    Gradient, 43–46

    No brush, 42

    Solid-color, 42–43

    Tile, 46–47

Brushes category, 18

Brushes editor, 42–47

    brush-centric properties, 42

    Gradient brush option, 43–46

    No brush option, 42

    Solid-color brush option, 42–43

    Tile brush option, 46–47

btnClickMe object, 98

btnFlip buttton, 65

btnMyButton, artboard, 102

btnRotate button, 65

btnSkew button, 65

btnStartAnimation UI element, 97

btnStartAnimation_Click() method, 116

BubbleThoughtsControl, 213, 215

BulletDecorator control, 134

<Button> element, 181, 186, 197

Button node, 117

Button objects, 65, 101, 104, 125, 136, 163, 186

Button template, 193

Button type, 172, 195

buttonCaption element, 185

ButtonChrome, 191

Button.Click trigger, 106

Button's background color, 339

buttonSurface element, 185

<Button.Template> scope, 182

byte data type, 229

■ C

C alphabetic token, 37

C# code file, 60, 77

C# code snippets, 21

C# (*.cs) code file, 20

Calendar control, 172

CallMethodAction behavior object, 157

Callout class, 40

CalloutStyle class, 41

camera

    controlling in code, 77

    using properties panel for, 73–74

Camera Orbit tool, 72–73

Canvas layout mode, 141

Canvas panel, 141

Canvas Silverlight layout manager, 316

Categories category, 26

cells, adding items to in Grid object, 142–144

Center Point option, 67

CenterOfRotationX property, 79

CenterOfRotationY property, 79

CenterOfRotationZ property, 79

ChangeCamera() method, 77

ChangeColor method, 146

ChangePropertyAction behavior object, 157

CheckBox control, 222

Checkout artboard, 337

Checkout screen, 332–334, 337, 340

circleOne object, 98

cleanup, of projects, 243

Click event, 65, 68, 97, 101, 117, 126, 160, 182, 245, 299

Click handler logic, 116

Click handler value, 115–116

code editors, integrated, 20–21

code files, 19

Code Samples link, 307

Collection node, 263

CollectionDataContext project, 236, 246

collections

    binding

        to DataGrid controls, 243–244

to ListBox controls, 240–243
creating custom, 236–237
manipulating at runtime, 245–246
color coding, of nodes, 318
Color Eyedropper tool, 43
ColorSwatchSL application, 10
ColorSwatchSL project, 9, 13, 20–22, 28
columns, defining in Grid object, 142
Combine menu, 48
Common Properties category, 18
CommonStates group, 209, 215
Component screen, 319, 329–332, 334
Component screen button, 329
Component screen nodes, 330
composite content
creating, 124–125
handling events with, 126
reusing, 127
configuration options, viewing, 19
ConstrainToParentBounds property, 159, 289
Content properties, 65, 102, 129–130, 150, 165, 186, 223, 227, 233
Content value, 186
ContentControl derived class, 24
ContentPanel Grid object, 286–289
<ContentPresenter> class, 187
Control class, 167
control content model, and composite content, 123–127
creating, 124–125
handling events with, 126
reusing, 127
control templates
containing data templates, 251–254
creating, 189–203
copying default templates, 189–193
creating templates from graphics, 193–203
role of in styles, 180–189
<ContentPresenter> class, 187
creating, 181–182
incorporating templates, 187–189
incorporating visual cues using WPF triggers, 184–185

storing templates as resources, 182–184
TemplateBinding markup extension, 186
in Windows Phone Application Project, from graphics, 289–291
control-to-control data binding, 222–227
creating new, 224–226
example UI, 222–224
viewing generated markup, 227
Controls category, 26
ControlStoryboardAction, 87, 96, 98, 115–118, 157, 305
ControlStoryboardOption property, 305
<ControlTemplate> element, 179–180, 188, 191–192, 197
<ControlTemplate.Triggers> collection, 185
ControlToControlBinding project, 222
Convert() method, 228–229
Convert to Motion Path option, Path menu, 99
Convert to New Resource option, Blend Properties panel, 182
ConvertBack() method, 228
Converter attribute, 232
converting data types
conversion classes, 229–232
creating, 228–229
viewing generated markup, 232
overview, 227–228
Copy menu option, 62
core namespaces, for Windows Phone 7, 280
Create a Screen menu option, Map panel, 332
Create Annotation menu option, Tools menu, 13
Create Data Binding dialog box, 225, 229
Create data source button, 237
Create Empty option, 173
Ctrl+W keyboard shortcut, 296
currentSelection Label control, 131
Cursor property, 161
custom collections, creating, 236–237
custom content, adding to sample project, 23

custom states, 211–212
custom templates, creating, 181–182
customListBox control, 128

■ D

data binding, 221–272
    control-to-control, 222–227
        creating new data bindings,
            224–226
        example UI, 222–224
        viewing generated markup, 227
    converting data types, 227–232
        creating custom conversion classes,
            228–229
        selecting conversion classes,
            229–232
    data templates, 246–254
        composite UI elements for, 248–251
        control templates containing,
            251–254
        editing, 247
        styling items in, 247
    Databound project templates, 270–272
    ListDetailsDataBinding project,
        259–262
        creating UI, 259–261
        viewing generated markup, 261–262
    modalities, 232–236
        data binding options, 233–234
        two-way data binds, 234–236
    to non-UI objects, 236–246
        collections, 240–244
        creating custom collections,
            236–237
        and Data panel, 237–240
        properties, 243
        at runtime, 245–246
    for relational database data, 269–270
    role of, 222
    sample data for, 262–269
        adding properties, 264–265
        binding to UI, 266–268
        inserting into project, 263
        modifying types and values,
            265–266

WPF XML data source, 255–258
    adding, 256–257
    and XPath expressions, 257–258
Data Binding menu option, 224
Data Context attribute, 241–243
    data template markup, 242
    quick project cleanup, 243
    viewing bound data context, 242
Data Context tab, 225
Data Field tab, 225
Data panel
    defining data sources with, 237–240
    in Windows Phone Application Project,
        287
Data property, 37
data templates, 246–254
    composite UI elements for, 248–251
    control templates containing, 251–254
    editing, 247
    markup for, 242
    styling items in, 247
data types
    converting, 227–232
        creating custom conversion classes,
            228–229
        selecting conversion classes,
            229–232
    modifying, 265–266
data values, modifying, 265–266
databases, data binding for relational,
    269–270
Databound project template, 270–272
DataContext attribute, 241
DataContext property, 262
DataGrid control, 236–237, 243–244, 266
<DataGridTextColumn> element, 244
DataStateBahavior behavior object, 157
days.hours:minutes:seconds.fractionalSec
    onds format, 95
default templates, copying, 189–193
    examining, 191–192
    style properties, 190–191
    using tools to edit, 192–193
Default.html test page, 7
Description node, 259, 261, 287
Description property, 243, 259, 261

design patterns, MVVM, 270–272

Design tool, 2–3

Design workspace, 31

destination control property, 221

Detail Page node, 319

Details Mode button, 259, 287

Details mode, Data panel, 240, 258–259, 261, 266

Device panel, 292

Direct Selection tool, 24, 35–36

Directional subnode, DirectionalContainer node, 76

DirectionalContainer, 75

display, zooming of, 11–12

Divide option, Combine menu option, 48

DockPanel, 133

Document APIs
    overview, 147–148
    WPF
        block elements, 148
        document layout managers, 148–149

document layout managers, 148–149

Document property, 151

documentation
    generating, 325–326
    for Windows Phone 7 SDK, 278–280

documentation system, 31–32

double data type, 227

double member variables, 80

DoubleToSolidBrushConverter class, 228, 231

Download the Developer Tools link, 274

drawing tools, 34–47
    Appearance editor, 40–41
    Brushes editor, 42–47
    Ellipse Tool, 38
    Line Tool, 38
    Pen, 36–38
    Pencil, 35
    Rectangle Tool, 38
    Shapes section, 39–40

DropAndBounceBall storyboard, Objects and Timeline panel, 111–113

DropShadowEffect object, 55

DynamicResource markup extension, 166

■ E

easing effects, 87

EasingFunction button, 111

EasingFunction drop-down list box, 111

Edit a Copy option, 172

Edit Additional Templates menu option, 252

Edit Current option, 172

Edit resource button, 247

Edit sample values button, 265

Edit Sample Values dialog box, 266

effects
    in animations, 109–114
        applying, 111–113
        executing at runtime, 114
        initial layout, 110
        initial storyboards, 111
        KeySpline editor, 113
    transition, defining, 209–210

Effects category, 26

Elastic Out effect, 303

Element Property Binding option, 233

Element Property tab, Create Data Binding dialog box, 225, 229

ElementName attribute, 227

Ellipse component, 204

Ellipse controls, 129–130

Ellipse element, 98

Ellipse from the Objects and Timeline panel, 132

Ellipse object, 92–94, 111, 288, 305

Ellipse style shape, 331

Ellipse Tool, 22, 34, 38, 49, 302

EllipseGeometry class, 37

ellipsis button, 297

emulators
    Windows Phone 7, 276
    for Windows Phone Application Project, configuring with Device panel, 292

Encoder tool, 2

event handling, with composite content, 126

Event trigger, 104

EventName property, 117, 305

Events button, Properties panel, 28, 97, 114

Events editor, 28–30

events, handling in Windows Phone Application Project, 291

<EventTrigger> elements, 94, 109

Exclude Overlap option, Combine menu option, 48

Export All button, 60

Export menu option, File menu, 59

Export to Microsoft Word option, File menu, 325

Expression Blend web site, 274

Expression Blend Welcome Screen, 5

Expression Design, 56–64
    exporting images from, 56–60
    for Silverlight applications, 60–64
        event handling, 62–64
        importing data, 61–62

Extensible Application Markup Language. *See* XAML

Extensible Markup Language data sources. *See* XML data sources

■ F

fancyShape name object, 50

Fill object, 42

Fill property, 42–43, 45, 47, 81, 93, 129, 186, 202, 229

Fill value, 206

finding objects, in Properties panel, 17

firstButtonStyle, 173–175

FirstName property, 263

<FixedDocument> element, 148

Flip value, 65

FlipHappyDude storyboard, 305

FlowDocument, 148, 154

FlowDocument containers, 151–155

<FlowDocument> element, 148

FlowDocumentPageViewer, 148–149

FlowDocumentReader, 148, 151, 153–154

FlowDocumentScrollViewer, 148–149

FluidMoveBehavior behavior object, 157

Focused states group, 210, 215

Folder button, My Feedback panel, 323

Fonts folder, 328

Foreground property, 247

Format drop-down list box, 59

FunWithDataTemplates project, 246, 254

FunWithSampleData project, 263

fx button, 339

■ G

Geometries, 47–50

GoToState() method, 216

GoToStateAction behavior object, 157, 216–217

Gradient brush option, 43–46

graphical user interface. *See* GUI

graphics
    templates from, 193–203
        adding interactivity, 200–203
        creating initial graphics, 194
        extracting, 194–197
        ListBox control, 197–200
        WPF triggers, 203
    in Windows Phone Application Project
        control templates from, 289–291
        interactive, 288–289

gray egg button, 303

Grid control, 182

Grid layout manager, 165, 241

Grid layout mode, 141

Grid object, 141–147
    adding items to cells, 142–144
    adding nested StackPanel objects, 145–147
    creating splitters, 144–145
    defining rows and columns, 142

Grid Silverlight layout manager, 316

grids, for Pivot Application Project, transforming, 303–304

GridSplitter control, creating, 144–145

Group Info option, 302

GUI (graphical user interface)
    controls, 119–123
        details of, 121–123
        locating, 120–121
        with Properties panel, 121
    replicating navigation, 334

■ H

Handled property, 126

handling events, in Windows Phone Application Project, 291
Header element, 140
Header properties, 93, 107, 140, 301
Height property, 224, 226–227, 229
Help tab, Expression Blend Welcome Screen, 5
Horizontal value, 129
HorizontalAlignment property, Properties panel, 182, 199
HotItem node, 258
hours:minutes:seconds format, 95
HoverAndCrashPoly storyboard, 111
HTML file, 342

■ I, J

IDE (integrated development environment), 1–32
  artboard visual designer, 10–14
    annotations, 12–13
    rendering effects, 12
    UI positioning with snap grid, 12
    XAML from, 14
    zooming in, 11–12
  code editor in, 20–21
  documentation in, 31–32
  Events editor, 28–30
  Microsoft Expression products, 1–5
    Design tool, 2–3
    Encoder tool, 2
    SketchFlow tool, 4–5
    Web tool, 2
  Objects and Timeline panel, 15–16
  options for, 30–31
  Project panel, 19–20
  Properties panel, 16–19
    categories of, 18
    finding objects in, 17
    naming objects in, 17
    options for, 19
  Results panel, 21
  sample project, 9–10
  templates for, 5–8
    Silverlight, 7–8
    Windows Phone, 8
    WPF, 6–7

Tools panel, 22–28
  adding custom content, 23
  Assets library, 25–28
  Assets panel, 25–28
  Direct Selection tool, 24
  Pan tool, 24–25
  Selection tool, 24
  Zoom tool, 24–25
Image control, 70–71, 80, 98
ImageBrush object, 71, 296
images, exporting, 56–60
ImageSource property, 46, 297
incoming object, 51
InkCanvas control, 143–145
inline elements, 148
InnerRadius property, 40
InsideAShape method, 50–51
Install Now button, Windows Phone 7 SDK, 275
integrated code editor, 20–21
integrated development environment. *See* IDE
interactive graphics, in Windows Phone Application Project, 288–289
interactivity, adding to control templates, 253–254
Internal Page node, 316
Intersect option, Combine menu option, 48
Inventory.xml file, 255–256
InvokeCommandAction behavior object, 157
IsChecked property, CheckBox control, 222
IsMouseOver property, 185, 202
IsPressed property, 203
items control model, 128–132
  adding ListBoxItem objects, 128–130
  finding current selection, 131
  Tag property, 132
  viewing XAML, 130
Items editor, 199
<ItemsPresenter> element, 198
ItemsSource property, 241, 257
ItemTemplate property, 241–242, 257
IValueConverter interface, 228

■ K

keyframes
    adding, 91–92
    SketchFlow Animation panel, 338
KeySpline editor, 113

■ L

Label controls, 77, 120, 128–129, 145, 227, 233, 248–249, 259
LastName property, 263, 266
Layout category, 18
layout manager, 132–138
    Border class, 134
    BulletDecorator control, 134
    changing type, 134–135
    document, 148–149
    nested, 135
    TabControl class, 134
    and UI elements
        grouping of, 136–137
        repositioning of, 137–138
        ungrouping of, 136–137
Layout section, Properties panel, 93
layout systems, creating tabbed, 138–141
LayoutRoot Grid object, 88, 285, 294
LayoutRoot node, 23, 27, 64
LayoutRoot object, 27, 62
Layouts, 302–304
LayoutTransform options, 67–68
LayoutTransform property, 68
leftEye object, 62
LeftMouseButtonDown event, 29
lighting effects, changing using light editors, 75–77
Line Tool, 22, 34, 38
LinearGradientBrush object, 46
Linked In node, 177
Linked To node, 177
List block, 154
List Mode button, 259
List mode, Data panel, 240, 243, 266
ListBox controls, 197–200
    binding collections to, 240–243
    binding properties to, 243
    Tool panel, 120

ListBox member, 131
ListBoxItem objects, 128–130, 132, 199
ListBoxItemSendToTop.cs code file, 20
ListBox's SelectionChanged event, 131
ListDetailsDataBinding project, 259–262
    creating UI, 259–261
    viewing generated markup, 261–262
Loaded even, 340
Loaded event, 102
Locations category, 26
LookDirection property, 77

■ M

M alphabetic token, 37
MainControl.xaml file, 10
mainMenuSystem, 106
MainPage.xaml file, 62, 115–116, 292, 295, 300
MainScreen node, 329–330
MainScreen option, 334
MainViewModel.cs file, 295
MainWindow.xaml file, 22, 101, 197, 229, 246, 256–257
Make Into Control dialog box, 290
Make Into Control option, 289
Manage Help Settings tool, 278–279
Margin properties, 141, 145
Margin Settings, 143
Margin value, 65
markup
    for data templates, 242
    for PanoramaItem objects, 295–296
    viewing generated, 227–232, 261–262
markup extensions, 186
Maximum property, 223
Media category, 26
Menu control, Assets panel, 106
menu items, assigning triggers to, 108–109
Menu object, 106
menu system, 106–108
MenuItem control, 107
MessageBox.Show() method, 63, 299
Microsoft Expression products, 1–5
    Design tool, 2–3
    Encoder tool, 2

SketchFlow tool, 4–5
Web tool, 2
Microsoft Word, generating documentation, 325–326
Microsoft XNA Game Studio 4.0-and Windows Phone 7 SDK, 276–277
Microsoft.Devices namespace, 280
Microsoft.Devices.Radio namespace, 280
MicrosoftDevices.Sensors namespace, 280
Microsoft.Expression.Drawing.dll library, 40
Microsoft.Expression.Effects.dll .NET assembly named, 56
Microsoft.Expression.Interactivity.dll library, 157
Microsoft.Expression.Media.Effects namespace, 56
Microsoft.Expression.Prototyping.Runtime .dll assembly, 343–344
Microsoft.Phone.Controls namespace, 280
Microsoft.Phone.dll assembly, 280
Microsoft.Phone.Interop.dll assembly, 280
Microsoft.Phone.Notification namespace, 280
Microsoft.Phone.Tasks namespace, 280
Minimum property, 223
Miscellaneous category, 18
mnuFile item, 107
mnuPause menu item, 107
mnuPlay menu item, 107
mnuPlay object,Objects and Timeline panel, 108
mnuStop menu item, 107
Mode attribute, 232, 235
Model node, 74
Model-View-ViewModel (MVVM) design pattern, data binding for, 270–272
ModelContainer node, 74
motion paths, 98–102
MouseDown event, 126, 216
MouseDownState, 216
MouseDragElementBehavior object, 157, 159–162, 288–289
MouseEnter event, 50–51, 217
MouseLeave event, 52
MouseLeftButtonDown event, 29, 63, 114, 335

MouseOverState, 211, 215
MouseWheel node, 316
MoveShapes animation, 102
MoveShapes storyboard object, 101
mrHappyGrid object, 303–304
MSDN Windows Phone sample projects, resources for Windows Phone 7 development, 306–309
MVVM (Model-View-ViewModel) design pattern, data binding for, 270–272
my3DCamera object, 77
myBrush file, 83, 85
myCallout name object, 50
myDocumentReader, 151
MyFeedback file, 323
myInkArea, 143
myListStyle style, 252
myPolygon object, 23, 28
myPolygonMouseDown method, 29
myRect object, 98
MyResources.xaml file, 83
myShape object, 68
myStar name object, 50
myStarMouseDown method, 29
myTabControl,, 141

■ N

Name property, 17, 132, 141
Name property text area, Properties panel, 98
namespaces, for Windows Phone 7, 280
naming objects, in Properties panel, 17
Navigate panel, 321, 340
NavigateBackAction behavior object, 157
NavigateForwardAction behavior object, 157
NavigateToScreenAction behavior, 157, 334–336
NavigateToScreenAction object, 335
navigation framework, 273
NavSystem component, 334–335
NavSystem node, 330
NavSystem screen, 330–331
nested layout managers, designing, 135
nested StackPanel objects, adding, 145–147
.NET class libraries, 7, 20

.NET code, 4
.NET object, 2
.NET tab, Add References dialog box, 40
New Item dialog box, 228
New Project dialog box, 5–8, 280, 284, 326
New Project option, Projects tab, 5
New Storyboard button, 303
No brush option, 42
nodes
    connecting, 319
    Start, 317–318
Normal state, 211

■ O

object parameter, 229
object resources, 81–86
    applying to UI elements, 85–86
    managing, 83–84
Objects and Timeline animation editor,
    304
Objects and Timeline panel, 15–16
objects, in Panorama Application Project,
    294–295
ObservableCollection class, 237, 245,
    263–264
OneTime option, 236
OneWay option, 234
OneWayToSource option, 236
OnlineStoreApp, 326–327
OnlineStoreApp_Production project, 345
OnlineStoreAppScreens project, 328, 344
OnlineStoreAppScreens.csproj file,
    343–344
Opacity property, 40, 51–52
OpacityMask object, 42
options, 30–31
Options dialog box, 30
Orientation property
    Properties panel, 125, 129, 145
    StackPanel control, 248
orthographic camera, 74
Oscillations property, 113

■ P, Q

Package SketchFlow Project, File menu,
    341

packaging prototypes, 341–342
Pan tool, 22, 24–25
Panorama Application Project, 294–299
    backgrounds for, 296–298
    objects in, 294–295
    PanoramaItem objects in
        creating new, 299
        markup for, 295–296
Panorama control, 281, 296
Panorama node, 299
panorama-style application, 282
Panorama type, 294
PanoramaBackground.png file, 296
PanoramaItem objects
    creating new, 299
    markup for, 295–296
Paragraph block, 152, 154
<Paragraph> element, 148
path animation, 87
Path class, 37
Path object, extracting, 47–50
PathGeometry class, 37
PCGamingSketch project, 314–315
PDC (Professional Developers
    Conference), 1
Pen tool, 23, 34, 36–38, 289, 302
Pencil tool, 23, 34–35
PersonCollection node, 263, 266
perspective camera, 74
phone page, 284
PhoneTextNormalStyle, 286
PhoneTextTitle1Style, 286
Picture property, 265
Pivot Application Project, 300–305
    animating layout for, 303–304
    controlling Storyboard for in XAML,
        304–305
    creating new PivotItem object for, 301
    designing layout for, 302–303
    transforming grid, 303–304
Pivot control, 281
Pivot node, 301
Pivot object, 300
PivotItem object, 300–301
PlaneProjection object, 79–80
Play button, 94, 304

PlaySketchFlowAnimationAction behavior, 340–341

PlaySoundAction behavior object, 157

PointCount property, 40, 194

Position property, 77

positioning UI, with snap grid, 12

Product node, 257

<Products> node, 257

Professional Developers Conference (PDC), 1

Program Files, 344

Project category, 26

Project panel, 19–20

project templates
    Blend Windows Phone, 281
    Databound, 270–272
    Windows Phone 7, 276

Projection property, 79–80

Projects panel, 61, 255

Projects tab, Expression Blend Welcome Screen, 5

properties
    adding, 264–265
    binding to ListBox controls, 243
    changing, 92–93

Properties panel, 16–19
    categories of, 18
    changing camera settings using, 73–74
    configuring GUI controls with, 121
    finding objects in, 17
    naming objects in, 17
    options for, 19

Properties tab, Properties panel, 31

property triggers, adding interactivity with, 200–203

Property1 property, 263

Property2 property, 263

prototypes
    feedback for
        adding to, 322
        exporting, 323
        importing client, 324–325
    incorporating interactivity, 337–339
    moving into production, 343–346
        modifying App.xaml.cs files, 344–346

modifying *csproj files, 343
        updating assembly references, 343–344
    packaging, 341–342
    for Silverlight, 326–341
        Component screens, 329–332
        creating screens, 332–333
        incorporating interactivity into, 337–339
        NavigateToScreenAction behavior, 334–336
        PlaySketchFlowAnimationAction behavior, 340–341
        project files for, 327–329
        replicating navigation GUI, 334
    testing, 320–326
        adding feedback to, 322
        exporting feedback, 323
        generating Microsoft Word documentation, 325–326
        importing client feedback, 324–325
        navigating screens, 320–322

PurchaseOrder class, 236–237, 246, 259, 287

PurchaseOrders class, 237, 246, 259, 287

PurchaseOrders collection, 237–238, 245

PurchaseOrders node, 240, 242, 244, 246

■ R

RadialGradientBrush object, 46

Rational Unified Process (RUP), 311

raw XAML, 13

rawButtonTemplate style, 190

Record Keyframe button, 91–92

Rectangle element, 98

Rectangle object, 38, 101

Rectangle style shape, 331

Rectangle Tool, 22, 34, 38, 49

RectangleGeometry class, 37

Refined node, 316

RegularPolygon class, 40, 42

regularPolygon object, 126–127

RegularPolygon shape, 49

relational database data, data binding for, 269–270

rendering effects, hiding and showing, 12

RenderTransform options, 67–68
RepeatBehavior property, 95, 106, 125
Resize and Skew button, 296
Resource Dictionary location, 82
resources
    applying to UI elements, 85–86
    managing, 83–84
    storing templates as, 182–184
    for Windows Phone 7 development
        App Hub web site, 309–310
        MSDN Windows Phone sample
            projects, 306–309
Resources panel, 329
Results panel, 21
Return scope to Window/UserControl
    button, 250
RichTextBox control, 148–149
rightEar object, 62
Ripple effect, Asset panel, 27–28
Rotate option, 67
Rotate value, 65
<RotateTransform> element, 169
RotationX property, 79
RotationY property, 79
RotationZ property, 79
RoundButtonTemplate, 183–186
rows, defining in Grid object, 142
RubberbandTriangle storyboard, 111, 113
Run as Administrator option, 275
Run button, Windows Phone 7 SDK, 274
RUP (Rational Unified Process), 311

■ S
sample project, 9–10, 23
Samples tab, 5, 8
Scale option, 67
Scale tab, Transform section, 253
scope, of animation services, 88
Screen1_.xaml file, 344
ScrollViewer, 133
SDK assemblies, 40
SDK (Software Development Kit), for
    Windows Phone 7, 273–284
    Blend Projects Templates in, 280–283
    Blend User Guide in, 282–283
    documentation for, 278–280

and Microsoft XNA Game Studio 4.0,
    276–277
    tools included in, 276–277
    Visual Studio 2010 Project Template in,
        283–284
Selected state, 253–254
SelectedIndex property, 131
SelectedItem property, ListBox control, 262
selecting objects, in Objects and Timeline
    panel, 16
Selection tool, 22, 24, 62
sender object, 51
SetDataStoreValueAction behavior object,
    157
Setter objects, 164–165
Setters collection, 164
shapes
    coloring, 42–47
        brush-centric properties, 42
        Gradient brush option, 43–46
        No brush option, 42
        Solid-color brush option, 42–43
        Tile brush option, 46–47
    converting to Path objects, 49–50
    modifying using Appearance editor,
        40–41
Shapes category, 26
Shapes section, of Assets library, 39–40
Silverlight 3D graphics, 79–81
Silverlight API, 204–212
    configuring transitions, 210–211
    custom states, 211–212
    defining transition effects, 209–210
    establishing state group transition
        timing, 208
    viewing generated XAML, 207–208
    VSM via States panel, 206–207
Silverlight applications, 3–5, 11, 21, 33–34,
    56, 63
Silverlight Button, 120
Silverlight control, 25
Silverlight Databound project type, 270
Silverlight for Windows Phone 7 node, 283
Silverlight for Windows Phone portal, 279
Silverlight Image control, 80
Silverlight project template, 7–8

Silverlight projects, 22, 34, 56

Silverlight proper, 273

Silverlight System.Windows.Controls
Namespace link, 122

Silverlight UserControl, 42, 80, 90, 97, 137

Silverlight3DExample project, 80

SilverlightRoundButtonTemplate
application-level resource, 205

Simple Styles, 175–180

Simple Styles.xaml file, 177

SimpleBlendAnimations example, 115–116

SimpleSlider style, 176–177

single property, 19

Sketch suffix, 330

SketchFlow, 4–5, 311–346
and application prototyping, 311–314
packaging prototypes, 341–342
prototype sample using, 314–326
Silverlight prototypes in, 326–341
Component screens, 329–332
creating screens, 332–333
incorporating prototype
interactivity, 337–339
project files for, 327–329
replicating navigation GUI, 334
using NavigateToScreenAction
behavior, 334–336
using
PlaySketchFlowAnimationAction
behavior, 340–341

SketchFlow Animation panel, 338

SketchFlow Feedback option, Window
menu, 324

SketchFlow Feedback panel, 324–325

Sketch.Flow file, 328

SketchFlow Map panel, 315–319
assigning transition styles, 319
color coding, 318
connecting nodes, 319
creating nodes, 319
Start node, 317–318

SketchFlow Player, testing prototypes with,
320–326
adding feedback to, 322
exporting feedback, 323
generating Microsoft Word
documentation, 325–326

importing client feedback, 324–325
navigating screens, 320–322

SketchFlowLibraries attribute, 345

SketchStyles.xaml file, 328

Skew option, 67

Skew value, 65

SLControlTemplate project, 204

Slider control, 77, 120, 176, 178, 223,
226–227, 229, 233–234

Slider objects, 80

SmallChange property, Slider control, 227

snap grid, UI positioning with, 12

Software Development Kit, for Windows
Phone 7. *See* SDK, for Windows
Phone 7

Solid-color brush option, 42–43

source control property, 221

Source property, 70–71

SourceName property, 305

SourceObject property, 117

SpinButtonAnimation storyboard,
102–106, 108

splitters, creating, 144–145

Springiness property, 113

StackPanel controls, 33, 64–65, 223, 248

StackPanel objects, adding nested, 145–147

Star object, 27

Star tool, 39

starButtonStyle, 195, 200

Start node, 317–319

Start screen, 320–321

Startup event handler, 344

state group transition timing, establishing,
208

states
adding visual, 215–216
custom, 211–212
transitioning
in code, 216
in XAML, 216–218

States panel, 206–207, 254

StaticResource markup extension, 166, 168

Storyboard class, 97–98

<Storyboard> element, 208

storyboard objects, 16

Storyboard property, 305

Storyboard1 storyboard object, 101
storyboards, 87
    controlling in XAML, 115–118
        ControlStoryboardAction behavior
            object, 116–118
        SimpleBlendAnimations example,
            115–116
    creating, 89–90
    executing at runtime, 114
    initial, 111
    interacting with in code, 96–98
    managing, 90–91
    properties for, 94–95
String data type, 266
Stroke object, 42
Stroke property, 47, 52
StrokeEndLineCap property, 52
StrokeStartLineCap property, 52
StrokeThickness property, 52, 99
Style class, 164
Style property, 165–166, 190–191
<Style> scope, 188
styles
    assigning Style property, 165–166
    constraining, with TargetType
        attribute, 167–168
    creating, 164–165, 172–180
        empty styles, 172–175
        WPF Simple Styles, 175–180
    default, 169–170
    empty, 172–175
    managing, 170–171
    overriding settings for, 167
    role of control templates in, 180–189
        <ContentPresenter> class, 187
        building custom templates by hand,
            181–182
        incorporating templates, 187–189
        incorporating visual cues using
            WPF triggers, 184–185
        storing templates as resources,
            182–184
        TemplateBinding markup
            extension, 186
    subclassing existing, 168–169
Styles category, 26

styling items, in data templates, 247
stylized templates, creating from graphics,
    193–203
    adding interactivity, 200–203
    creating initial graphics, 194
    extracting, 194–197
    ListBox control, 197–200
    WPF triggers, 203
Subtract option, Combine menu option, 48
SuperPreview, 2
System Styles, for Windows Phone
    Application Project, 286
System.Collections.ObjectModel
    namespace, 237
System.Windows.Controls.Navigation.dll
    assembly, 344
System.Windows.Documents namespace,
    147
System.Windows.Shapes namespace, 37
System.Windows.Style class, 164
System.Xml namespace, 255

■ T
tabbed layout systems, creating, 138–141
tabBehaviors, 141
TabControl class, 134, 139–140
TabControl component, 138–139
TabControl node, Objects and Timeline
    panel, 140
TabControl object, 140
tabDocs, 141
tabInk, 141
TabItem objects, 139–141
TabStripPlacement property, 139
Tag property, 132
TargetType attribute, 167–168
TargetType property, 197
Template property, 182–184
TemplateBinding markup extension,
    185–187, 192
templates, 5–8
    control
        creating, 189–203
        role of in styles, 180–189
    incorporating, 187–189
    Silverlight, 7–8

storing as resources, 182–184
using Silverlight API, 204–212
    configuring transitions, 210–211
    custom states, 211–212
    establishing state group transition
        timing, 208
    transition effects, 209–210
    viewing generated XAML, 207–208
    VSM via States panel, 206–207
Windows Phone, 8
WPF, 6–7
Text category, 18–19
Text property, TextBox control, 233, 235
TextBlock controls, 248–249, 259–262, 292,
    303, 332
TextBlock UI control, 316
TextBox control, 120, 169–170, 235, 331
This document location, 82
Tile brush option, 46–47
TiltButton style, 171
timeline editor, zooming, 96
Timeline panel, 23, 27–28
TitlePanel layout manager, 292
ToolBar controls, 149–156
    loading document data, 155–156
    populating FlowDocument containers,
        151–155
    saving document data, 155–156
Tools panel, 22–28
    adding custom content, 23
    Assets library, 28
    Assets panel, 25–28
    Direct Selection tool, 24
    Pan tool, 24–25
    Selection tool, 24
    Zoom tool, 24–25
TotalCost property, 243, 259
Transform category, 18
Transform section, 253, 303
transformations
    applying at design time, 66–68
        LayoutTransform options, 67–68
        RenderTransform options, 67–68
    applying in code, 68–69
Transformations WPF application, 64

transforming grid, for Pivot Application
    Project, 303–304
transition styles, assigning, 319
transitions
    configuring, 210–211
    effects for, 209–210
    establishing state group timing, 208
    of states
        in code, 216
        in XAML, 216–218
Translate option, 67
TreeView control, 267
<Trigger> element, 185
triggers
    controlling animations using, 102–109
        adding, 103–106
        assigning to menu items, 108–109
        menu system example, 106–108
    WPF
        property, 200–203
        visual cues using, 184–185
Triggers panel, 103–106, 203
two-way data binds, configuring, 234–236
TwoWay binding mode, 235

■ U
UI element
    applying resources to, 85–86
    grouping of, 136–137
    repositioning of, 137–138
    ungrouping of, 136–137
UI (user interface), 138–156
    binding sample data to, 266–268
    binding to elements, via XPath
        expressions, 257–258
    composite elements for data templates,
        248–251
    creating, 259–261
    example of, 222–224
    Grid object for, 141–147
        adding items to cells, 142–144
        adding nested StackPanel objects,
            145–147
        creating splitters, 144–145
        defining rows and columns, 142
    positioning, with snap grid, 12

tabbed layout systems, creating, 138–141

ToolBar controls for, 149–156

    loading document data, 155–156

    populating FlowDocument containers, 151–154

    saving document data, 155–156

WPF Document API, 147–149

    block elements, 148

    document layout managers, 148–149

    inline elements, 148

UIElement base class, 51, 79

UniformGrid, 133

Unite option, Combine menu option, 48

Uri string, 345

User Guide menu option, Help tab, 31

user interface. *See* UI

UserControl, 3, 80, 88, 163, 213, 216–217, 315, 329–330

<UserControl> element, 15

UserControl objects, 16, 127

[UserControl] tree node, 340

UserControls, generating, 212–219

    adding visual states, 215–216

    transitioning states, 216–218

    VSM, 218–219

■ **V**

Value property, 225–227, 229, 233–234, 236

ValueChanged event, 77, 80

VB code, 21, 60

VB (*.vb) code file, 20

vector graphics, 33–86

    2D graphical transformation, 64–69

        applying, 66–69

        building initial UI, 64–66

    3D graphical transformation, 69–81

        in Silverlight, 79–81

        in WPF, 69–79

    combining geometries, 47–50

    drawing tools, 34–47

        Appearance editor, 40–41

        Brushes editor, 42–47

        Ellipse Tool, 38

        Line Tool, 38

        Pen, 36–38

        Pencil, 35–38

        Rectangle Tool, 38

        Shapes section of Assets library, 39–40

    Expression Design, 56–64

        exporting images, 56–60

        for Silverlight applications, 60–64

    and Path objects, 47–50

    Shape objects, 50–51

    stroke for, 52–54

        dash patterns, 53–54

        end caps, 52–53

Version 1 node, 319

Version 1 screen, 320

Version 2 node, 319, 322

Version 2 screen, 320–322

Version 3 screen, 320

Version Approved node, 316–318

VerticalAlignment property, Properties panel, 182, 199

View object, 7

ViewBox, 133

ViewCart screen, 332–334

ViewModel class, 7, 295

ViewModels folder, 295

Viewport3D elements, 79

Viewport3D node, 75

Viewport3D object

    changing using artboard tools, 75

    elements of, 71–72

    transforming with Camera Orbit tool, 72

visual cues, 88

visual effects, hiding and showing, 12

Visual State Manager and States panel, 291

Visual State Manager (VSM), 8, 206–207, 253

visual states, adding, 215–216

Visual Studio 2010 Project Template, for Windows Phone 7, 283–284

VisualStateManager class, 216

VSM (Visual State Manager), 8, 206–207, 253

■ W

Weather Forecast Sample project, 308
Web tool, 2
Welcome Screen menu option, Help tab, 8
Width property, 93, 226–227, 229, 249
Width value, 65, 171
wigglyListBoxStyle, 197–198
Window objects, 102, 133, 175
<Window> tag, 232
Window/UserControl, 68, 329
Window.Loaded event, 104
Window.Loaded trigger, 104
Window's artboard, 184
Window's code file, 155
Windows Forms framework, 34
Windows Phone 7, 273–310
    Blend Panorama Application Project
        for, 294–299
        backgrounds for, 296–298
        objects in, 294–295
        PanoramaItem objects in, 295–299
    Blend Pivot Application Project for,
        300–305
        animating layout for, 303–304
        controlling Storyboard for in XAML,
          304–305
        creating new PivotItem object for,
          301
        designing layout for, 302–303
        transforming grid, 303–304
    Blend Windows Phone Application
        Project for, 284–292
        artboard for, 284–285
        configuring emulator for, 292
        creating control template from
          graphic, 289–291
        Data panel in, 287
        handling click events, 291
        interactive graphics in, 288–289
        System Styles for, 286
    core namespaces for, 280
    resources for
        App Hub web site, 309–310
        MSDN Windows Phone sample
          projects, 306–309
    SDK for, 273–284
        Blend Project Templates in, 280–283
        Blend User Guide in, 282–283
        documentation for, 278–280
        and Microsoft XNA Game Studio
          4.0, 276–277
        tools included in, 276–277
        Visual Studio 2010 Project Template
          in, 283–284
Windows Phone 7 emulator, 276
Windows Phone Application Project,
    284–292
    artboard for, 284–285
    configuring emulator for, with Device
        panel, 292
    creating control template from graphic,
        289–291
    Data panel in, 287
    handling click events, 291
    interactive graphics in, 288–289
    System Styles for, 286
Windows Phone Application template, 281
Windows Phone Control Library template,
    281
Windows Phone Databound Application
    template, 281
Windows Phone Developer Tools, 274
Windows Phone Development MSDN web
    portal, 306
Windows Phone Marketplace, 309
Windows Phone node, 280
Windows Phone Panorama Application
    project type, 294
Windows Phone Panorama Application
    template, 281
Windows Phone Pivot Application
    template, 281
Windows Phone project template, 8
Windows Presentation Foundation. *See*
    WPF
Windows Start button, 276, 278
Windows Update, performing, 276
<Window.Triggers> collection, 109
workspace layout
    for animations, 88–96
        adding keyframes, 91–92

capturing object property changes, 92–93

creating storyboards, 89–90

managing storyboards, 90–91

storyboard properties, 94–95

testing animations, 94

viewing markup for, 94

zooming timeline editor, 96

customizing, 30–31

Workspaces menu option, Window, 31, 88

WPF 3D graphics, 69–79

camera settings for

changing with properties panel, 73–74

controlling in code, 74–77

changing lighting effects using light editors, 75–77

mapping 2D images to 3D planes, 70–71

Viewport3D object

changing using artboard tools, 74–75

elements of, 71–72

transforming with Camera Orbit tool, 72

WPF project template, 6–7

WPF Window/Silverlight UserControl, 82

WPF (Windows Presentation Foundation), 98–109

controlling animations using triggers, 102–109

adding, 103–106

assigning to menu items, 108–109

menu system example, 106–108

Document API, 147–149

block elements, 148

document layout managers, 148–149

inline elements, 148

motion paths in, 98–102

Simple Styles for, 175–180

triggers, adding interactivity with, 200–203

visual cues, using triggers, 184–185

XML data source, defining, 255–258

adding XML data source, 256–257

binding to UI elements via XPath expressions, 257–258

Wpf3DExample application, 70

Wpf3DExample project, 77

WpfControlsApp WPF application project, 138

WPFMotionPathApp WPF application project, 98

WpfStyleByHand project, 164

WpfStylesWithBlend project, 172

WpfTemplatesByHand project, 181

WpfXmlDataBinding project, 255, 258

WrapPanel, 133

www.microsoft.com/expression/try-it

Key attribute, 168, 170, 188

Key value, 169–170

Name attribute, 50, 60

■ X

XAML elements, 17, 21, 60

XAML (Extensible Application Markup Language)

controlling storyboards in, 115–118

ControlStoryboardAction behavior object, 116–118

SimpleBlendAnimations example, 115–116

editing, 14

transitioning states in, 216–218

viewing, 14, 130

viewing generated, 207–208

XAML files, 19, 22, 57, 60–61

XAML formats, 56

XAML Silverlight 4/WPF Canvas option, 59

XamlReader object, 155

XamlWriter object, 155

XAP binary, 342

XAP file, 345

Xbox LIVE Marketplace, 309

XML-based grammars, 3

XML Data Source option, Data panel, 255

XML (Extensible Markup Language) data sources

adding, 256–257

for WPF, defining, 255–258

XmlDataProvider resource type, 257
XPath expressions, binding to UI elements
    via, 257–258
xVal variable, 77

Y

yVal variable, 77

Z

Z alphabetic token, 37

ZAM 3D tool, 78–79
Zoom tool, 22, 24–25
zooming
    display, 11–12
    timeline editor, 96
    zVal variable, 77

You Need the Companion eBook

Your purchase of this book entitles you to buy the companion PDF-version eBook for only $10. Take the weightless companion with you anywhere.

We believe this Apress title will prove so indispensable that you'll want to carry it with you everywhere, which is why we are offering the companion eBook (in PDF format) for $10 to customers who purchase this book now. Convenient and fully searchable, the PDF version of any content-rich, page-heavy Apress book makes a valuable addition to your programming library. You can easily find and copy code—or perform examples by quickly toggling between instructions and the application. Even simultaneously tackling a donut, diet soda, and complex code becomes simplified with hands-free eBooks!

Once you purchase your book, getting the $10 companion eBook is simple:

❶ Visit **www.apress.com/promo/tendollars/**.

❷ Complete a basic registration form to receive a randomly generated question about this title.

❸ Answer the question correctly in 60 seconds, and you will receive a promotional code to redeem for the $10.00 eBook.

THE EXPERT'S VOICE™

233 Spring Street, New York, NY 10013

All Apress eBooks subject to copyright protection. No part may be reproduced or transmitted in any form or by any means, electronic or mechanical, including photocopying, recording, or by any information storage or retrieval system, without the prior written permission of the copyright owner and the publisher. The purchaser may print the work in full or in part for their own noncommercial use. The purchaser may place the eBook title on any of their personal computers for their own personal reading and reference.

Offer valid through 8/11.